TALKING TO EXTRATERRESTRIALS

"Whether or not we are being communicated with from outer space is no longer the question. That question has been answered long ago. The current question is, what are we being told? What wisdom are we being given? What assistance are we being provided? What insight are we being offered and what answers are we being supplied? In *Talking to Extraterrestrials*, through information received in a remarkable way by an extraordinary human being who has had the courage to come forward and reveal an intimate and personal process which has taken her consciousness to the deepest reaches of the universe, the above questions are answered."

— Neale Donald Walsch, author of *Conversations with God*

"The insights this book contains cannot be ignored. We are blessed to have this knowledge. I urge you to read this book."

— Joel Rothschild, author of *Signals* and *Hope*

"Read this book. Be done with the language of victimization. Be as brave as Larkins; step up to the cliff of the mind, and let the wings of the heart unfurl. Hear the resounding choral call of destiny: prepare for global contact."

— Dana Redfield, author of *Summoned* and *The ET-Human Link*

"Our worldview is being transformed. We are entering the era of the Universal Human, a being whose identity is independent of nationality, religion, or ethnicity. Lisette Larkins now takes us further, to show our kinship with even those from other worlds. Join in this exciting journey and let her introduce you to our new, Universal Community."

— Walter Semkiw, M.D., author of *Return of the Revolutionaries: The Case for Reincarnation and Soul Groups Reunited*

TALKING TO
EXTRATERRESTRIALS

COMMUNICATING WITH
ENLIGHTENED BEINGS

LISETTE
LARKINS

HAMPTON ROADS
PUBLISHING COMPANY, INC.
for the evolving human spirit

Cover design by Marjoram Productions
Cover art © 2002
"Face of an Extraterrestrial Alien"/
CA/Corbis Images

Hampton Roads Publishing Company, Inc.
1125 Stoney Ridge Road
Charlottesville, VA 22902

434-296-2772
fax: 434-296-5096
e-mail: hrpc@hrpub.com
www.hrpub.com

If you are unable to order this book from your local
bookseller, you may order directly from the publisher.
Call 1-800-766-8009, toll-free.

Library of Congress Catalog Card Number: 2001099308

ISBN 1-57174-334-0

10 9 8 7 6 5 4 3 2

Printed on acid-free paper in Canada

Table of Contents

Editor's Introduction

An Offer We Can't Refuse

Just about everyone thinks that the human race is in *some* sort of trouble. What kind depends on your point of view. Environmentalists focus on the damage we are doing to the planet. Bible fundamentalists believe that Armageddon is close, and that famine, plague, and war will soon destroy the majority of humanity. The political right believes that the political left is taking us on a path to disaster, and vice-versa. Others believe that we about to undergo a quantum evolutionary leap, a spiritual awakening that will compel us to re-examine our place in the universe, and to re-discover who we really are.

The fact is, we are such a fractured and divided world that people murder each other in the name of whatever God they believe gave them—and only them—the correct rules to live by. Somehow "love your neighbor" got misplaced. We allow children to starve, and poor people to go without medical attention.

We have merely to look around us to observe what is happening. Notice the ozone layer; the percentage of people in the industrial world who get cancer; the AIDS epidemic; global warming; the destruction of the rain forests to raise cattle for fast-food restaurants;

the pollution and depletion of our ocean resources; and much, much more. It is easy to point fingers, to find enemies, to waste our resources building weapons instead of working to repair the damage.

Lord knows, we need help.

And this is a book about getting help.

We've had an offer we can't refuse. It's from our neighbors. The ones who live off the planet, who see what's happening on a global level. They've lived through much of the same process. And they admit that they have on occasion destroyed much of their civilization, too.

They don't want it to happen to us.

They are offering help, if we'll accept it. This book is one of the ways they wish to convey that information. Oh, I know that many of you will think that this communication process is a distorted and unproven means of conveying information at best, and at worst a complete fraud. I know many will say that if they really wanted to help us, they'd land in a public place and announce that they are here.

But think about that.

What would really happen if a race of more highly evolved beings actually landed on the planet? How would it affect our religious beliefs, our economic, military, and political structures? Would they be treated as God's messengers, or shot at as alien intruders whose "real purpose" is to take over the planet? We are exceedingly primitive beings with a technology that can destroy ourselves and the planet. And there are people out there *right now* who believe that the God they worship intends for us to do just that. They are going to help make it so in any way they can. There are people out there *right now* who are attempting to build atomic or nuclear weapons so they can take out Tel Aviv or New York City. There are people out there *right now* who danced while their messengers flew airplanes into buildings and killed thousands of people.

If you were from off-planet, and unarmed, and incapable of killing, would you come here and show yourself? Would you beam a radio or television message that would be widely rejected as trickery and Hollywood special effects? They have showed us that they exist. They occasionally allow their craft to be observed, and they often interact with people in many different ways. And what has been the net result of those encounters? Skepticism, dismissal, denial, government cover-ups, and a general consensus that such events are "unproven" or are evidence of mental illness. Those involved in attempting to have governments disclose information and evidence encounter the same resistance. (Many think that the government *itself* doesn't control it, but groups of super-secret organizations whose purpose is to reverse-engineer the technology and control access to the information.)

But our friends in space are not going to play the good guy-bad guy game here. Sure, there are black-ops groups who have hidden information from the rest of us. Sure, there is technology that could be made available to the people that would change the direction of human development. Sure, there are those who want to control access to ET contact, who want to preserve their own power base, and who apparently seek to preserve the current paradigm of fossil fuel technology. And sure, that path may eventually pollute the planet in such a way that it sets us back hundreds of years, or maybe destroys us altogether. But even if there are power-mongers, and men in black, and international corporations more concerned with stockholders than with the health of the planet—they are not the bad guys. They are only human beings, like us, acting out of their own view of the world. And to a large extent, they are serving what the rest of us want. Do you think the drug cartels would exist if millions of people didn't crave the stuff? The point is that, we cannot play the good and evil game; we cannot blame others for the condition we find ourselves in. It is *true* that we have met the enemy, and they are us. We really are one, all part of the same energy source which created the entire universe. And on this beautiful, green and blue planet called Earth, we are in control of our destiny, we are, all of us, at cause in the matter. Therefore, we can change it.

And they are here to help. They want to mentor all of us—if we desire it. There's still the matter of free will (the *universal* prime directive), and could it be that it takes a critical mass of people to *ask* for help before they are willing to show up and render it more directly?

This book will tell you what has been going on: who they are, why they are here, what their purpose is, and how we all can participate in a way that benefits everyone. It will introduce Lisette, describe her encounters as an "experiencer" (not an "abductee"), and the difficult process by which she came to accept her role as a communicator for physical beings from another planet. You are of course free to consider the information and accept or reject it based on what it says to you individually. You will find in the patient and kind tone and content of these words, a concern for all the peoples of the Earth, that most would not have expected from these enlightened beings, who are much maligned, feared, and misunderstood by the vast majority of us on this planet.

So, for what it's worth, here it is, the result of having been *Talking to Extraterrestrials*.

—Robert S. Friedman

Author's Preface

One does not normally fall asleep wondering if the night will bring a face-to-face encounter with extraterrestrials—the gray ones with large black eyes—or if one will awake floating through the air, being transferred from a strange craft to more waiting extraterrestrials below. These certainly were not ideas that I had growing up. But one night in 1987, I sat up in bed with the eerie feeling that something was not quite right. As a young mother, depressed, and in my third year of an unhappy marriage, I wouldn't have believed that my life could have gotten any more challenging. But that night, as my seven-month-old child slept peacefully in his crib, I was blasted from above by a white funnel of light that shot through the ceiling and pierced my whole body with an electrical vibration. My hair billowed around my face as though I was standing in a wind tunnel but the curtains lay still against the bedroom wallpaper. My life has not been the same since.

The mysterious lights and vibrations came visiting almost every evening after that; yet I had no idea what was happening to me. Following each burst of light overhead, within seconds, I would float to sleep. Such a strong and sudden repose would overcome me that it reminded me of when I was anesthetized to have a tooth pulled. It was a seemingly induced sleep, initiated precisely because of—or despite—the screaming terror of my mind. After almost two years of this chaos, finally in my desperation, and with my then-husband's encouragement, I admitted myself to a psychiatric hospital. During my short stay there, I lost custody of my son, and because of the fury that I felt over that injustice, I vowed to get to the bottom of what was coming through the ceiling over my head.

By the time my hospital stay ended three weeks later, I had a sense that I wasn't crazy, but I knew that I needed help. Over the next four months, I regained full custody of my son and I became committed to finding out everything that I possibly could about my experiences. Perhaps if I had been more spiritually and emotionally grounded during the initial experiences, I might not have been so traumatized. But by this time I was motivated to unravel the mystery. So for the next few years, I was counseled by a wonderful therapist who helped me to delve into my lingering trauma. After much testing and evaluation, he assured me that I was psychologically sound.

Eventually, I healed emotionally and I became determined to find an explanation behind the paranormal phenomena that had routinely filled my nights. I had a feeling that, whatever it was, it was not of this world. Other strange things began happening too: the electric car windows would go up and down by themselves, even when the engine was off; electrical appliances would constantly malfunction when I used them; my head would strongly vibrate as though it were plugged in to a socket, and worse, would spontaneously move on its own just as the vibrations would descend on me from above.

Throughout those first few years, the idea of extraterrestrial encounter phenomena seemed foreign to me and so I did not seriously consider that this was what was occurring, until finally I "awoke" during one encounter to find myself face-to-face with a group of extraterrestrials. My heart was beating so hard I wondered if I would have a heart attack. All I could think of was my burning desire to return home and to tell somebody what had happened. Suddenly I understood why I had been experiencing episodes of "missing time." As I stared in disbelief at the beings in my midst, they began to speak to me, although their mouths never moved, nor I believe, did mine. They seemed to speak from their mind to mine, but the words were as clear as though you were speaking to me across the room. This communication has continued to this day and makes up the content of this book.

Despite my initial terror at seeing extraterrestrials in front of me, they seemed oddly familiar, as though I were greeting a beloved uncle who I had known as a child but had not seen in years. They spoke to me, and I spoke to them and I cannot explain how it was that they seemed so strangely familiar. Inexplicably, I felt tremendous love for them, and I could feel their absolute love for me. Through my conversations with them that evening, as well as many communications since, I have come to understand that my encounters—and the encounters of other people worldwide—are part of a magnificent, universal plan.

From that moment on, as my understanding about my experiences changed, I changed and the experiences were transformed. I began to develop, rather than to fear, certain newly acquired abilities that I later found out, come with the territory, such as clairvoyance and clairaudience, clairsentience, and materialization. They began sending me colored bursts of light that I eventually was able to decode, which provided gentle guidance and suggestions at moments of confusion or lack of clarity. In general, my whole world changed. Once in a while I could "hear" the thoughts of animals.

I have come to understand that these beings have not "abducted" me, for I have never been kidnapped. I understand that this term has been given by a culture which does not understand, and which greatly fears these otherworldly neighbors of ours. For as I changed my idea of what had been occurring to me, and refused to accept the label of victim, I began to tell one person, and then another, about my experiences. Before long, I had formed a small group. I advertised and invited others to come and speak about their encounters, for I remembered that there had long been no one in whom I felt I could confide. As people came to my group, I learned that there is tremendous shame and embarrassment surrounding this phenomenon. There were many times just after the group ended for the evening, that a new participant would take me aside, and with wide eyes and a tremor in the voice, would say, "I, too, have had those experiences but I have never told anyone."

I now recognize that there are many, many of us who are having identical experiences, but few of us feel comfortable talking about them. In fact, I've come to believe that our culture demands that we silently agree to keep our collective voices quiet and not speak of such things. Should we dare to, we blow open the idea that we are not here alone and that we are not separate from other inhabitants of the universe. Despite the prevailing attitude of governments and society, most of us sense that we are indeed universal humans, having brethren somewhere close by.

I now understand that despite the initial trauma related to my early encounters, it did not mean that something bad has happened. Trauma was my initial reaction, based on the way that I have grown up in my culture and the understandings that I had adopted. But I no longer choose trauma as my reaction, and as soon as I made that contextual shift in my perspective of the experiences, I brought curiosity, wonderment, and most of all, an inquiring mind to this whole phenomenon. Now that I have made a shift in the context of how I hold these experiences in my perceptions, I am emotionally free to go to the next step. I decided that it would be most interesting to interview these extraterrestrials and to find out things from their perspective.

I wish to share some of the communications that I have had, and am having, with these enlightened beings. They describe themselves as enlightened, and that is in fact my experience of them. Even among UFO buffs, this is not a popular stance. But there is a ring of truth to their communications. I find that I simply feel the heart and soul of them, and resonate strongly with them. Those who walked with Jesus had a sense of who he was. They had a sense of his light, and although I may take great ridicule for this seemingly unpopular perspective, I state unequivocally that I experience these beings as enlightened.

The extraterrestrials remind us that you can tell the tree by the fruit that it bears. As a result of my contacts with them, I am left with the feeling of peace and hope. Their words resonate with those of the great masters who came before them. Their mentoring over the last fifteen years has helped to transform my life, for if you had known me in 1987, you would not recognize me now as the same woman.

Most of us need to believe that something extraordinary is possible for ourselves, for our loved ones, and for our planet. Astonishing things have happened to me, and so I know where miracles live. They live in your ability to believe.

There is nothing unique or unusual about me. If I can experience the seeming miraculous, so can any one of us. Physical contact with extraterrestrials may be more common than you think. For where is it written in the sky that the supernatural happens only to Tibetan monks or fishermen who hung out with Jesus? An ordinary redhead like me can attest to what is possible when the Universe opens her curtains and we get a peek backstage.

Except for this small matter of talking to extraterrestrials, I'm just like you. You probably don't consider yourself to be delusional, or a liar, and neither do I experience those qualities in myself. So don't distrust me because I say that I have friends who are gray. I'm trying to come out of the closet too.

I'm really not a new age freak. You and I probably have more in common than not: the same challenges; similar hopes and dreams; a microwave oven that needs cleaning; and kids who outgrow their shoes before their attitudes and eat more junk food than should be possible.

There's this dilemma of the stigma associated with declaring that one has had encounters of the fourth kind. If I ask anything of you, dear reader, I ask that, as you read this book, you notice how many assumptions you have as to what is, and is not possible. I might gently point out that just because you limit yourself as to what experiences are possible, does not in any way limit my own. Perhaps that is why I talk to extraterrestrials and you don't (at the moment). But I'm getting ahead of myself.

I do understand that it doesn't seem believable, all this ET stuff. I can really relate to that because I've never even liked science fiction—

until my own experiences changed all that. When my life turned topsy-turvy that evening, I had no way of knowing that it would take me this long to finally be comfortable with telling you the truth about it. And I probably wouldn't bother at all, except for the fact that I'm betting that tens of thousands of otherwise ordinary people out there have had similar experiences, but like me, have never told anyone. It's been our little secret. But that's all about to change.

I'm a late bloomer. It's taken me decades to find my rhythm and I've been late to mature emotionally. I've been so concerned with what you'll think of me, that I had to really grow up and grow older and get good and cavalier, until I don't care any more that you can't believe the experiences of my own life. Well, okay, my timing may have something to do with my son's age who, at fifteen, is probably too old now to have custody taken away from me over this. So I've thrown caution to the wind and I gotta tell you, it feels great to speak my truth. I will probably ignite the fury of much of the UFO community, who insist that gray "aliens" with large black eyes are really kidnappers—and worse.

This book declares that extraterrestrials are enlightened beings—an oxymoron in some paranormal circles. So, you see, I don't even have the approval of the UFO crowd. And if you know anything about current UFO literature, you'll know that such claims are considered blasphemous, or dismissed as a symptom of my having been brainwashed by the ETs.

Aside from alienating myself from "respectable" UFO groups, it's also not easy in social settings when you bring up the "E" word. Of course you already know what the general opinion is about such claims. Those who do believe that extraterrestrials probably exist somewhere can't accept that you've met one. Or a whole group of them. Do you see how slippery this is? The Standard Cultural Norm is at work deep in our belief system, dictating What Is Possible. It's politically correct to admit to seeing a craft from afar, but never to have had a personal relationship with the occupants. It's perfectly acceptable at the kids' scout meetings to say you've seen a UFO in the night sky while camping in Santa Fe, but you can't have come face-to-face with those who are flying that very craft. It's safe to say that you've observed signs of ET life from afar but there should be no communicating going on between the species. If there is, it can only be limited to squeals of fright as you helplessly become "abducted." At least that version of an encounter will get a baleful nod in the UFO journals, or the tabloids.

Of the UFO groupies who do agree that maybe you've been contacted, and that perhaps it may be possible for there to have been some sort of telepathic communication going on (some ufologists agree that ETs probably don't use their mouths to speak), such telepathic communication is only valid to them if the extraterrestrials in question are positioned some arbitrary distance to that of the human. So you can receive telepathic communication if you say that you're lying on a tabletop in a spacecraft being dissected and that the being is three feet seven inches from you. That, they say they can believe. But not if you're across the room, or across the street, or the craft is overhead or above the house, or above the galaxy, then it's no longer possible to "hear" anything telepathically. Never mind that astronauts use devices to keep in touch with NASA back on Earth when they're out and about in space, and no one thinks a thing of it. Your great-grandmother would think that this is a miracle. Apparently, it's not believable to consider that beings who are far more advanced than us in every aspect can figure out a way to stay in touch.

I've set the stage for what I'm up against here because this is not an easy task. There's not a whole lot of dignity in my line of work. There may be more entrenched preconceived, negative assumptions, and stigma associated with UFO phenomena than any other field, period.

But although this work can be lonely, it is not without reward. The pioneer spirit is alive and thriving in my household and inspires those of us who have been holding on to a secret for too long. I bet that you accept that the world is not flat. Some of us know right now that extraterrestrials contact humans. And that contact does not fit into just one type, style, mode, or pattern. To insist that it must because you haven't heard about it before, doesn't make it invalid. The spectrum of universal experience does not fit into only two or seventeen categories. There's no finite number of potential miracles and in addition, even the aspects of miracles would have to be miraculous.

Just who are these extraterrestrials and why would they want to know us? Or are we just lab rats to them, running around in a maze on our freeways, and periodically being beamed up to be inspected?

Here then, is the first of several dialogues that I share with you. Come with me on an adventure, even though your mind may protest that such communications from other physical beings in the galaxy cannot really be possible. But join me anyway. Perhaps for the first time, so many of our questions will be answered. Assume nothing, and bring yourself to this communication with an open heart and you may find that you too are growing fond of these neighbors who we once called, "alien."

[*A Note to the Reader:* Each chapter begins with my voice. This commentary is always in italic. The indented questions to our E.T. friends are also in italic. And the E.T.'s responses are always in a regular font. L. L.]

CHAPTER 1

Preparation

Have you ever been in the middle of cooking breakfast, or talking on the telephone, and suddenly your whole body freezes for a moment, as you stop what you're doing and pause because you can feel that you're about to sneeze? If it's a big sneeze it feels as though a sudden burst of energy moves right through you and out your nose and mouth. Now pretend that the process just up to the point that you sneeze lasted for twenty minutes, or an hour and a half and your entire body felt as though you were holding onto a metal knife that you had stuck into the toaster. You'd feel electrocuted. Your hair would stand on end and one of your legs might involuntarily begin twitching. Your scalp might feel as though it's being peeled back, and the crackling is so loud that you can't understand how no one else hears it. Most embarrassingly, your head would move back and forth as though you were a human satellite dish. These are some of the sensations that accompany both my physical encounters with extraterrestrials, as well as sessions in which I sit down with a tape recorder and interview them when they're not right in front of me.

Because I am human and I have human friends and family, of course I know how ridiculous this all sounds. I don't know which has been more challenging for me, accepting that I have had encounters with ETs, or dealing with the emotional residue from others' reaction to what I do. Nonetheless, I'm getting braver every day and I thought you might like to begin by reading one of my questions about how I receive these communications.

> *Most people who channel information and record it for publication are very careful to differentiate between information received while in trance or in an altered state and what is added later as their own commentary; however, after coming out of whatever state that I'm in when I "hear" you, that I've captured on a tape recorder, I then sit down to transcribe the tape. But then even during the transcription process, I continue to receive input and information from you, which helps me to better clarify your communications. In fact, it's really a two-part process, and I can't see how it makes sense to attempt to separate the information received from you during "trance" and that which is received by you while I compile it all at the keyboard. But there's no doubt that both processes make for a fuller, richer communication; yet, I'm concerned that others will feel that somehow I'm "cheating" if I include your input here that I have received during the second part of this communication process.*

This process is not received like traditional channeling as you understand it, and so it will be different, for you are involved in active communications with us—not channeling. You are not channeling disembodied spirits, you are communicating with other physical beings off of your planet. You are in a unique position with respect to receiving information from a source from another location in that, unlike "hearing" from disembodied spirits, you have had physical encounters with us during which telepathy was the mode of communication. At those times you are not in "trance" either. We are physical beings and you have been transported at times to other locations through our assistance and with our technology. This makes our association unique and has set up different requirements and aspects to our ongoing communications.

During those face-to-face encounters in the past, you have had conversations with us which have entailed a process of something like mind reading, which is telepathy. In addition, you have a genetic connection to us, so you have a cellular understanding of us. Not only do you perceive as though you were channeling, but we are also sending you a telepathic voice from afar. In addition, you receive images and flashes of light which you have learned to decode and now understand their meanings and so you see and hear constant prompting to keep you on track in order to help your confidence level and allow you to notice when you are receiving what we have sent. You also receive "input" via your scalp, which produces cues and prompts which you have learned to decode.

We do not expect that this process could be done by us alone. This is a joint effort in which you bring your skills, your genealogy, and your vocabulary to the table. We believe that this work is best enhanced by your personal contribution, both while in an altered state and out. Remember, during physical encounters, you hear us clearly, telepathically, without any special ritual or routine. When you sit in your home during this process, you are undergoing the same telepathic process in which you translate our words into your own. But this does not invalidate it as any less valuable than other traditionally channeled work or communication.

You have likened your role to that of a translator in which you receive incoming communications, and then you unravel those communications to your own language. This you do quite effectively, but this process has several other layers to it. Imagine if you were translating somebody who spoke Italian and yet not only are they not sitting across from you, they are not even on the telephone. They are across the galaxy in some cases. So you are not only translating, you are actively translating telepathic communications while simultaneously receiving additional clairaudient and clairvoyant input. As you know from your encounters, this communication is not limited to your moments in an altered state but also you receive clarification and encouragement through the transcription process as well. You also receive further input during the night hours which is why you reach for the tape recorder and record those sentences or paragraphs that you "hear" and then add it to the body of your work.

We wish to suggest that there is a new paradigm opening in which many of you will begin to understand that communications between you and others in other realms, dimensions, or physical locations are not limited to channeling disembodied spirits. Extraterrestrial beings are physical beings. We are actively alive right now, but are not standing across from you. Many of you are also growing in your ability to hear us and others like us at different moments of the day and night.

Is this work infallible? Suppose I make mistakes, choose the wrong words or hear you wrong? I don't want to mislead anybody.

No, this work is not perfect, nor is it without distortion. But you and others like you bring a high degree of integrity and interest in contributing ideas from other realms. But even though this process is not without the challenges of any other communication, it does not minimize the importance of what you and many others are beginning to experience, which is active associations with us and others like us. The type of communications that you are receiving will also spearhead an expanded movement of published material coming through humans from *physical* beings off of Earth. Many of you have grown accustomed to hearing of and reading about mediums who have contact with angels and spirits. The next generation of this type of material includes communications with physical beings who live elsewhere. It's a very exciting time for you. So in many cases, as far as the general public is concerned, this process is somewhat "new." What you consider to be traditional channeling with disembodied spirits has been in "production" through publications, etc., for many years and now many of you are introducing the idea that physical beings can speak to you and through you and provide input with you.

Also, the intention and integrity of the "interviewer" and producer of this work is all important. But to insist that it be brought through in one manner, and is valid only if it is brought through in one rigid way, is to invalidate important aspects of this and others' work. Beethoven was inspired and received direct input and communication from a divine source. He then "collaborated" with his higher self but did not "disclose" that this note was channeled and this other set of notes came to him in his sleep, any more than Einstein "disclosed" the manner in which his formulas were received in an inspirational way. Should he have clarified that this equation just popped into his head, but this other idea over here came to him another way? Yet we understand that when it comes to "inspired" writings from others, there is a cultural expectation that it be dissected and inspected, so that the reader is clear as to what purportedly came from where.

But inspiration and divine communication can come through in myriad ways and it would be of benefit to allow changing and emerging ways for such "mentoring" to be brought to your species in whatever form that it comes. You did not demand that Einstein or Beethoven identify from where their inspiration came, because you did not recognize that they were inspired from a higher source. But you are now beginning to understand that Divinity connects all of us. Divinity connects the one-source with angels and spirit guides; spirit guides and angels with humans; God with extraterrestrials; and therefore extraterrestrials with humans. And so what is needed on your part is a desire and intention to receive inspired information and ideas without allowing the intellect to demand a full analysis of how, where, and why those ideas and information came through. Since this material is not traditionally channeled, nor traditionally translated, it may not meet the "normal" standards of delivery for either—but our announcement is that it does not strive to.

There are those who will demand that it be specified as to what is heard versus seen or what is dictated. But those demands come from those who do not understand the nature of these communications, or who attempt to dissect and analyze the manner in which the divine one-voice can be manifested. And so begin with this work to recognize that the theme throughout is that we are closely connected—you, your species and us. Continue to meditate and pray and hold your highest intention that this material be closely aligned with the divine seed. This process must be done within you. There are those who cannot or will not believe your claims of face-to-face contact or experiences with extraterrestrials, and that is okay, but those very encounters have prepared you for the work that you are doing now. This has been your greatest desire for your life, to be able to provide humankind with messages from us and your encounters and your "modifications" have helped facilitate this process. The three cannot be separated. Yes, you read that correctly. Lisette and other experiencers do have bodily implants and modifications in some cases.

You mean we're really going to say that here for all to read? Not only does it sound outrageous, but also it seems unnatural at the very least. Even if others believe it, it makes me sound like a freak.

When you have an ache in your tooth you go to a dentist where a procedure ensues that may replace, rebuild, or repair a diseased, broken or worn tooth as a result of your eating tendencies, overall general health, environmental factors—or a combination of all of these—to enable you to chew your food effectively. Your digestion process does not then protest that the tooth which chewed your food was not a "real" tooth. You do not protest and disallow that nutrition by demanding that the food be chewed on a "natural" tooth. Your cultural mind seems to accept "enhancements" only when the body is diseased or ill. When you accept "adjustments" only under these circumstances, it allows you to cope and "forgive" those enhancements.

Well, it does seem okay to receive a physical enhancement when the original organ is damaged or diseased. That we can all accept without any problem. In my case and other encounter experiencers, the use of implants to simply keep us in touch seems, shallow. And besides, if you're enlightened, then we humans should be able to facilitate this process without anything being added or altered.

Why? It is okay with you if your politicians and leaders receive organ transplants or mechanical devices within their physical being which helps them perform and live out their mission on Earth. You do not protest and say, "That procedure is not natural." If a pacemaker or hearing aid or other device allows one's body to better perform the stated purpose of that soul, you honor that enhancement and find value and marvel in the very technology that allowed you to stay alive or to perform more effectively. And regarding enlightenment, we may be, but you are not yet. You still experience illness, disease, and breakdown while your body is virtually brand new.

The purpose of this book is to confront some of your societal assumptions that do not serve you. One of the main points is that "extraterrestrials" exist and that, gasp, they even have ongoing contact and communication with some of you. In some cases, implants or devices make those communications and contact more effective. You understand this concept when you track and help facilitate the care and nurturing of some of your endangered animal species. You tag birds and sea life, track lions and elephants and even relocate them to more suitable locations. You mark them, put implants in your dogs' ears to better identify them if lost, and generally, have found an altruistic use of physical implants or adjustments. But if we do this with you, you call foul. If these ideas cause you too much discomfort, simply put this book down.

When one of you actively chooses to enhance a process whereby the highest communication is made possible between us, that you protest. You say it seems unnatural or Frankenstein-ish, or worse, that we use these devices to manipulate you to do our bidding. Who is to say that Einstein or Beethoven didn't choose to be "enhanced," which allowed them to better receive divine inspiration? You do not know of all that has and is transpiring in your world and other worlds. And by the way, all of you are potentially Einsteins and Beethovens. Not just one or two of you. The only difference between those two and all of you is that they were willing to be "used." They were willing to be conduits. They were willing to be a vessel through which great truths and universal ideas and inspiration could come through. You do not know of the process by which Thomas Edison brought through his ideas. How do you know that he was not an encounter experiencer? If someone were to have a near-death experience, and during their time on the other side received wisdom and communications and then came back and disseminated it to the world, would you then say that it should be disallowed for the information did not come from this realm, and further, that the process by which the patient had "returned" to life had been facilitated by adjustments, implants, or techniques of "modern" medicine? You do not claim that the person had been a victim and had been manipulated unfairly because techniques were used which allowed him to continue his life as efficiently and effectively as was stated by that soul's agenda.

Remember that it is not necessary for you to believe any of what is written here. It is not necessary, nor does it require your acceptance and agreement. This is offered as a result of Lisette's chosen path and mission, and ours. The decisions that she has made and the processes that she has undergone are her own choice and should you choose to condemn those choices for whatever reason, you may wish to notice that each of your paths is personal and has been deeply considered and chosen by the soul. Simply because you cannot comprehend it, nor believe it, does not make it invalid or false. Because you call it evil or bad, does not make it so.

This work represents a team effort between a group of "extraterrestrials" as you refer to us, Lisette through her encounter experiences, as well as the contribution of publisher and editor Bob Friedman, who has overseen both the production end of this project as well as provided emotional and technical support and encouragement through an often-challenging process. We bring this material through as a team. In some cases the questions are asked by Lisette in her own voice and we have answered. In other cases, Bob Friedman queries us and engages with us in a dialogue after Lisette enters an altered state. This is a collaborative endeavor made possible through a combination of the right skills, intention, and soul plan of Lisette, Bob, and us.

Expand your idea of what is possible and notice where the intellect feels threatened at the very suggestion that Divinity has joined in this undertaking. It is not "perfect" any more than a conversation is "perfect" between any of you, but the intention and integrity of the participants in this project are motivated by a deep love and compassion for your people and planet Earth. Accept this communication as the gift that it is, and remember that Divinity is not relegated to be expressed in only one way or another. Allow life to unfold and express herself in new and creative ways. Allow the Beethovens and Edisons to step forth confidently and find in your society a "safe" place in which to provide inspiration. There are other Einsteins and Edisons among you, waiting for an opening to be heard. This message hopes to act as an encouragement for them to step forth now. As you are willing to be open to their new ideas that confront deep societal assumptions, in so doing, you allow the Einstein within self to emerge. This is how you evolve individually and how you can elevate your entire planet, when you become willing for the soft whisper of Divinity to replace the resistant, self-righteous denial of your mind. We are a team. We all are a team. Those of you who would like to join with us, let's find a way to bridge whatever dilemmas face your species and together co-create a wondrous tomorrow.

CHAPTER 2

Who We Are, Why We Are Here

I'll always remember the first time that I saw them. So frightened was I that I began to shiver uncontrollably. My heart had never before caused me to notice it, except for the occasional aftermath of robust Mexican food, but at that moment, my chest had gone wild. My heart was hammering inside of me with rare intensity, like a pacemaker gone bad, warning me that my senses were on overload. Having one's beliefs shattered is never comfortable.

Despite my shock at beholding extraterrestrials before me, I momentarily considered my plight: it was possible that I might drop dead like a stunned parakeet. I was still curious, but deeply scared at the same time, at least initially. My whole physiology responded as my college biology textbook had taught me that it should. I was being readied for fight or flight—until common sense prevailed—yeah right, as if I was gonna go anywhere. There I was in deep space, probably in a black hole somewhere and my autonomic nervous system was readying me for escape. Leaping into the night galaxy from the portal of their craft didn't seem like a viable option. Besides, a greater dilemma presented itself: I couldn't move at all. At least not until I calmed down.

Now I'm no Steven Hawking, so don't ask me where I was. It was very dark and even colder than it was late. There were no clocks or steaming cups of hot chocolate. I'd been plucked from my bed on a warm summer night, and although I'd been wearing a soft cotton nightgown, it was nowhere to be found. My nudity unnerved me at first but in the context of the Milky Way and life beyond Earth, I got over it. After being moved several times, from one craft to another area, I settled in, as would a proper guest come to visit, and eventually we "talked" for a long time, the ETs and I, but not with our mouths. It just goes to show you that what they teach you in high school is so outdated. There I was having a perfectly nice conversation with foreigners, and I never needed to fall back on my foreign language requirement, because telepathy doesn't require knowing either German or Spanish.

There was an emotional transition made somewhere in which my fright left me—as I might imagine that all my friends might be less fearful after reading this story—but there I was as intrigued as you please, gazing in wonder at their strange gray skin. It was like that of a dolphin's, both in color and texture, and perhaps this commonality that they shared with such peaceful creatures of the sea helped me to reconsider them. I was trying to be brave as I sat having my encounter in the nude, and I reasoned that it was not so impolite of them, as they weren't wearing any clothes either. There was no Star Trek suit or special weapons belt, and I surmised that it seemed proper enough, since you wouldn't see a dolphin show up in a Hawaiian shirt and trousers. Except that they were not animals, I knew that. Their language was directed cleanly into my mind and I could "hear" them with precision. And for another thing, in so many ways they seemed very much like you'd imagine any other sentient being. I marveled that I could understand them. Imagine that, I thought, having never taken a workshop on telepathy. I would have made Henry Kissinger proud, the way I stepped up to the plate so quickly, and bantered like a United Nations delegate.

Then the voice of reason—and the entire UFO community— came crashing into my consciousness and I glanced suspiciously around for an operating room or kitchen, wondering if I'd end up either as an experiment or as pot roast. But I soon forgot about

*modesty and recipes, and before you could say "ET go home,"
complete understanding burst into my awareness. We are family. I
felt it, and I next understood that within the context of a universal neighborhood, I was visiting their home, and it was high time
that we began to see more of each other.*

*This is the juncture where ufologists and others would state
that brainwashing had no doubt taken effect. In other words, if
fright gives way to an understanding of mutual connectedness, and
if thoughts of fear, judgment, and suspicion transform to sublime
peace and awe at beholding kinship with another, then I've been
messed with. That's okay. Such ufologists might need a workshop
of their own in making practical the ideas of spirituality and universal one-ness. I don't know what types of seminars they've been
going to lately, but in the personal growth arena in the last thirty
years, love, acceptance, and non-judgment are not considered to be
states induced by brainwashing. It's suggested that this is the natural state of things. We're only taught by our culture to be aggres-
sive, to hate each other, and to think the worst of others, especially
if they're different from us.*

*Now before you argue that there are similarities between some-
one who has been kidnapped and brainwashed—like Patty Hearst
for example—and me, I might add that no one is convincing me to
rob a bank, take up an Uzi, kill anyone, or even spread unkind gossip. So what result has brainwashing induced? A feeling of fellow-
ship and camaraderie? A sense of wonder and connection with
other foreign beings from "native" tribes? Then the Red Cross and
United Way are brainwashed too, and ought to recognize their
naiveté and stop spreading messages of brotherly love right now.
Would closer examination reveal that theirs is the kind of message
that could really destroy you? Love your brother, help your neighbor, and cease your judgments and feelings of superiority. Boy,
that's dangerous!*

*In short, during that encounter, I felt deeply honored at meet-
ing intelligent beings from far away, and the end result was that I
didn't care how different they were from me in appearance or cus-
tom. I felt a degree of camaraderie that I hadn't felt in years. It was
a unique field trip, not to the backwoods of the Ozarks, or the*

islands of New Guinea, but to the outback—the way outback— beyond our planet and even farther. After my initial surprise wore off, I did eventually get around to asking some pertinent questions.

Who are you? What is your name and where are you from?

Our name, the name of our group, is spelled and sounds much like your word, "sphinx," but this is only one of the words that you might label us with, just as others may refer to you this time around as a woman, mother, experiencer, Caucasian, American, earthling, etc. There is not just one of us here; there is a group of us. Where we are located is outside of your "jurisdiction," as you would say. We live in a place that is neither here nor there, for we jet from one galaxy to another. We communicate with you right now, not from a physical planet. At this moment, we are on a large craft resembling an entire neighborhood in size. And yet, if you are asking us about our original planet, we will tell you that it no longer exists—but then we are speaking of many thousands of years ago. That planet we destroyed, which propelled us to an understanding that we might want to awaken if we wanted to continue and further our species, and so we did. The name of that planet was Pluterous, but it no longer exists.

Pluterous was located outside of your solar system, and we had developed it into a state of technology similar to your own, in which our technological ability far exceeded our spiritual development. Through accidental mutations of certain technology, we literally blew ourselves asunder. At the time, we had the capability to travel intergalactically, and we did. We have moved from place to place as a group family, and we have lived on other physical planets, including, at times planets in close proximity to your own. Now you understand why we mentor you. You could say that God has sent us to you, like angels in a sense, to watch over you.

We do not carry weaponry. We carry only substantial technological apparatus that enables us to come and go as we please and facilitate all manner of physical healings with certain members of your species.

We first initiated contact with you many years ago. When we say "you," we mean your group there on the planet, and through trial and error somewhat, we have narrowed down our contact to a few hundred thousand of you. There are many other groups who have contact with many others of you. This contact ranges from full face-to-face encounters, such as the type that you experienced, as well as those to whom we come while they are in altered states of consciousness through meditation or during sleep. You personally will know us as we communicate, because you also feel a very strong energy, which seems to settle over you, while you are receiving.

Our world is grossly under-populated from where you stand, and yet we have a comfortable ratio of beings to our resources, even though those resources are on a vast ship. When we dictate like this through you, we do so as a result of eons of intention between your lineage and ours. We don't pretend that you and your kind feel no resistance at all to us, coming through like this. We understand that you may feel some resistance. When we speak to you, we speak of worlds that are far different from yours, worlds that tear asunder your entrenched ideas of how life must be. To be travelers like we are is akin to your older citizens who take to the road with their motor homes in order to explore the vastness of your country; and we too in our maturity, although we are not in the last years of our life, have taken to the "road" in order to meet neighbors such as you and others, to mentor, and to communicate in order that we too may fulfill our highest destiny.

Atlantis, before you, and our planet before us, are histories of what a species can do to itself when left unchecked. Do not assume that Atlantis was a myth, for many of you were there and experienced first hand the diatribes to which a few industries adhered and proclaimed as gospel. If you believe in the concept of a Holy Grail, you are believing in an idea that says there is always hope. Does it seem hopeless to point you in the direction to which we have been pointing you? When we speak of laying down your sword and feeling brotherly love, does this seem unrealistic? We tell you this: the more unrealistic it seems, the closer you are, potentially, to giving it a full examination. The reason for this is that you are running out of different ideas, different avenues, individually and culturally, and this is when one does come upon an enlightened path and step onto that path and find your way home.

When God bestowed upon us the ability to reach other nations in other galaxies, as we are doing here, we rose to the occasion and took our mentorship quite seriously, in that we are overjoyed to communicate with you and also to lend a hand in whatever way we can.

Our Connection to You

It is a naturally occurring phenomenon to reach out and love those who are close to us and with whom we are one. This is the reason behind our contact with you. We cannot experience our oneness without including you. As so little is known about us, we make this contact with you now in this way, so that more of you can hear from us. There is much contact going on with many of you. And yet what is unique in this case is that we would like to disseminate this information more broadly. As you receive invitations from family members and dear friends to break bread together, and to enjoy one another, you have an understanding that your mutual love and compassion brings you together and keeps you together, even though, at times, great distance separates you. There is a connection between us that has been established and get-togethers are a natural part of families, are they not?

We are beginning to suggest to you through the latest communications through others and here, that we are your family. Some of you have a hard time believing this because there has been so much media exposure about how we have bothered you. So in many cases, we come to this experience with your minds already turned against us, but that is okay. As with any prejudice, we are willing to continue to love you despite your preconceived notions about us. We are enlightened and not offended by your lack of wholeness in your perspective. We delight in knowing you and in being able to conduct communications with you. We yearn for the same opportunities that you yearn for. We yearn to have a solid connection in place for our mutual collaboration and communication, just as you seek out those friends and family who bring you to a sense of connection to your lineage.

We have a connection with you. Come picnic with us. Come break bread and we will share our bounty with you—encouragement and an offer of friendship. We have seemed to be such a great mystery and secret to you, and yet these walls between us are crumbling now as the walls between East Germany and West have fallen. There was a time when many of you could not ever imagine such a crumbling of that divided country. But that is only the beginning. We would like to engage with you emotionally, so that you may know who we are and understand that we have no harm in mind for you.

We have the highest ideas about our relationship together. Can you allow your mind to rest momentarily, and put aside the cries of warning from others concerned about your safety? Do their cries ring true with your awakened ideas of spirituality and oneness? Are their ideas of mistrust and suspicion consistent with what the masters have taught? When we can all come together and see the Divinity in one another, no matter how imperfect, only then do we approach enlightenment. We do understand that it is merely fear that captures the imagination of our most outspoken critics. It does take bravery to pierce through the veil of prejudice, and this is no exception.

If you are spiritually ready to embrace the idea that we are all one, then come with us as we show you the magic of our universal connection. You will know the tree by its fruit. Respond in this way to one who warns you of your impending victimization by us. Listen to our words and notice that we choose for you your highest path, according to the highest part of you, not another. Does another who sells opinions to you ever ask and invite you to look into your heart and your soul, and to come to your own conclusion about us? This is a wonderful test when you are attempting to determine the type of tree, for you can tell the tree by its fruit. Come and taste of our words. Come and hear our ideas and you may soon discover that your soul remembers us.

Gravitate now toward your yearning for connection with us. Learn of the unthinkable, as deemed by some members of your culture. Limit yourself no longer. Bring yourself to an understanding of what lies beyond your cities. Let myths no longer be perpetuated, and instead believe that we are connected deeply. Was it your thinking that you would grow spiritually and yet continue to feel split off from your universal counterparts? Those of you who are asking about us will find our response.

Clearly there is something going on. As more and more of you see signs of our visitations there, as more of you are awakening to the limitlessness of the universe, you make an invitation possible by this willingness to loosen your limited thinking. Open-mindedness is everything when it comes to experiencing other realms. Would you like to know us? We do not begrudge those of you who warn others about us; as we said, we are not the only ones who have experienced prejudice, and we understand deeply how fear motivates this thinking.

When you consider that many of you have had face-to-face encounters and that no harm has befallen you, you begin to understand the expansiveness of true potentiality. If "abductions" are really kidnappings, why are experiencers returned to their homes? Many of your children already know us, but dare say nothing, for they know immediately what response they would be met with; and so they enjoy the camaraderie, but say nothing in order to refrain from risking a fearful adult's reproach.

Listen to the wind in the trees, and you may hear us. Watch the night sky, and you may very well see us. For we come from afar to relate to you on a more and more individual basis as you call these experiences to you. You can count yourself among the many, many of you who know our kind personally.

We Come In Peace

With regard to our choice to not arm ourselves in space, you must first understand, in order to comprehend our position, where we are in our own spiritual evolution and development. We recognize fully that we cause our own experience. If we are enlightened beings and we own wholeheartedly that all of our experience is called to us by us, then for what reason would we arm ourselves? At this juncture we are not conflicted in our creations, that is to say we are not creating at one level and creating something different at another level of consciousness. We are integrated. We are united in thought, word, and deed. We are a unified whole, literally. And so we would no more slay an attacker than we would be an attacker.

This is difficult for you to understand, for you live within an ideology in which you are so used to seeing yourselves at battle with someone else, whether it's your next door neighbor, your mother-in-law, your ex-wife, your ex-countryman—or even us—that you cannot imagine being at war with no one. We are at peace with ourselves and others. We have no reason to cause ourselves to be armed, for we are armed with our own causation. In other words, we take full responsibility for what we are creating and so, should we create adversaries that arrive on our front step, we would first understand that we are in the process of creating that. There would be no surprises. When

16

you are at cause, you manifest from pure intention, and so we have long since lost the desire to protect ourselves from something. There is nothing to protect oneself from. If we were to be confronted with losing our life, we would gladly do so. What is there to fear?

You mean if an adversary approached someone you loved, you would do nothing?

We would do something, but it is not the something that you would do. We would, as would our loved ones, heal the moment as it is occurring. We would send love and resist nothing.

This may be almost impossible for you to understand, and that is okay. But by the same token, we cannot adjust our response to your question simply because you balk at the response. Suppose that there was nothing to protect any more. Suppose you were at peace, and really did see your adversary as part of yourselves, and you took full responsibility for that adversary and that adversary's behavior. It puts your action and response to that other in a whole new light, doesn't it? And so we don't carry weaponry because we no longer utilize those tools. We have outgrown them and the need for them, just as your dentists may outgrow outmoded tools of dentistry and take on more efficient means of producing the same outcome. We have produced the same effect as you have attempted to produce with your instruments, but we do so, by necessity, without weapons.

We instill peace by noticing how our thoughts create peace. We ensure harmony with ourselves and others by noticing that we are fully at cause and through our thoughts, words, and actions, we take responsibility for the peace, or for a state of conflict, that we have created. But then if we should create conflict, we do not then call it bad and attempt to disown it, pretending that we had nothing to do with it. That is insane. If your left hand slaps your right hand and your right hand then demands that the left hand be cut off, how then is the whole affected? Does that not, too, affect the right hand, having then no left? And so your question is understandable, given your present context.

There is nothing to protect, and even if there were, weapons could not protect it. Safety or lack thereof is an illusion. You are all inherently safe. An environment where peace reigns is created by the

17

inhabitants of that environment. If two inhabitants out of a group of one hundred attempt to create peace, but the other ninety-eight are war driven, those two are in a place of deep spiritual challenge, we would agree. Do you think that those two have not called that precise challenge to themselves? Perhaps once they were part of the majority that precipitated hostilities, and so a greater perspective is needed, and they may have called themselves to that minority position in which to always remember how precious peace is.

Having had our experiences with "losing" our planetary home as a result of our own aggressions, we find peacefulness is a coveted state of being. By the way, we travel about not as nomads, but as scholars. We give the example of your senior citizens to show that in one's maturity there can also be a greater sense of awe at one's surroundings, as exhibited by much of your elderly, in which they recognize that perhaps they have fewer years left then have come to pass. And with this same deep appreciation for our galactic surroundings, we have undertaken a scholarly mission. We are not just simply tourists. We are universal anthropologists, and we have a great understanding of civilizations near and far; and so we come to you having this deep understanding of other species and a deep appreciation for where you are in your evolutionary cycle.

You might consider us a group of Margaret Meads extraordinaire. We are not homeless as a matter of victimization; we are actually beyond demanding that one tiny pinprick of a location is our home. We are evolved to the point that we understand that the space in which we stand is our beloved home. Our family is all of our brethren, including you.

When we come to a place where we recognize that there is nothing to protect—there is nothing so sacred that requires destroying another—there is a tremendous freedom in this. Can you imagine all of you simply one day laying down your weapons and taking them up no longer? There is an incredible understanding that says that nothing anymore belongs to you and only you, or is worth protecting. Your safety is guaranteed, for you are one of God's children and owners and inheritors of the universe. And so how can this possibly be taken from you?

Yes, we are adept at making these ideas practical, which is why we are encouraging this communication, so that you can begin to ponder the implications of living in such a way, for it is your next step, believe it or not. Did you think that you would evolve over eons and still be carrying weapons around in space? Are you thinking that we have burglar alarms upon our flying craft? This is our universe as much as it is yours. And if someone would insist on taking our craft from us, before they could take it, we would cause them to have it. For we would simply need to consider how it was that they had been created in our reality. Granted, these are advanced ideas, to your way of thinking, but it is our truth, and we live that truth every day.

We are one group of scholars who travel and study, yet there are many other groups as well who have taken up observation of your species. Most of those groups are benevolent, and we are familiar with many of them, for we have even studied them. We observers could almost be referred to as a crowd, with respect to the attention that is being given to you on your planet. There are many reasons for this, many of them obvious, such as noticing that you are at a critical juncture in your evolution, and it is a marvel to remember that moment in our own histories, in which we too made the conscious choice to evolve or to devolve. And this is a great observation, to also be a part of history on your planet, to help where we can, just as you send groups to the most impoverished areas of your planet, whether to build houses or to provide medical supplies. There is a deep satisfaction in seeing a group of you rise from spiritual poverty, despair, and sickness. And you can understand that, even in your own present state of evolution, this is still an important and revered way for many of you to spend your time and resources—helping those who are less endowed. What makes you think that that quality ceases to exist elsewhere? You are our children of Tijuana. Our efforts are our "Concert for Bangladesh." You are the reason for our airlifting of medical supplies to the outback. It is an honor to serve you in any way that we can.

There are other groups who have different appearances, and many with similar appearances to us, who have as much to do with you as we have. There are some striking similarities. There are far fewer "kidnappers" in the galaxy than you might imagine. When you consider how many of you in your neighborhoods watch over each other's homes, children, pets, and even front lawns, the "deviant" is the rare exception. Most of you on the planet there, the masses of you, would help in any way you could, given the opportunity. And this ratio is duplicated in the universe as a whole. There are very few "deviants," considering the overall population of all that is.

And just as your one assailant causes the majority of the reason for the morning news, when 99.9 percent of the world has undergone a peaceful evening and did not make the news, so it is with your relations with one potential deviant in the universe. That is the story that makes the Hollywood release or the television show. That is an incredible minority of all experiences and all contact. And yet that is what you focus upon. For right now, that is your way of the media, but that will change soon.

And so, yes, there are other groups who are in concert with you and who mentor you as well. We are anthropologists who have dedicated our lives to the studying of species. If we were caused to give up our life, we certainly would for we have no fear of transitioning. Nor should you.

The sun always comes up.

Why We Are Here

When we have contact with you, we do not do so as a result of fear that you might not be around tomorrow. We contact you because you and we are from the same universal family. It is a natural state of affairs for families to know one another, is it not? We have long awaited more and more of your developing awareness, so that you might become aware of us. There is more than one way in which to do this. You may argue that if we would simply bring our ships into your backyard, then you would know us. But awareness means being able to consider more than one avenue of expression regarding communicating with us.

We have come to your people to attempt to provide a format for ongoing discussions in which we can introduce ourselves. When you doubt that we are able to communicate with you like this, you simply hold your old ideas in place, which is fine with us. We have no need for you to evolve more quickly than is comfortable for you. We too had this luxury; we too evolved at our own pace, but it is interesting that so many of you, because you are not ready for contact yourself, then doubt others who are ready, and are indeed having contact. This cultural denial explains why we are not more accessible on a wider scale.

In the "past," we also have had contact with some of your so-called black groups—that name being given to groups associated with your government who do not hold themselves accountable to anyone, and therefore there is no accountability to the people. We see the budding angel behind each seeming sleepwalker, and so we do not assume that certain people are not worthy of our communication. Some are ready for our communications, and yet may not have the consciousness to be motivated by thoughts of healing the planet, for the fear is too extreme. There is a genuine idea amongst them that, should the status quo be shaken, their very lives would be in danger, along with their livelihood. We don't even judge them, as you do, for we see aspects of denial in each of you; some simply have them to a greater degree.

We do not currently have contact with that segment of the population, for we have no need to. We are here on a mentoring mission, and the people involved with your cover-ups, for right now, are opposed to this option. Those beings who do entwine with certain groups of your government also share the same level of consciousness. They have attracted one to the other, but just as your neighbor who robs a bank does not necessarily represent you simply because you live on the same street, other beings do not represent us simply because they live as we do, outside your galaxy.

However, as the masters have asked you to do, approach the bank robber or the "deviant," and send them your blessings and your love. Are they not precisely the ones who need your love and forgiveness? These beings, both human and extraterrestrial, fear lack of identity and seek to connect unconsciously with a species that reminds them of themselves. They connect in this way, although they do so unwittingly and do not recognize that they are asleep. That is the characteristic of sleepwalking. If there were consciousness, one would be awakened.

Our groups here, and there are several of them, wish to communicate that there is no reason to contribute to a further sense of victimization by suggesting that there is anything to fear from any species, anywhere. Simply remind yourself that fear is not who you are, and should you feel fear, acknowledge it and bring yourself to a place where you feel God. Like does attract like, and so if you hold fear and paranoia as your primary thoughts and feelings, you will attract, not repel, a like vibration.

You have not traditionally seen us or considered us to be an enlightened species but that is due to your own limitations. Do you want to individually choose to shift to a greater relationship and a better quality of communications?

Why don't you just involve me in more face-to-face physical encounters like you did years ago?

During this embodiment, you have chosen to be fully immersed within the human visage in order to accomplish your stated life's work. This decision requires you to operate within the illusion of your own realm, in order to call to yourself all the challenges and opportunities of that realm. Too much exposure outside of your illusion would render you less effective in relating fully to that of a human. And this has been your choice this time, to embody, and therefore embrace, all of the challenges and opportunities relative to humanity at this time and in this place.

In addition, it is not easier for you when we come there frequently and speak with you and others face-to-face, for when we do, we are limited by your emotional reaction to our different countenance. And so our communications would be lost for some time, while you process the experience in seeing us before you. Experiencers themselves can attest to this, as can you, for it sometimes takes years to develop the countenance to withstand public pressure about the meaning of one's encounters and to then come to some peaceful resolution about them. This kind of communication allows us to connect without jarring the psychology of the human, although we have in fact jarred the psychology of *this* human, and you have now healed from that. But even that "trauma" has been part of your chosen past. However, this process, in this way, you have called to yourself, since through this communicating, there is a great deal of physical and spiritual benefit. This benefit is what your soul is seeking, among other things. When we communicate through you, notice the waves of energy that come. These are the electromagnetic frequencies that touch you and help you to touch us.

We can feel you at any moment of the day or night. We know what you think and we know how you feel, and we know what the greatest of your soul's desire is, because all this information is readily available to everyone, everywhere. All we need do is simply pluck it from the universal consciousness, and it is there for the taking. And yet we do not abuse one another with this information. We use it only to "catch up," as you would say, when we have not seen our loved ones for some time; for example, we can simply tap into the universal knowledge, and we know the status of a loved one. But most important, we are connected to you through all of these different ways constantly. If this is not a demonstration of how we are all one, we don't know what is.

When we play the instrument of your physiology by utilizing your energy and frequency, and when you allow us to come through like this, we have set up a grand experience in which we demonstrate that you and we are one. Simply ask any channeler, and they will tell you what a glorious experience it is, because one's Divinity is not easily forgotten. Otherworldly phenomena and related experiences bring the experiencer home over and over, to a place where one remembers that all is possible. Do not mind that it has taken some time, although not too much time, for you to emotionally adjust to this process. You have had to work on issues of confidence, and we understand.

The Real Meaning of Contact

The free flowing of ideas from us to you is the first step in utilizing all that we know, and is how your species can benefit from our relationship and the furthering of our intern relationship; because we don't have any preconceived ideas as to the nature of how you might best utilize the information that we provide. We come to you with an open heart, not with a vested interest in how you must benefit from knowing us. Recognize that it is important to not be insistent that you respond in any particular way, and this alone keeps our relationship clean. We concur with some UFO investigators, in that we do have a vested interest in some areas of your evolution; however, that is a guaranteed outcome. Species evolve after a length of time—and yours will too. It is just a matter of whether you will do so here and now or at some other point in the planet's history. Do you see how we are completely patient? It does not have to be now that you awaken, although we would thoroughly enjoy your awakening, because that would enable us to immediately benefit from the dialogue together; and also there is a richness in the communion of family, but it is not a necessity. Of course we benefit in your evolution, inasmuch as to the degree that you are joyful and at peace, we are joyful for that. We are delighted for you.

When we first came through you as a conduit, we did not know if you would be willing to simply allow the words to come as they do, not knowing where this communication is going; and yet by your willingness to allow these words to come through, we are working with your throat center more and more every day to bring more and more concepts and ideas. Don't be discouraged because the voice of us is not as loud as it would be through a megaphone; you're improving constantly and readying your mind, body, and spirit for a more complex relationship with us. By this we mean that you are preparing yourself even as you prepare others who are reading this. To expand your thinking and include the processing of ideas from beyond—this is an example of how one might evolve simply by being willing to move from the routine and consider new ideas. In your case, by exposing yourself to electromagnetic frequencies, you change your very physiology for the better. Congratulations. It is a challenge and a journey, but one that you will find rewarding on several levels.

As you continue this process, be willing to allow others their response to this. We do not believe that one soul helped is too few, and so be willing to help even one soul and know the magnificence of the universe by inviting her to consider that we exist, and therefore others exist too. As you deepen your ability and understanding of this process, you will deepen and broaden our communications. We emphasize that you will see great rewards with the transformation of your own being, simply as a result of the very process of communicating itself.

Brush away the last remaining cobwebs of your doubt about your own ability and the ability of others to grasp the material in whatever way best suits them and their souls. We are not invested in the outcome, nor should you be. Simply be a vessel for the communication and allow for life to unfold.

Do not be alarmed that we have come to you in a manner that seems to have no investment in the way that your species responds to or accepts us. Our gift is the offering of friendship. Your gift is the freedom to choose any way in which you as a group would like to respond, if at all. Of course your returned love is an added benefit and would be deeply satisfying to us, but it is not a requirement, and there is still great benefit in simply providing this communication as one more option. Through books and discourse, ideas can be presented to you all, and those of you who resonate with it will find it; those of you who cannot or do not resonate, will not find it.

When one day we visit your home for all to see at the dawn of your awakening, you will look back and notice that these and other communications of this type were the predecessor to global contact. When you ask us for that date, we withhold that information by necessity, since it is not set in stone. You, for example, are scheduled to be at work this morning. It is a probable outcome. But should you change your mind at the last minute, you will not arrive there, although you will eventually arrive, but perhaps by the most circuitous route. And again we remind you that in many cases we *are* landing there, through our demonstration with your crop circles and with contact with other experiencers. We just have not done so publicly, with cameras on us, at least not on a general scale. There have been plenty of sightings of our crafts. What more proof do you need? There are thousands of photographs circulating in books, through clubs, on the Internet. Consider how it is that we are able to readily contact you through these communications. When you suspend your ideas that contact with us must look one particular way, you open yourself up to allowing life to unfold as life would like to, instead of insisting that contact with us initially must look only one way. Be willing to notice that sometimes the process of evolution takes a route that is different from what you might demand or expect, but this does not mean that there is no value, nor does it mean that we will not all get to where we are wanting to go.

Beneath the veil of denial of many of you is a deep soul-longing to embrace us and to remember our connection. Just as the little child begins to crawl and yearns to walk, this yearning is not necessarily conscious. The child is just compelled by the soul's desire, and so it is with you collectively. You may not think that you demonstrate collectively a willingness to adopt a relationship with us, but we know differently. It might be helpful to consider who we are and why we commune as we do, than to dismiss it outright as impossible. Then, the knowing of us would be aligning you closer with the soul's desire.

CHAPTER 3

But Is It Fun!

There are some things that were never meant to go together. Like Martha Stewart in a messy, overcrowded bachelor pad; or a redhead without sunscreen joining a Bedouin tribe; or Donald Trump applying for food stamps. For whatever reason, certain things just don't seem to mix well. When you try to force them, you often get a questionable outcome, a mixed bag, or just a plain weird result. At the very least, you're left scratching your head, wondering, "What's that about?"

Take for instance the human memory as it applies to extraterrestrial encounter phenomena. The two seem to be in a constant juxtaposition. You've seen enough movies and read enough books on the subject to know what I'm talking about. My encounter experiences have been no exception. On the one hand, I've captured fabulous detail about "the Group" in the recesses of my memory, and lived to tell about it. On the other hand, some incredible phenomena, too obvious, or certainly too important, to miss or forget, I can't recall for my life. Hypnosis is helpful at times, but not at others.

During one particularly vivid encounter, I was placed in a small, open flying craft, which moved me from one area to anoth-

er. Although I couldn't move my body at all—lest I jump out I'm certain—I'm one hundred percent sure of what I was thinking at the time. Looking up above me, and down below, I took it all in with my eyes with an intention to transcribe it all later. Federal Express doesn't offer an overnight package fast enough to deliver the account of that evening, which I intended to send to National Geographic just as soon as I returned home. Even while my heart continued to go thumpity-thump, I was no idiot. I knew a journalistic opportunity when I saw one. This was going to make the cover of the New York Times.

Okay, so I really didn't expect anyone to believe it, but I certainly expected to bring the images with me into old age, to have something to tell the grandkids by the fireplace. But noooooooo. I can remember the extraterrestrials' skin, the little badge that one of them had on his chest, a few snatches of telepathic conversation, some sheep that hung from the "rafters" in the distance, and a few bell jars containing fetuses, but that's it! What the heck's going on here? As I was returned to my bed that night, my memory of the encounter faded away as fast as my hopes for a Pulitzer Prize.

Either way, memory or not, it's a nightmare, because you can remember snippets of one thing, but not another. Talk about a reality check for Alzheimer's. What you do remember is never enough, and the fragments haunt you like the plague since no one believes it anyway, and you're left exasperated, like being offered just one spoonful of strawberry Haagen Daz with nothing else to quench your craving. It's enough to make you admit yourself to a mental hospital. Actually, been there, done that. That's no help either. . . .

Now, I know what you're thinking. "Just ask them!" you insist.

Let's get something straight between us. Do you have any idea how many questions there are left to ask? I no sooner find a free hour between carpooling a teenager and walking the dog, when I steal away to a quiet chamber and ask question number 274 from a handwritten list that's as long as my VW Jetta. I capture it all on a tape recorder, then find another few hours between the grocery store and getting my brakes fixed to transcribe the whole thing. Then it's time to be back at work and schedule an eye exam, during my lunch break, to increase my contact prescription. Are you getting the picture? No sooner have I submitted another wonderful question and answer to Bob Friedman for this book, when he's asking, "But why didn't you ask them such-and-such?" I'm doing my best here. And in many ways, the ET's answer, in part, to this question is found in the previous chapter. We're all subconsciously blocking, so scared of what we're going to see and how we'll process that into our daily lives, that there's probably two things going on: the mind goes on overload and conveniently "forgets" some parts of the encounter to help prevent reconciling what we're seeing; and the ETs themselves place some type of hypnotic suggestion that the memories trickle out a little bit at a time, so as not to overload the mental circuits. In other words, there's so much darn ridicule going on with this phenomena in our culture that the intellect refuses to cooperate and steps in where it must.

At least my intellect has. You cannot imagine how difficult this process has been for me. In truth, just between us, it's really not simply an issue of finding the time to sit down with a tape recorder and communicate with them. I admit it, I'm conflicted. There's still a part of me that doesn't want to make any mistakes or to do it wrong, or be ridiculed—like I've picked a profession where that's gonna stop. But the other part of me is brave and loves myself for at least trying. The bottom line is that mine can be a hostile audience, and I'm still working on issues of feeling like an outcast. Gee, but that internal struggle couldn't have anything to do with my not retaining full memories, could it?

If you have any doubt that there's lack of cultural support out there should you offer full details of an encounter, just try a little experiment. Get together with a panel of your family members; throw in your co-workers, your accountant—and be sure the in-laws are there for good measure. Schedule it during the holidays when everyone's emotional and exhausted, and tell them you have an announcement. After you spill the beans with all the glorious details of the encounter you've just had with your ET friends, look at their grim expressions. You know that there's going to be an awkward silence that rivals the time a friend of mine told her family that she was scheduled for a sex change operation.

Now, in the midst of all that admiration and genuine respect, do you feel good about yourself and all your wonderful memories? Come on, you hardly just announced that you graduated from Harvard cum laude. If you're recently engaged, I hope you're not too attached to your beloved.

In any case, there's no lack of questions to ask the extraterrestrials and I suppose this is as good a reason as any for a sequel. But since one of the images that many experiencers do remember ever so clearly is the extraterrestrials' signature eyeballs, let's find out about their trademark, unforgettable, huge black shiny peepers. I asked them this question a few months ago, and you can see how we seemed to get off track a little.

I've seen you and other extraterrestrials in person many times, particularly in 1992 during one significant encounter. I have so many questions as a result of that evening. Let's start with the easiest question. How does your gray skin suit your adaptability to your environment?

Our skin, as you refer to it, is balanced between something like a skin and a hide, to enable us to withstand freezing temperatures. Our skin is quite resilient to habitual—if you will—"time zone changes," which facilitates our coming and going through multi-dimensional, and other, travel. It is quite resilient and has evolved over time. The color, yes, like that of one of your dolphins, has helped to prevent damage from various sources and tends to absorb ultraviolet and other rays through a process much like photosynthesis in your plants. We have a heightened sensitivity to light, and yet our skin or outer covering facilitates a better protection than does yours.

During that same encounter, one of your associates, comrades, flight crew, whatever, had some kind of badge or nametag or something on the left side of his chest. He didn't appear to be wearing any clothes.

The badge that you saw represented his place in relation to our ranking of airmen. You observed a proud moment for him when he was witness to your being brought to this area.

But not everybody had one of those badges?

That is right. A newly designated airman is identified much as your newly trained drivers are identified in some areas, so that other drivers know that there is some level of inexperience to the driver next to them. It is much the same process that allows those of more experience to keep an eye out, so to speak, for a less experienced comrade.

You mentioned photosynthesis. Is this the only way you receive nourishment, from sources of light, and does that include the sun, or do you ingest anything else?

We don't like to ingest substances through the mouth, although we are able to, much as you may not prefer to receive sustenance through your vein, but you can, if you are hospitalized. Preferably, a light source, such as a sun, not necessarily the sun that you know of, provides ample nourishment for our growth and sustenance.

What about water? You don't drink water? You don't get thirsty?

We rarely require liquids in the manner that you require them. We absorb what we need through our skin, much like some of your animals.

Can you tell me about your eyes?

Our eyes are one of our greatest sense organs, for we not only take in some nutrition through our eyes, but also absorb impulses almost like the process of biofeedback—but resonate this through our eyes. The larger surface area prevents overuse, so to speak, and allows for a transfer of data from many sources, including general knowledge, nutritional requirements, and pleasurable sensations, the way your ears would bring pleasure to you while listening to beautiful music. Those types of pleasurable sensations would be, for us, more of a feeling of connecting through an energetic communication, where our energies are exchanged. We utilize our eyes for multiple functions. Not only do we, of course, use them for vision, but our eyes also act as radar.

Is it always dark where you travel; are your eyes like a cat's eyes that allow it to see in the dark?

We are able to have excellent sight in the dark, but that does not fully explain the large size of our eyes. Predominantly, our eyes are a multiple sense hub where myriad tasks are going on all at the same time.

Why don't you have hair anywhere on your body?

Hair will eventually go out of "fashion" with you, too, although it has provided your species with a covering for warmth and protection against the sun and as a screen to cover openings. In our case, the requirement for hair disappeared when our species gave up the need for identification, and you might find it strange to hear that hair is no longer needed.

Excuse me for a minute, but I may need to stop for a break. I can't be certain that I'm "hearing" you correctly. This whole communication is very subtle and it leaves a huge margin for self-doubt. I don't want to mislead anybody because I'm not even sure if I'm hearing you correctly.

To have had waking encounters with us has been possible only as a result of your basic courageous nature, and after you strengthened yourself emotionally, our contacts with you resumed, even though there have been gaps in those face-to-face encounters. Much of the last fourteen years has been peppered by instances of your pinching yourself, because many of your experiences have not been shared by anyone that you know. This is the emptiness that you feel often. You feel as though you are alone within your own emotional reaction to these contacts and communications. There is no need to feel alone in this work. We have been with you for your whole life.

But this transmission is so quiet. There's so much room for error. I'm not sure that I can do it. Especially when I'm asking you the question, "Why do you have the eyes that you have?" I almost can't hear you. I so don't want to get it wrong. At times, it feels as though if I blink my eye I can't hear you, so then how can I be so egocentric as to think that perhaps I can hear you clearly enough to represent you to others? Perhaps I have a . . . I am seriously considering if I'm having delusions of grandeur here. What makes me think that I can do this?

If not you, who?

Well, maybe we should wait for the evolution of our species until the time—in ten or twenty years—when you just fly out here, and you can sit across from me and I'll interview you. How's that?

That won't happen unless someone like you involves himself or herself in a process such as this.

Why is that?

Because work like this serves as an introduction. It would be too jarring to just show up there. You know that. Work like this, which you are doing, is making our entrance possible in the long run.

And you don't think that I should consider that I'm having delusions of grandeur?

To have an ability to articulate these communications is not a delusion but an empowerment. Many people create for themselves very grand opportunities for self-statement, and you don't have to feel guilty for calling this opportunity to yourself.

I don't think I feel guilty.

You feel unworthy.

I feel incompetent. I feel unable to do this, because at times I can't hear you loud enough. It was during our communication that you were talking about your eyes and I suddenly wanted to stop because the reality of what I'm doing just hit me very strongly. I think that's the reason why I've somewhat avoided starting into other questions. I keep blaming it on you, but it was me. The responsibility feels overwhelming. Even if I give this to nobody else, I don't even want to delude myself; can you understand that? I just don't want to delude myself, either.

If you want to be true to yourself, then love yourself enough to recognize your special place in the world.

I don't want to lead—I mean mislead—anyone else and I don't want to mislead myself.

Yes, you can replay the tape recorder to see if you really made that "Freudian slip." And there you have it, if you want to drive to the heart of the matter. You just said it yourself. You don't want to lead anybody else. You're frightened to lead.

I don't see myself as being afraid to lead.

You cannot help but lead because of the ideas that you express and the ideas you have as a result of your encounters and the personality you bring. You cannot help but lead, but you have not gotten in touch with the discomfort you feel in doing so.

I've just felt that that discomfort was because I don't want to mislead anybody.

When will you take your rightful stance and lead the way to this material?

I only want to do it if there's certainty that I'm not providing nonsense to people, that I'm not passing on wrong information; if that is so, then I have no desire to participate in this.

You keep confusing the order. Your ability will follow your confidence, not the other way around. You keep thinking you'll have more confidence when you ascertain if the material is perfect.

Okay, whatever. Let's change the subject. So do you fall in love? I really want to know that, because, if you, as enlightened beings, can't fall in love then what's the point?

Yes, we love deeply but not jealously, possessively like you do— meaning like all of you do. We enjoy deep bonds with one another. You know, you are capable of achieving deep bonds with others.

Fortunately, you are clearing up some personal issues that were inevitable before you proceed much further with this. You can look now at your own issues about leading on a grander scale. You have created an amazing opportunity for yourself, in bringing forth some ideas that are very healing to a population that is also very conflicted about the idea of sharing the universe with other beings. And in you they have a spokesperson who can finally offer some ideas about what it's like to have neighbors and, in some ways, you are showing by your example that it's safe to go next door and borrow a cup of sugar, and that you can come back in one piece to talk about it. There's so much fear on your planet that other inhabitants of the universe are somehow going to hurt you or harm you or are out to get you, promulgated, of course, by your media and some UFO investigators. This is an opportunity for you to offer a new way to look at us, more important, a different way to *feel* about us. You are making *real* for people the idea that we are no longer a concept that needs to be relegated to fantasy, that we are real, that our contacts are real. Because of who you are, you can move this out of science fiction and into households that have the same questions that you are asking.

Well, okay, we're in agreement that it's a great idea. I'm not really sure that I'm arguing that. What we're talking about here is how practical is it for me to sit here on this little spot on this planet with you over there and for me to . . . how practical is it for me to think that I can accurately bring in this information? Based on my experience so far with these communications, it's fun, and it's fine enough when I'm asking certain types of questions that are not for publication. But when I start asking you questions whose answers represent your whole species, I want to be sure that I'm representing you accurately. And it's so subtle. There's no loudspeaker here. It's like feeling a soft feather touch my cheek while I'm fast asleep and then awakening and wondering if I really felt it.

It need be no less fun when you're asking us about us than when you're asking us about you. Can you bring the same playfulness and confidence to those questions? Why do you become so doubtful?

It's about putting on a different hat. Collecting information that will be held to scrutiny and that may never find approval.

But Is It Fun!

We appreciate your vigilance in desiring to represent us as accurately as possible, and that is all that we can ask for. That is why we have chosen you, and you have chosen us, in the first place. Many are called, but few choose themselves in this field, for all of the reasons that you are mentioning, and other reasons that you haven't mentioned. To allow yourself to understand that this is a fallible process will be healing for you. You are doing the best that you are capable of doing. Can anybody fault you for that? Many lawyers wake up in the morning and do the best job of which they are capable. Architects wake up and design and oversee the building of the best project of which they are capable. And you too will do the best job that you can do. Why are you so hard on yourself?

All of a sudden, when I was asking you those questions, I couldn't hear you anymore over the protests of my own mind. I started choking on my own self-consciousness.

Move into a place in which you allow yourself to recognize that this is not a perfect science. For that matter, recounting your conversation with anyone else is not a perfect science. Love is not a perfect science. Bring back your playfulness. Bring back your understanding that you will do the very best that you can, and if anyone faults you for not doing a better job, invite them to try to contact us, and let's see how well they do with this.

That's really funny. I like that one. Okay. But they'd have to go through the whole enchilada. You know, getting snatched from their beds, the whole floating-through-the-air thing; not knowing what's going on, losing the respect of family and friends, and then admitting themselves to a psychiatric hospital.

Now do you feel better?

Yes, when you put it that way. Let somebody else try this. It's so easy to criticize. Somebody else should try this and sit down and dial up Galaxy 847 and look you in the eyes and not have the hairs stand up on their arms . . . sorry, no offense, you know there's a whole lot of stuff that goes along with this. Have you looked in the mirror lately?

35

Your laughter heals you.

I haven't laughed that hard at you yet.

If anyone else out there thinks they can do a better job of contacting extraterrestrials and interviewing them, please raise your hand. Step forward, purchase a tape recorder at Radio Shack, and begin this process. We hereby send this proclamation to the planet Earth, and invite anybody who would like to give this a try. There. You see? No one.

Very funny. Radio Shack's already closed at this hour of the night.

It doesn't have to be perfect. The intention to do well just has to be from your heart. The integrity is there. Your intentions are honorable and so go forth with this, and *we* will even forgive you if you get something wrong. Okay?

You will?

Yes, of course. You've already gotten something wrong.

WHAT? What did I get wrong?

You assumed that our appearance is frightening to others everywhere, but you are speaking for a very tiny segment of the universal population when you refer to humans on Earth. This is simply a prejudice on your part for, believe it or not, certain other species who share your present spiritual development would be equally jarred by the sight of you.

Okay, I guess I was just referring to us low-level consciousness people over here who don't know how to respond to gray skin and no hair.

Yet you find your dolphins loveable.

Yes, but your eyes are ten times larger than theirs. There's something about your ratio of eye space to face size . . . I'm just not quite sure what to do with that. You know I'm playing with you now, right?

Yes, where we come from, these are attributes of great honor, unlike species who have beady little eyes.

Touché and goodnight for now.

Goodnight.

CHAPTER 4

Coming Undone

As many encounter experiencers can attest to, the physical world seems to go all funny when exposed to the energies of otherworldly phenomena. I can only imagine what the physical body must go through, but what has been of great intrigue to me, and has also been exasperating, is the ongoing "stressors" that are seemingly placed upon ordinary household mechanical devices, machines, and apparatus. If you are just beginning your journey with encounter phenomena, do yourself a favor and don't purchase a thing without also buying a warranty to go along with it. Believe me, you'll wish that everything from your toaster to your computer came with a ten-year warranty because you'll go through several of everything a year, once the encounters begin. Shortly after my encounters began, lights flickered as I walked by, the answering machine would replay on its own, and my pooch would sometimes run from me when her hair stood on end. Everything from your treadmill to the motor in your hot tub, all of it is in jeopardy once you enter the realm of the paranormal.

At first, it's cute when car windows go up and down by themselves, or your computer begins printing out messages on its own, choosing from your cache of saved documents to spit you out a sentence or two of something that fits the moment or your current dilemma. But more important, all of your "stuff," no matter how brand new, will come grinding to a halt. Eventually you may grow weary of the breakage. The expense notwithstanding, you would do best to not touch anything that doesn't belong to you. House sitting is not recommended.

In easy-to-understand lingo, can you tell me what the heck is going on? I've gone through more tape recorders than relationships. My household appliances are in an uproar.

We represent a frequency far different from your own, and those frequencies are light years apart, literally and figuratively, and so if you bridge those two frequencies through your encounters or your ongoing communications, you begin to emanate a cloud around you—something like that of the Charles Schulz cartoon, Pigpen, except, of course, your cloud is not from lack of showering, but from an abundance of pulsations that you are "picking up" from our realm. You begin to carry it in your presence.

Bob keeps saying that we should find a way to bottle it and put it to some good use.

Our feelings exactly.

How do you mean that?

In time, you will better harness these frequencies and put them to use, rather than simply turning your appliances into shambles.

What are some of the potential areas?

This seems somewhat obvious—anything that might benefit from heightened electrical pulsations.

Now let's keep this book clean. . . .

We are referring to healings of all kinds.

I remember at the chiropractor's office he used a little machine that sent electrical or whatever sensations into affected areas of the body. So how could I get these pulsations into somebody's body?

You tell us.

Oh boy, this is getting silly.

You'll look back on this particular communication one day and note how this is one of the most important ones you've done because of where you and others can take this if you choose.

Okay, so back to the appliance problem first. It's not just the toaster. It seems to be hot tubs and computers and the floor lamp and the car radio. The list seems endless. My question is, is this my imagination or do other experiencers also cause constant malfunctions like this in the things around them or is this just Taiwan not manufacturing things like it used to?

Don't blame this on Taiwan.

Hold on, I'm laughing pretty hard.

You didn't think that you could laugh while you "channel"?

Well, it wasn't too long ago that I was pretty exasperated during these communications as I learned to "hear" you.

Yes and now you're a lot more playful with this. By the way, this would work for lovemaking too.

Laughing would work in lovemaking?

Being playful and bringing these energies through to your touch.

Oh no, you mean experiencers might start damaging their lovers?

Fortunately, there is not an adverse effect on the human body, as there is on your toaster.

Are you sure about that? Things could get pretty dicey in a person's love life.

Yes, we hope an experiencer's partner would have springs that are wound a little tighter than a toaster's.

Yeah, unlike your garden-variety motherboard. Well seriously now, it wouldn't harm anyone, would it?

Define harm.

You know, HARM, as in OUCH as in causes pain.

No, we are just eliciting your laughter. In truth, these energies are wonderfully healing and—

Wait. I can't find a word in my vocabulary that translates to the word you just sent me. "Sparkly" is the best I can do. So these are healing, "sparkly" energies?

Yes, close enough. They enliven and cause a speeding up of atoms. We do not see a problem, although if you set your intention, you may harness this in a way that will bring pleasure and beneficial effects.

Okay, I'll give that some thought. In the meantime, can you tell me more about my toaster or my tape recorder? I mean, what this represents. Really, what is going on?

Electrical impulses and vibrations that are not suited to products manufactured in your realm will be affected. These effects show up in any number of ways. Their circuitry is either sped up or impacted in such a way that causes the entire mechanism to cease functioning. As far as what you feel throughout your body, static electricity has a sound to it. When you take your clothing out of the dryer and it's stuck together and you separate it, you can actually hear it crackling, can't you? This is what you feel in your scalp and throughout your body. They're just pulsations, surges. It does not have to trouble you, although it can wreak havoc on a tape recorder.

Okay, so does that mean my tape recorder is fried again? And what about my computer? My son's gonna have my hide. This is the third one of his that I've gone through, now that I've made my way through my own. Is it kaput or should I stop using it for forty-eight hours and let it cool down?

Our recommendation is to place it in the refrigerator after use.

Put the Gateway in the fridge? Very funny. I can just picture my roommate coming home from the grocery store and opening the refrigerator door.

Our recommendation is to allow for certain changes to occur with your machines and appliances that you come into contact with.

Or purchase product warranties and return things every twenty-seven days.

Better first read the fine print to see if there's a disclaimer for encounter experiences.

Speaking of encounter experiences, I've found that I've always tended to avoid reading books and articles about UFO abductions. Friends assume that I'm well read on the latest UFO literature, but I find that I seem to resist it. Why?

It appears that you are sensitive to "alien bashing." You are sensitive to this prejudice, like nationalism, when one blindly heeds a cultural belief, no matter the relative truth or falsehood to that belief. In your case, you seem to avoid what we'll refer to as "dimensionalism," a word we can use to describe a fixed standard as to the way a culture insists upon perceiving events associated with certain otherworldly dimensions. You have felt that much of what is written about encounters seems slanted to one particular belief, so you have felt justified in refraining from giving it your attention.

Well how can I be sure that I do have this right, that is, the way I feel about you? I mean, my positive slant and all.

The mind is a wonderful thing to waste when it sabotages you like yours does. Your intellect alone will not, cannot *ever* reconcile these experiences, or how you feel about your experiences. You're asking the mind to do something that it cannot do.

Well then, what am I to do with my mind? I have to take it along with me.

But you don't have to allow it to have the best seat in the house—front and center. And every time it stands up, you can't see where you're going.

How do I get it to take a back seat?

For starters, heal the part of you that assumes that your mind is better informed than your soul. You don't recognize this, yet. You know it some of the time but not all of the time. Secondly, when your mind begins to protest, send it the love as you would a rebellious, but uninformed teenager who knows no other way. What did Jesus say? Forgive them, for they know not what they do . . . so forgive your mind, for it knows not what it does. It doesn't understand that it is attempting to divide you from the path that is of your highest calling. It doesn't understand that it's making turmoil of your ability to fully embrace this process, so forgive it. And once you forgive it, you will see it for what it is. Your mind is a tool that you can use in other areas, but when it attempts to direct this area, you will at some point confidently stand tall and announce that you have another path and that path follows a higher ideal. You will no longer wrestle with your mind for control. You will understand that your power, when it comes from within, need take no stand. Simply put, confidence will generate a new stature within the split-off parts of yourself and you will firmly take the helm of your own vessel, but not by force. It will be a matter of a light bearing truth, and all aspects of the mind will have no choice but to begin to defer to you. Do you have another question?

Let's see. This is kind of becoming fun. What can I ask? Do you have any ideas as to what I should ask you?

Now we've gotta come up with the questions, too?

No, but you're the all-knowing, all-wise, entities, aliens, check-the-one-that-applies, right? I just thought, gee, you're so quick to jump in and offer your two cents, but now that I ask you this, you're all shy.

That may be the first time someone there has referred to us as shy.

Okay, here's a question. Is there any way that I can control my, uh, cloud, my Pigpen cloud or whatever you call it? Because I'm trying to be sensitive to other people's belongings and also, I would like to use these energies in a positive way.

As with everything, play with it. Practice using it. It doesn't take too much imagination to see how one could use these energies to enliven a sore arm, a toaster, or a lover.

God, there's a book title there. "How to Enliven Your Toaster or Your Lover."

The point is that you and others are learning how to hold your own counsel, rather than constantly deferring to the "professionals," or your next door neighbor who purports to have a better take on your own experiences than you do.

Some of you have more inherent tendencies for confidence than others, for many reasons. Take Bob for instance. He has more experience than do you in stating aloud his own truth, no matter how others feel about it.

So in other words, I'm a wimp and Bob's not.

Bob holds his own counsel, which is exactly what you are now choosing to do, too. Bob has not had issues of fear in speaking out and speaking up. This is what Bob has helped you with.

And what will I help him with?

Through your friendship and through your collaboration here, you are helping him with a different type of healing. See how perfect it is when you bring complementary characteristics to one another?

Okay but do you think he'd be irritated if I was ever at his house and his toaster broke?

Naw, he won't let you anywhere near his toaster . . .

Yes, I suppose I have long been tackling issues of my own self-confidence.

Unlike you, we do not have issues with credibility. There are those who would say, "How do we really know that this is not just you? How do we know that we are really hearing from extraterrestrials and that you are in fact relating what is being said?" Of course, the highest response to that is that it is okay to doubt. No one needs to attempt to convince anybody of anything. Those people who are looking for what other beings in the universe might have to say, they will find you, and they will bring themselves to your work. Those people who need proof, or feel that credibility is an issue, will not find what they are seeking through this work anyway; and so, see if you can find a place of self-confidence within yourselves to offer this to those who would like to hear it and be at peace with those who question it.

There is a certain degree of faith that is required when you embark upon this work. There are often more reasons available to the mind and its reasoning system to refute or deny divine phenomena than there are reasons to hold it as true. Therefore, as you proceed with this work to develop a stronger connection with us in whatever way that may manifest, your intention will dictate the degree of pleasure that you find in this process. If you find yourself eager to prove that this work is "real," or are desperate to respond to your critics, then you are approaching our work from a defensive posture. Rather, seek a stronger communication for reasons of your own satisfaction and for those others who seek a strong connection with you in spirit. This way will you keep this process filled with joy and wonder.

Before the advent of many of your scientific instruments, there was doubt as to the existence of what you now hold as fact. Do not worry that this work will never be proven as "scientific," or that people will never know us or see us, for that time will surely come, just as your species saw flight when most of you thought that you'd never get off the ground. Be as pioneers, strong in your conviction that the part that you play is very important. Pioneers are a hardy bunch and bring a strong inner conviction that what they know is the truth for them.

You would not feel desperate to prove to another that there is life after your physical life. You would simply be puzzled if another were to suggest that there is no "proof," for you would not be able to relate to such a limited perspective of what seems to be so obvious in these times and days. And so bring that same acceptance to those others who doubt and criticize this process, for these are indeed the early days of contact, and it is, in fact, contact. Take pride in this contribution, no matter that it seems less than what you and others seem to be demanding. All things in their time.

Each success in the literary world sets up the next success. There is a perfect unfolding of what the culture is hungry for and reads, and one success with one book sets up what the culture can digest the year after. And you are bringing and heralding the next wave of this type. What would you suppose would be next? Physical contact is not as far away as you might think, although we will not give you a date at this moment, for as you well know, there is too much free choice on all of our parts to attempt to answer such a question.

We are not the only beings who are your brothers and sisters. We do not use that term loosely. We are of the same Divinity. You are so isolated from your heritage. There was a time when you were so connected to the other beings on your planet that it could have been considered that the very animals there were your brothers and sisters in many ways. Now you are eating them. There is much memory to retrieve. Don't worry, we're not concerned that you will attempt to eat us, but the degree of superiority thinking in which your egos are involved in some cases is considerable. It is just a mask for isolation, for if you truly felt connected to the other animals and to the other humans, you could not allow your present state and conditions to continue. Things would change very, very quickly, which in fact, is the direction in which you are heading.

There is a kinship between us and other beings in the universe, and those beings would also like to know you and to relate to you and no doubt they shall, just as we shall.

Some time ago there was an agreement made in which those of you who have a heavy influence off of Earth agreed to play this role in the human visage, so that your connection would be in place despite potential ridicule and doubt from all sides. This way the decks would be stacked, so to speak. Your connection to us would be so strong that you would continue this work no matter what, because someplace in your genealogy and your memory, you know the truth of what you speak. And you will connect with other people with the same genealogy, other humans who have resources at their disposal through many different avenues, and the group of you will connect. It will be a very natural process. Not everybody in mainstream media is cynical. Even there we have our "plants," as you recognize the meaning of that word, meaning there are those of you, throughout every walk of life, strongly connected to us.

It would not further our mission or yours to have every experiencer on top of the mountains in Tibet. Rather, they are spread throughout the globe in various positions of influence and those people will gain the courage professionally to both "mentor" other experiencers in spreading this type of message throughout the world, and one day to be able to admit to their own encounters. This will occur as this type of subject matter gains greater respect.

When we come before a people like this—and yes, this is not the only time we have mentored in this way—there are certain levels to the involvement, certain degrees of involvement that change with the ebb and the flow as our relationship continues.

As you currently observe there to be spiritual retreats, in which groups of you come together in celebration of the remembering that you are creating your own life, and that you do not have to walk the path that holds no joy for you, imagine creating gatherings in which you celebrate together your understanding of your relationship with us and others from off your planet. Imagine a time when groups of you would gather at remote locations where visitations and encounters occur. This would be some kind of retreat, would it not? Just as at your retreats today you do not necessarily take photographs of each other as you find your bliss, fall in love with self again, and get in touch with the Divinity inside, because it is a very personal moment and a very personal experience. This is not something that is needed to be "sold" to the media or to anyone. And those experiences and encounters at such retreats could have the same feel to them, because your confidence will be so great that you will be joyous simply to experience the wonders of the universe. Your maturity will be such that you will not feel the need to be believed or to prove anything to anyone. Of course, just when that need is surrendered, will you do just that anyway.

Picture an elite club. There is no fee. The only requirement for membership is a deep faith that there is more to the universe and to its inhabitants than what most of you accept right now. Such membership links you to others who share in your memory of the universal one-soul. Actually, all of you are members, but only some of you will remember that you are. Imagine small groups of you not only having encounter experiences together, in which you might enjoy the camaraderie associated with experiencing something so wondrous and having another with whom to talk about it, but also taking short excursions with us here or there. Through your faith it shall be done.

As you begin to describe this type of event through your art, through your storytelling, through your books and your movies, you begin to create this outcome. This is inspired storytelling at its finest. For the most part, encounter experiences have been characterized by a certain degree of isolation, due to the fact that, by their very nature, encounters often happen individually; and the events seem so "far out," the experiencer does not necessarily have an intact support system in which to share and discuss, or even to be debriefed. This will begin to change, too.

Imagine a time when you will no longer need to rely on UFO theories, or other "experts," but you will begin to decide and define for yourself the glory of the expansiveness of the emerging universal human, as evidenced by your own extraterrestrial contact and by experiencing firsthand your expanding neighborhood.

CHAPTER 5

Count the Stars, Count the Ships

One morning while I was in elementary school, my teacher made an important announcement. The annual science fair was upon us, and we were all encouraged to dream up some technical device or scientific demonstration to display at the fair. There would be prizes for all who entered. And to kick off the event, we would be taking not one, but two, field trips: one to the Los Angeles Griffith Park Observatory and the other to the museum of modern technology.

As much as I liked the idea of escaping Mrs. Ricard's classroom, I did not join the uproar of enthusiasm that erupted, as though we'd just been given the next two years off. Instead, I slumped in my chair with my head in my hands and moaned.

Not only do I not particularly like science, I think I actually have an aversion to it. Don't get me wrong, I love and appreciate the night sky, but just don't ask me to study it or contemplate how it all works. I don't have that kind of mind. I'm not a simpleton. There are other areas in which I have plenty of talents, but when it comes to technology or principles of science of any kind, my brain clicks off. Perhaps I'm sort of dyslexic, as it were, with machines, or planets, or anything resembling a VCR. I can use my dryer, and the clothes come out fine, but don't ask me if it runs on 120 or 240 or 360 volts. The marvels of science and technology I am in awe of, but let's keep it simple and just point me in the direction of the "on" button. If I want it to stop, I'll just unplug the sucker, which brings to mind the question of why my computer is on the fritz, seemingly every other weekend.

When my auto mechanic had me looking under the hood with him while he tried to explain why he was charging me $725 to make the car go, I had to stop him in mid-sentence. "Wait. Stop. Just tell me if you connected all the dots. Is there a warranty? Yes? Here's a check. Have a nice day."

Everybody wants the formula for a flying saucer. More than one friend has asked me incredulously why I haven't yet gotten the details on how the ETs traverse thirteen galaxies over cocktails. One astronomy student expected me to provide a map of the universe, including planets unknown to humankind, to use as the basis for his thesis.

The pressure! I'm stuck on contemplating the irony at work here. Somebody please check if ever there were an astronaut who was afraid of heights, or a politician with an aversion to public speaking, or a surgeon who had issues with the insides of the human body. I can't be the only anomaly who resists, and is left dumbstruck about, aspects of her professed line of work.

Believe me, I've tried to ask these scientific types of questions during sessions, and I've had some marginal success. But what happens is that I end up with a huge clump of technical information during the communications, and the words and sentences come at me wound up so tightly that I have trouble unraveling them. It feels like my vocabulary and limited understanding of science affects what I can bring through. And then I panic and get frustrated and end up one more time saying, "I can't do it."

Granted, I've only been receiving communications in this way for less than a year. And I have heard of a case in which, after an "abduction," an ordinary housewife began spouting quantum theory. So maybe mine are growing pains. But there you have it. I'm a sissy. When it comes right down to the stuff that every scientist really wants to know, I choke. I've got more issues than a Vietnam POW returning home. But these are the facts, and you might as well know them. Every time I've been in the process of asking a technically oriented question, and the answer begins to sneak over the horizon toward me, I start into my typical downward spiral, feeling ill equipped to continue. Abort! I can hear my mind scream. The airplane of my communications has stalled, tipped on its wing, and is spinning out of control. Boom! It's enough negative energy to have turned off Edgar Cayce from ever conducting another life reading.

So what to do? For starters, this is an introductory book. Perhaps I'll return later when I'm more proficient at this. Maybe I won't get to the good stuff until volume 23—if you'll stick around that long. But since confession is good for the soul, I feel a lot better. Now let me try again.

> *Please describe for me how it is that you're able to travel such great distances so quickly. In addition, our people would like some concrete schematics for building flying craft and formulas for curing diseases. And while you're at it, the winning lottery numbers wouldn't hurt.*

When you feel you must capitulate to be all things to all people, you will feel torn. Let us remind you of the path that your soul has communicated that it would like to embark upon. Each of you, prior to your incarnation, chose a path for yourself. You don't always reach your highest goal, but you have an idea; the soul has an agenda of what it would like to accomplish, and how. You have stated and described your mission as one in which you wish to inspire others who are about to, or are in the process of, having encounter experiences, and like you at one time, do not know what is happening to them; they do not know what to expect, are embarrassed by the things that have happened and the things they have seen and heard, and do not know where to go from here. In this way are you a beacon to them. You have gone before them in the context of "UFO encounter phenomena." Your role, as perceived within a limited paradigm, which states that these experiences are happening to one or two of you, once in a while, makes no sense to you. But within this emerging new paradigm of the New Human, who is evolving and is becoming increasingly aware of his and her universal neighbors, there is a call for those of you who have gone before the masses and have bridged those challenges—significant emotional, psychological, physical, spiritual, and intellectual challenges. There is much to address.

You are adept at communicating what those issues have been for you, and many will find your words and take refuge in them.

You have focussed on the emotional and practical sides of the phenomena. You have decided to hold yourself up as an example of all of the ramifications involved in being a new experiencer, and the implications of "coming out of the closet" within a culture where it does not feel that safe to do so.

This does not mean to say that you couldn't do both, but for many reasons, right now, you have blocked the ability to bring through clean details as to the inner workings of scientific data. However, that does not render your work useless, for you have a different mission as stated by your own soul. Like the Russian tourist who finds himself in America, a foreign land, attempting to communicate with Americans, there are challenges to that mission. There may be emotional, physical, perhaps intellectual, challenges. If he does not readily speak English, there are additional obstacles as he attempts to bridge the communication gap. In this you have been a tourist, but really much more than that.

You and all other experiencers are leading your people toward a future that involves interaction with physical, otherworldly beings on a day-to-day basis. How could you think that your collective future would involve anything else? Some, like you, have gone before the majority of you in meeting physical beings from elsewhere, and are now choosing to describe that process and what it was like for them. There is a reason for this. The souls of those experiencers, and the souls of those who find this work to be valuable, have found each other. There is great pioneering work here. Even when Lewis and Clark stepped forth into the new frontier, there were considerable emotional, psychological, and physical challenges for those who were willing to brave a new world. You speak of those challenges. You trumpet the idea that addressing those challenges is the precursor to more experiences of this type for more of you. There is no shame in refusing to feel inadequate by specializing in the articulation of a very difficult process.

You may find at a later time that you do branch out into more technically oriented material. Or perhaps you would prefer to host and sponsor others who are more technically minded, and provide a forum for them. In any case, simply because you know us, simply because you have met us, and simply because you continue to have ongoing dialogue with us, does not mean that you also must prove yourself by bringing through technical data, as demanded by certain others. It is a natural query, yet you must decide if this is your responsibility. If it is not, yours is no small undertaking. In fact, in many instances, the work that you are doing is making it possible for the more "left-brained" of you to address their own emotional, psychological, and spiritual issues in order to prepare for their own communications and visitations with ETs. Do you now understand the perfection of your work? Somebody must start the ball rolling. There are others who already have, and you are continuing with it. But there is no need to minimize or trivialize the contribution that you are making. Just ask someone who has found this material, someone who is deeply troubled by what he has experienced, and does not know what to make of himself or what he has seen. Just ask this of the teenager who feels crippled and questions her own sanity. If you can reach her through your voice and this work, how trivial is it then? So you may not provide her with a schematic to our ship. She needs something else from you, and it is precisely this that you are gifted at providing.

You are able to articulate to your species a very complex emotional process, transcending the idea that you are alone and what happens when you discover that you are not. You are a symbol; you are modeling the process through your story, and it is an important contribution, particularly to those who still suffer in silence. Lead them home, and your work will have been valuable.

As for the lottery numbers, are you asking us to help you cheat?

Well, uh, I just thought that you could give me a heads-up . . . Okay, forget it.

Do you understand how it is that this process is helping others to move into a greater understanding of the universe and its inhabitants? You are helping others to recognize this and to begin thinking of this. For how else do you suppose you will all move into more of a relationship with us and your other universal neighbors?

But everybody wants a soil sample. Even Lewis and Clark and the astronauts returned with soil samples.

Place your emphasis on bringing back our voice. Return with a message. Plant the seedling of our ideas in *your* soil, and you won't need to bring any of our soil back.

Getting To Know You

Your world has expected that, should it have contact with other-worldly beings or extraterrestrials, the day would simply arrive when we land there. But this is not the way the universe works. Before such an abrupt event were to occur, does it not make sense to you that we would first introduce ourselves in a more gradual, less dramatic way? When you question if these communications could be real, does it not make sense to you that if we have the technology that we have, and if we have the enlightenment that we have, we would first contact some of you, rather than your whole planet at once? This way, experiencers can raise their hands and voices and announce to your world the nature of our contact. This way, together we begin a slow and gradual marketing campaign to announce our existence.

So much of this early contact has been refuted by most of you. This type of resistance to new ideas has been the case consistently within your history, with respect to every introduction of ideas that are considered to be new thought. On the one hand, you intellectually recognize the psychological pattern of this type of denial, and yet, when it comes to this phenomenon, you still have doubts.

Contact with you on a grander scale is approaching a time when more of you who hold responsible positions of worldly influence will begin to come forward as experiencers—those of you who, as seen by society, potentially have too much to lose to make something up. More and more of you will begin announcing what you know about us to your friends and families. And what many of you *do* know about us is that we are here. We have been speaking to you through your dreams, through your meditations, or contact, and there are some of you who only have lingering, fragmented memories of us.

It is part of the desire of the universe that we should all move toward ultimate union with one another. Does this idea hold merit for you? If not, then how else would you suggest that we begin to know you? We begin through these types of communications. We begin through having our ideas and our words expressed through certain humans. We begin by having contact with those of you who have agreed, prior to incarnating there for reasons of your own backgrounds and souls' desires, to do so. Were we to be taken more seriously by more and more of you, you would hear of more so-called paranormal phenomena with more of you. This is due to the fact that as you expand your awareness to include those things that seem to be not of your world, you open yourselves to a host of phenomena. Religions label this type of phenomena as evil. To suggest that only the planet Earth and certain individuals on the planet who subscribe to certain religions have been awarded God's grace is hypocrisy. The very teachings of the masters that those religions follow teach that God's love is ever present and is withheld from no one.

Well, we are someone. We don't look like you do, and we don't live where you live, but we are living in the same universal home. Do you think that we are the only ones out here? We have news for you. First, adjust to us, and then perhaps you'll be ready for others. At the very least, we have the physical appearance of those to whom you have been exposed through your tabloids and on some magazines and book covers. But there are many, many other beings, who are part of your universal neighborhood and who have a completely different appearance from us. If you are jarred by our physical differences, you might be shocked to see what others look like. This is simply a prejudice on your part.

Depending upon your level of tolerance for those different from yourselves, will you be able to be tolerant of others who both exist off the planet and are different from you? Notice your own level of tolerance for others who look different from you, and who speak different from you, and who hold perhaps different abilities than you do. If you find that you do not have much trouble with those of your own species who are different, then you will find that you do not have much trouble knowing and accepting us.

Our young are raised in a way that allows them to have the advantage of having visual contact with other species in the universe. From a young age, they have seen what you look like, and they have seen what others in the universe look like. They understand that their own physical appearance does not make them better, worse, superior, or inferior. They understand that they and others have physiological appearances based on certain variables of environment and other things. They are raised and exposed to the idea that physical appearance is subject to a host of variables, and therefore no one is superior to anyone else.

When your young are small, you take them to zoos and expose them to all manner of animals. You might show them the two-headed snake, for you have one. You might show them the baby orangutans and note how similar they are to you in some ways. Yet imagine introducing your young to the idea that there are as many physical beings in the universe, with as many varying physical descriptions, as there are animals on your planet. This idea exposes young children at an early age to have tolerance for others' differences. In this respect, you are all quite isolated. Each culture finds the culture on the opposite side of the globe to be somewhat strange.

Our young benefit early from those teachings that matter the most. Your system is set up to provide just the opposite. What matters most are the universal ideas that we are one family, all of us. Your great masters—Buddha, Jesus, Gandhi—have invited all of you to love one another and this is what we teach our children above all else, and we equip them with the tools with which to be able to love one another. Those tools are the tools of empathy, compassion, tolerance for differences, and an understanding of just how many differences there are, and we actively make those differences personal to them. You may wonder if our young study you. Yes, they do. We attempt to expose our young to as many different cultures and beings as possible, so that they understand that they are not alone in the universe with just their own species, and also, we expose them to the idea that God has made myriad others who make up the universal one-family, and that they are not only children.

One hundred years ago, you would have had a hard time believing that conversations such as this would be possible. But my friend, they are here to stay and will be expanded upon henceforth. Yes, there are other species besides us, of course. There is effort among all of us to gently and slowly bring an awareness of ourselves to you. There is a group effort to slowly introduce one species at a time. It is time for our introduction, and this is no accident or coincidence. Our physical appearance has been bandied about in much of your media, although admittedly, much of it has been negative. But at least the idea of our physical appearance is not too unfamiliar.

When we come to your people like this, as we mentioned before, we come to you as a group. The youngest of us represented here has lived many thousands of years. It takes a certain amount of wisdom to be eligible to have contact with you. We have agreed, through our own modes of consensus, that those most demonstrating the highest levels of tolerance, patience, and empathy have the privilege of communicating with you. Other species in the universe are aware of these exchanges and await eagerly news of the ongoing process. Picture your *New York Times* and *Wall Street Journal* announcing that contact has been made, and what a glorious moment that is. We, too, have our version of this media coverage, but our morning paper is not predicated on the cutting down of trees and processing printed matter on a physical object. We can simply place information in the ethers and send it out, much like your Internet, but without a keyboard or monitor. There is a certain knowing that comes with spiritual development, which makes instant understanding possible. This is why we say that all information is available to everyone, everywhere.

The "prime directive," as discussed in your *Star Trek* films, suggests that no interference may be made with other species. To suggest that any kind of contact is necessarily interference does not allow for the idea that we are all one, does it? If we are separate entities, then this makes sense. But we are not, so it doesn't make sense, any more than it makes sense how you divide your globe into sections with imaginary lines drawn and then you must fill out paperwork you call passports to cross over the line. As you dissolve those ideas and become a one-globe, and allow your people to travel freely at will where they will—as these boundaries dissolve, and you realize the absurdity of attempting to hold one group in one place for so many days and then allow them to pass over the line to another part of the globe, but only for so many days, prior to receiving a stamp of approval—as those ideas dissolve, so too will your idea that the universe is sectioned off into areas that require a certain approval to visit.

The approval that we seek is on a different level and comes not from an arbitrary authority who rubber-stamps our visit and allows us three weeks to sightsee, and then turns his back. The approval we seek is motivated by a spiritual awareness that we do not wish to jar you, nor emotionally harm you. So look to your highest selves first to see if you have invited us. This is why we have contact with some of you at a time, rather than all of you at once, for all of you at once have not invited us. The higher selves of you collectively do not wish to know us, at least not at this very moment, but this is something that is about to change.

Does it seem like the highest idea of the universal heartbeat to suggest that we should all stay to our geographic sections and mind our own business? What kind of globe would you have, even with your current system of requiring visas, if no mixing between your cultures occurred at all between you? When you love others, you look to see what their wishes are. Even if their wishes are different from your own, you honor those, and we, too, honor your wishes. Some of you have forgotten, or are not aware of, the wishes of your higher self, which is why you are sometimes upset over certain occurrences and experiences in your life, but it does not mean that your higher self has not brought you to those experiences.

We, too, know the aroma and subtle beauty of a delicate flower petal as it basks in the sunlight, with dewdrops sparkling under the blue sky. We know of this beauty on your planet and others. These nuances are not lost to us. Sometimes when you consider us, you do not make your awareness of us personal, which is the purpose of these dialogues. We would like you to understand us personally, who we are, and why we are contacting you. Our young send their greetings. They, too, are excited about the potential of meeting you. You might wish to know that our young do not always resemble us, for we have agreed to sponsor the young from other species, who in some cases have been cast out, or are unwanted. In some cases, our young do not resemble us at all, and yet we raise them with love. We are a relatively small colony, in that we have chosen to be anthropological scholars and so, by necessity, we travel quite a bit. We do have a physical planetary home, and yet many of us are involved to a point where this work is our greatest desire and idea of service, to be part of this huge involvement with you at this time.

Much like the way in which you plan your own futures with respect to your benchmark times for certain events—for example, the time for graduating from college in the early twenties, and the time for marriage and childbearing, and the time for retirement—we also have looked to this time in our lives, the time in which we go to the next step in our communications with you, with great anticipation. Thirty or forty years is a blink of an eye for us and so if you have had the feeling that you have been contacted since you were a child, or you feel that you have had a certain affinity or feeling of consciousness for us, this would not at all be unusual.

We wish to deliver a keynote address to you and it is this: If you would like to know us, simply hold that desire and share your understanding with another of these greater universal ideas of our existence. Just as the masters have said, send love, spread love. We are suggesting that you spread and send the idea, if you believe it in your heart, that there is more to this universe than just humans struggling on your planet. Spread that word. There may come a time when you will look back and be proud of the way in which you initially joined with this band of troupers and helped spread the good news on your planet that you are not alone. We don't have to tell you of the implications of this transition, for as a species, as you can accept us, there are more and more applications available for our mutual benefit. Those of you who are scientists, open your imaginations and look to see how willing you are to be a conduit from us to you, to bring in new technology that you can apply as a system that makes sense to your ecology. Conglomerates will not have a stranglehold on your planet forever. There will come a time when ethics reign supreme, and the health and quality of your lives and the ecosystem is paramount. Do not think that the highest ideas can be suppressed forever.

Opening A Channel

As you try to understand how it is that you comprehend our language, think of these communications as one of a language of the soul. This is the closest definition of what is occurring. We do not necessarily speak your literal language, and you do not necessarily speak our language. We have joined through a telepathic voice that feels as though it's heard in the area of the head, but it is more closely described as a resonance that permeates your entire being. It can be described as a language that connects us through a long lineage, but the process is similar to that of a "downloading" of information from one type of port to another. You bring certain abilities that enable you to translate this incoming data. You do something that is beyond translating from one language to another, you absorb the frequency of our communication that occurs simultaneously through an energetic transfer as well as a telepathic one. When we transmit to you, we transmit on more than one level or frequency. You decode our data. Prior to this decoding, it would resemble gibberish, as you once heard many years ago, that sounded like two computers talking together.

The process is actually quite complex, which is why it has taken many years for you to establish and maintain a frequency that complements ours. This is part of the reason for the blast in energies, which is experienced by you as a strong electrical sensation. You have been slowly acclimated through a bombardment of energies and frequencies, which now enables you to withstand our differing channels, so to speak. We have found a technique to bridge those differences, which has formed a union between us. Think of it as a funnel, which has a broad opening at the top, allowing an enormous intake of fluctuating energies and electromagnetic frequencies. Through the process of fine-tuning an adaptation, we have funneled all of this into a manageable application that helps transfer to your words.

Through the process of providing you input, we recognize that you are only as limited as your mind tells you that you are. The more expanded you believe that you are, the more expanded will be your experience of us coming through to you. You are growing rapidly every week in your confidence and your ability to cease second-guessing what you hear. The arguing is growing quieter, and even when you hear it, you are finding a way to simply step aside from the mind's need to thwart this process. In the past, the voice of your protesting mind was distracting, hindering you from progressing. But now you are moving nicely in the direction of allowing your mind to have its say, but that say is not expressing the higher part of you, inasmuch as you no longer defer to the intellect. Your soul better identifies and quiets the part of your personality as it is expressed through your ego and your mind. This process will become easier and easier and as it does so, we will step up the contents of this communication. You seem to be well pleased with this progress, as are we.

Deepen and strengthen your frequency through your fasting, and we will continue to adjust things from our end.

Your alphabet makes the building blocks for your language, and we send you these communications via a transfer of information that comes to you from our language and is decoded by you through a process remembered from other incarnations. You have come here and decided to meet with us like this. This has been your choice, not ours, although we have chosen it with you.

Telepathy is not fully hindered by distance, and yet this is more than telepathy, for it involves a sending of an electromagnetic current that you "download," in a sense through the back of your head. The sweeping movement of your head ensures that there is an even flow of energies and the movement also prevents a build-up. You have noticed that the rapidity of your head movement changes from time to time, and this depends on many, many factors, including what you have eaten, the weather outside, the energetic interference of your surrounding area, and your emotions and mood. We make adjustments from our end.

The process of this communication is not really understood. In this case it is a bit more complex for it is not just simply a knowing within you, although you certainly do have this knowing, but there is a direct communication, with us sending waves similar to radio waves. For example, you understand that you don't understand how the television works. You simply allow your lack of understanding to be okay without refuting that what you are seeing and hearing is real. And although you may not quite understand how this process works, we can assure you that it is real and that you are hearing from us. At some point in these readings, you will feel that you are hearing the ring of truth and feeling the ring of truth. This is because many of you have connections to us as well, either directly or through another lineage. Just as you may not have been born in the United Kingdom but have parents who were, you therefore have an ancestral lineage to Great Britain through your parents. In this same manner, many of you reading this work have an ancestral lineage to us and our species, which is what has brought you to these pages. If you feel a stirring in your soul and an excitement in reading this, this is your sign, for you are touching into your own heritage of life off the Earth.

Don't be surprised after reading these words, or soon thereafter, when your own dreams or memories begin returning. It would be very healing if you have unresolved emotional issues surrounding these to gently allow yourself to look at those memories.

We bring glad tidings that the complexity of the interactions between our species and individuals there have a great purpose. Our interactions with you are not as a result of a hobby. We are not merely scientists looking for another lab experiment or for information to conclude some thesis. We seek a relationship with you, if it is also your desire, because you are also part of our universal neighborhood, and meeting one's neighbors simply makes sense.

As you awaken to our presence, from deep within you may emerge questions. We delight in the communications between us, because as more and more of you recognize and resonate to these dialogues, you contribute to a new world in which your species finally embraces others of us who look different and who live in a different location.

We have come to these dialogues at just the right time in your evolutionary history, at precisely the right moment. We would like to help facilitate a healing of any of your unhealed issues from encounter experiences, and we welcome the opportunity to bring clarity. When you doubt that we are really speaking to you, ask yourself why it is so impossible to consider that we are here with you as part of your universal family and that we have agreed and have made agreements with certain of you, such as Lisette and others, prior to incarnation, to provide a means and a way to continue contact that is not constantly threatening.

There are those who will tell you that if you develop a positive take on your experiences, you have been brainwashed, and yet no spiritual master would ever respond in this manner, were you to declare that you have found peace and that you feel love for another. You will know the tree by the fruit that it bears, and so look to see what part of our communications feels out of integrity with your highest idea of that universal law and the teachings of the masters.

It is okay to believe in the magnificence and the diversity of your universal neighborhood and its inhabitants. It is not stupidity. It is not nonsense. It is perfectly understandable that you and others have an intense curiosity to know about us and about your universe. Truly, a lack of curiosity would seem less natural, wouldn't it? Bring your questions, and we will help where we can. Bring your concerns and your fears, and let us speak with you about them, for we await your communications with enthusiasm; how could we not?

It is as though we have been like your Helen Keller, awaiting a manner in which to speak with you, communicate with you, for you to see us and feel us in your hearts. This process has enabled that bridge to occur between us and we are deeply grateful for it. Do not judge the process if you do not understand it. Simply let this miracle take place. We are overjoyed at our meeting and would like to show you more signs of us if you are ready and willing. It is time to cease being afraid of the dark and know that you have brothers and sisters, brethren in the sky.

These communications help us fulfill our life purpose for everything that we are—all of our experiences have brought us to this moment as well. Allow your imagination to be freed from restraint and come to this process of pure counseling where we provide you an opportunity to finally ask your questions, to bring your confusion and let us help you unravel it.

We Are Not Alone

Beyond your time and space, there are places that are called home to groups of beings on different spheres, or globes, and they fulfill their incarnations in some ways much like you do, depending on the particular development of their spiritual growth. We say this to you because we want to introduce concretely that there are other neighborhoods close to yours. Just because you don't have the technology to notice them, doesn't mean they're not close. To us, you're very close. It's all a matter of perspective, isn't it?

If you are bound to a wheelchair, it may be very difficult to get yourself in and out of the wheelchair. The grocery store a quarter of a mile down the road seems a great distance if you are needing to rely on your own physical resources. Navigating the aisles, finding a way to reach the items on the top shelves, carting those groceries to the cash register, and then getting them home might be an ordeal. And so, you look at our distance from the viewpoint of a person who is limited in some ways physically. You try to see us but you can't. Yes, it could be argued that you are evolving spiritually, and we are attempting to show you how your sense of isolation comes from your own perspective. It does not come from reality.

There are beings who have bristles for hair, much like a porcupine.

If you were to meet such a being tomorrow at 9:00 A.M. at the corner coffee shop, would you be alarmed at their physical appearance? Then why do you wonder why you haven't met them yet? If they showed up with a small black nose and more limbs than you would expect, what might you have to say about that? Supposing this being is highly intelligent, highly spiritual, and completely loving and accepting? This confronts some of your ideas and beliefs about seeming qualities only assigned to animals such as the ones we describe. As you expand your horizons in scope and thinking, begin to ponder the purpose of our mission. We are attempting to break the ice; we are attempting to inform you that, as you can accept these ideas, they will be made real in your experience.

Dozens of cultures throughout the universe have gone through the transition that you are about to experience. Namely, that transition is a move from an isolated state of understanding that one is the sole inhabitant of the universe, to an understanding that one's neighborhood is simply that: a neighborhood located at a particular juncture in the universe, a particular quadrant of time and space. Only your fear prevents you from knowing more neighbors. Whether or not you can accept that this particular conversation, for example, is really occurring between extraterrestrials and a human, it is going to be more and more difficult for you to deny that there must be other living beings who just might have more technological know-how than you. They are aware of you although you may not be aware of them. You can only refute this for so long.

We too were as you are now. There was a time when we were isolated in our thinking also and we could not believe that there were other beings in the universe. And if they were there, they certainly wouldn't or couldn't be contacting us, because we figured they'd just show up on a mass scale, and that would be the end of the mystery. Then as one or two of us began declaring that we had seen them or heard them, or seen some sign of them, we would ridicule them. We'd say, "How ridiculous. That is so woo-woo; you are so on the fringes; you are so out-there in your thinking; you belong in a hippie colony with a nose ring." Then over time, as will be your experience, more and more and more of us began to have experiences of many different varieties, which created a thunderous voice in unison declaring that, in fact, others exist, and they don't live on the same planet.

How would you like to be one of those people? How would you like to be one of those humans in your historical evolution who invite more paranormal experience to yourself, which will enable you to raise your own hand and declare what you know? And then you will be joined by another who was waiting for someone else to speak first. And somebody else who was waiting for two voices in the room will join you, and then a dozen more people who were waiting for at least a whole group of their fellows to make such an announcement will also finally say, "Yes, this too has been my experience and I'm not crazy because I hold a position which many deem to be one of great responsibility, and I have everything to lose by stating this, but instead, I want to be part of that voice that moves the collective forward in their understanding."

The only way to move that understanding forward is to start speaking up. You also speak up by what you purchase, what you read, you speak to the culture by how you spend your dollars. So become more aware of what's going on with your brothers and sisters, so that you can become more confident and comfortable, and you too will then have your own voice and add it to the others. Does this seem like a ridiculous challenge?

We have ventured to your planet many times and have had encounters with many of you. Those of you who have healed from those "charged" experiences are now ripe for stepping forward. Do you think that this is all just an accident? Do you think that we're just working from our own agenda because we want to convince you of who we are, and that we're somebody in particular? It is true that we are undergoing an image adjustment, but it is an image transitioning from one of gossip and falsehood, to one of clarity and truth. Do you fault us for attempting that transition in your eyes? It is not that we are concerned or upset by your negative opinion of us. Please don't misunderstand. The souls of you are calling the souls of us, and so we are fulfilling our part of the agreement and you are fulfilling yours.

It will help you expand your consciousness as you begin to understand that so much of your world and so many of your beliefs are an illusion. Many of those ideas that your culture holds dear are blatantly false. When you begin to understand that your own government desperately suppresses what it knows, you begin to rely less on government and more on your own knowing. Then one day, your own government will simply be asked to move aside, because you will no longer see any need for it. There is a certain parental quality to your political set-up. Yes, of course it's obvious that most of the power rests with a few, but do you see how you've deferred your own power to a parental authority? More and more laws are passed that take more of your freedoms away. One day, you will have had enough of it because you will realize that wisdom does not lie in them. The wisdom lies within you. And you will become leaders and say, "Get thee behind me, for I have our people's interest at heart and you do not." And others will join you shoulder to shoulder and you will move forward into the millennium with confidence.

If you so choose, you can begin to experience those glorious paranormal, magical moments that others have had, that you may have read about or heard about. When you experience these, you too will have doors thrown open in front of you because you will see the limitless nature of the universe and it will deeply excite you.

Imagine falling in love with someone across town, or across the galaxy. Who might be more motivated to know us, the person who denies our existence, or the person who is deeply in love with another who lives elsewhere down the street, across the star system. It's a funny concept, isn't it? But this is the way that miracles happen. Space brothers and sisters, all of us together, have a wonderful opportunity to know each other and travel amongst each other. One day, you will create a way to do so without needing to get permission from NASA because NASA will still be looking for us with their satellites and their sophisticated equipment, and you will be talking to us while you sit in bed. Now do you understand in whom the wisdom lies? How many billions of dollars did it take to establish this very communication? Only the cost of a tape recorder and blank tape on which to record it, perhaps eighty-nine dollars. So you see, you do not need great sums of money or grants from space programs. You only need a consciousness that says, "I too would like to know my neighbors, and if they are talking, I'd like to hear them."

We would like to hear you, too. We are just as interested in knowing you as you are in knowing us. Don't think that this is not possible. Because it is. It's possible right at this very moment. Just try to hear us, and you may. Just desire to know us and you will. Even if your intellect refutes it, for a second you wondered if it could be possible. And if it were possible, what would that mean to your world? What would that mean to your whole perspective of things? What would that mean to your children and your children's children?

Count the Stars, Count the Ships

Many of you enjoy your children growing up in an integrated neighborhood so that they have an opportunity to see others who do not look identical to themselves. And, of course, to others, that idea brings fear, so you stick to groups who are exactly like you. But those of you who embrace differences and teach your children to tolerate physical differences, and teach them to even be comfortable with them, you will be the first to experience differences outside of your planet. Because you have laid the groundwork where others have not. This is tolerance extended beyond Earth.

As you see signs of prejudice in your children, talk to them. Remind them that there are others who are different on this planet, that it is important to get beyond that type of thinking so that they might get ready to embrace other children who are off your planet and who may be blue with green stripes and who may have a tail, and who may have mastered telekinesis. Help them explode open their imaginations. Do this with your children and you will prepare them to know us. Surely you can imagine how beneficial this would be. You open them up to receiving more of our ideas. Your children who would be scientists can be provided with ideas of science, which they can bring to all of humanity. So it's not just about getting beyond labeling your child as an "abductee," it's about noticing the new frontier that is unfolding in front of your eyes with this very transmission, for you may well be bringing the very next transmission through.

Don't keep to yourself. Speak to the heavens. When you count the stars at night, count the ships that you see gliding by. Have your children join you in this. Believe that somewhere out there, there is in fact a ship. Not all shooting stars are shooting stars.

CHAPTER 6

First Contact

If you're like me, in your fantasies, you'd probably prefer to toss your luggage from the curbside into a sleek black airport limo rather than trundle to the overflow parking lot in a rickety airport shuttle. I bet you'd prefer a trek to the high country snug in your hiking boots to a schlep through the gutters in a used pair of sneakers from the Salvation Army. And along the spectrum of evolutionary experience, I'd rather have a tofu bake on a neighboring planet with my friends, family, and the ETs rather than sit here alone and be zapped by them from afar. As grateful and as excited as I am about the nature of my encounter experiences and how those encounters have given new meaning to my life, I want more, not only for me, but for all of us. Let the "little gray buggers" (as Bob refers to them) meet up with us in the shopping malls or at Mount Rushmore, or at the very least, let me take a group of you to a soccer field somewhere and get a tour of a spacecraft and a joyride to Jupiter. Patience is good as far as it goes, but let's get to the good stuff, sooner than later. I've heard of stalling, but this is ridiculous.

So when will you get here, for all to see?

The winds of change are blowing, creating a way to bring a softening of your species' hearts and an acceptance of what might be possible in a universe filled with diverse peoples. When you first undertook this project, perhaps you thought that the goal was for us to provide concrete physical proof of our existence by simply arriving there. But experience with other species in the past who share your present level of denial (although many of you are awakening) shows that this is not the best way to jump-start your understanding.

Currently, we have contacts all over your world: some in the Himalayas, some in the cities, and the more representatives we have, the potentially greater awareness there is, for where there is a spokesperson among you, and then an experiencer among you, there is one who lights the torch of the dark path. By dark, we do not mean evil, we mean the path that is so dark that it is hard to see where you are going. When you light the torch on the path, you illumine the way home.

Why is it the way home, just to know other beings in the universe?

As you broaden your ideas about from where you receive inspiration and technological help, then many more of you can begin to increase your sensitivity to receiving such inspiration and direction, and therefore you unleash a powerful new human who actively encourages communication and relationships with others who can help. And then you can meet them. Before you know it, you too will be encouraging lesser evolved beings in the universe, as we are doing with you. This is how you return home, by experiencing and being love.

Are you going to allow us to announce in this book that some sort of visible contact will be made through us, and, if so, what kind and approximately when?

We would have thought that by now you understand that we are allowing or disallowing nothing.

We don't want to announce something that is not going to occur.

We do understand the intent of your question, but still we ask that you notice the choice of your words, which can set up a misunderstanding that somehow your experiences and creations are at the beck and call of our supervision, and this would not be accurate. Do you understand this clarification?

Yes, but may we announce that such an event is to occur?

You ask the question that all of mankind asks: When will extraterrestrials be among you face-to-face in a way that can be denied by no one. This is the question?

Yes.

Although you have qualified the question somewhat by asking if this book project will somehow announce such a first contact, inasmuch as "first contact" means an encounter of worldwide understanding, we will answer the question thusly:

Have you ever had your child or adolescent come to you and ask you, "Dad, Mom, will I or can I win the lottery and have ten million dollars when I am fifteen and a half so that I can buy a car and travel the world and have instant wealth, and can this please happen on, or before, my sixteenth birthday, when I can obtain my driver's license?" A wise parent might respond with an answer that gently causes the youth to notice that yes, all things are possible, and simultaneously, life unfolds best in a way that is most beneficial for all who are involved in the unfolding of life. That is why the question presumes that an event unfolding as you are asking and requesting in the very near future, such as next week or next year, would be at the behest of the souls there and would be in all of your highest good.

Life, and the events and circumstances in life, unfold in a way that life knows best how to do. It would seem that the obvious solution in the case of our introduction would simply be a sudden arrival, and therefore an instant understanding and awakening as to who we are would ensue on your planet. But this is an assumption that you have made. You have invented that. You are operating from your thinking processes, although in many cases duplicated by others, in which one assumes that if our goal is to know you, and if we have the technology available to know you, then the mystery as to why there seems to be a delay would seem to be unsolvable. This is not understandable as long as you are willing to stay completely, one hundred percent, within the illusion. Living within the illusion demands that you cease noticing that there is a grand perfection to all. Maintaining and living within the illusion requires that you resist noticing that there is a universal synchronicity to the spinning of the planets and the shining of the stars and the tides of your oceans. As you agree to look under the curtain, having for so long been a member of the audience watching the theatre production because you have not wanted to step out of the illusion, you will venture forward and declare a grander awareness. As you do so, you are peeking behind the curtain and are now able to catch a glimpse of what is happening backstage. Suddenly you realize that while you thought you saw intense drama from the perspective of the theatre seat, you now have a different vantage point for you have decided to finally notice what is going on behind the scenes. Now you understand that there may be a magnificent timing to the evolution of your species and how that is playing itself out.

We will not even tell you what food you should eat for breakfast tomorrow, although we may brainstorm with you your choices and inspire your grandest ideas about those choices. But it is not our place, nor our role, to send you a message of your incompetence by telling you how and when you should invite us for dinner—for this is the context of your question. You assume that you have nothing to do with the timing of that invitation. For us then to demand that you meet a certain timing would undermine everything about who you are growing to understand yourselves to be. We provide encouragement but we won't predict your future. We are not in a position to tell you if you will eat cantaloupe or cereal for breakfast tomorrow morning. How do you think then that we could justify making a determination as to the date and manner of your co-creation with us in our first joint meeting? This is a co-creative process. It is not simply up to us for it takes two to tango, do you remember?

This is an evolutionary step, the meeting of your species with ours, or any other. If you can step back for a minute from your seat in the theatre production and consider how grandiose this transition is to that of a galactic participant, it will allow you to have a greater appreciation for how many souls and divine properties there are involved in such a paradigm shift.

At every turn, there is a juncture in the road. All of you make decisions that can drastically change the direction of your near future, and you embark down a different path. At every moment, each of you behold numerous possibilities in the direction of your life. Even though you say that you understand this, it is difficult for you to apply this and comprehend how we cannot provide a definitive answer to this question. We are not the only souls involved in such an interaction as inter-species communications.

Furthermore, your question continues to dismiss the degree of impact and importance of the contact that we are *already* having with you.

As you insist on focusing on what is yet to come, you deny yourself the magnificence of what is happening right now. That is okay. It is a question for the material, but it is also characteristic of the egoic mind, demanding that events play out in a certain way to meet with expectations or one's experience will be unsatisfactory. And so we would like to use this example again to show you how your question may encourage you to, time and again, bask not in the present magnificence of our current relationship.

It may seem as if it takes great wisdom to balance an attitude of peaceful acceptance of what is and a surrendering to the present while also yearning for a grander tomorrow. There may seem to be a very fine line between the two. You will know the difference when you have crossed over from a deep sense of feeling of accomplishment and appreciation to one of gnawing angst over what should happen tomorrow. This difference may help you identify where you are in your perceptions.

We cannot tell you when you will have us for tea for you are half of the equation. When you insist that you are not, you disallow what is so. From the seat in the audience, the illusion says, "I am responsible for none of this; I have created none of it and it is all happening to me." Therefore, the question does make perfect sense from the depths of your illusion. But from the perspective of the awakened human, you are beginning to understand that your relationships are *your* responsibility and have been co-created by you. You might as well ask us, "When will I find and locate a suitable romantic partner and develop a thriving, loving relationship?" That is created by you through your consciousness at several different levels and so is the grand paradigm shift from that of your species' current understanding to that of an understanding better suited to an awakening universal participant. That is the whole point of this exercise. You don't recognize that you answer your own question by the very work that you are doing with this book. Your soul is intent on creating the answer to that question, but your mind deflects this understanding, asking you instead to go outside of yourself and to ask somebody else how your future will be and when will it be so. So if you allow this indulgence, we would like to ask you the same question in order to make our point. When is it your intention to meet us and have us there on your planet for all the world to know and accept us?

We are awaiting your response to our question.

Next summer would be a nice time.

Okay, thank you, so noted. We will pencil you in.

I'll have my people talk to your people.

Which of course is exactly what is occurring at this moment.

Today on your calendar is July Fourth, which in your country represents a celebration of independence. How this relates to this work is profound and remarkable. Do you understand clearly what is transpiring when you consider the efforts presently undertaken by NASA and other governmental space programs to contact us? It should cause in you peals of laughter. We certainly are enjoying it from our end, for the holders of the "sophisticated technology" seek to catch a glimpse of us and to hear a word from us, and yet all the while we are happily chatting to you and others while NASA grinds its collective teeth at its lack of progress in this area. This is so perfectly typical whereby the wisdom of the sages is not sought because the bureaucrats are certain that they have the answers.

But we do not even have the benefit of having the last laugh for NASA would never recognize this communication and others like it as the very "contact" that precedes the worldwide contact that they are pursuing.

73

Not yet they don't, but even so, their recognition is unnecessary for your planet will evolve gloriously, in any case, as you take your place at the universal peace conferences as universal beings, and you will have done so through the flowering of your individual souls. Move to a place in your understanding where it is irrelevant to you if the bureaucrats recognize this work, and other work like it, for what it is. You will not have been encouraged by your government. You will have been encouraged by your brothers and sisters on an individual level. As you awaken magnificently, your governments will come behind *you,* and you will form new groups comprised of those who are beginning to have a sense of where the wisdom lies and where true power is located. In some cases right now, if your government is sanctioning it, it may not be that which embodies the highest of universal principles and ideals. Be glad of it for you are all pioneers embarking on the healing of your globe and you may recognize that your governments may not do it themselves, despite having wrested financial resources and power from the lot of you.

You are creating the grand Boston Tea Party. You are recreating that amongst you, leaders all, in which *you* show the bureaucrats how you can grow wings and fly on your own. Let them attempt to catch you and they will soon find that true power is not owned by any one person or panel of grim faces, but is developed through love and trust. Other species in the universe are not gleefully pursuing relationships and communications with such groups, but rather with individuals such as yourselves who represent your collective idea that a global healing is necessary and possible. With a little help and mentoring from others who have come before you—we, if invited, would be honored to help where we can.

One of the most telling behaviors of jealousy is to ignore someone, which is why your government flatly ignores the statements of experiencers about their encounters around the world. They have little to tell in comparison. This should have you giggling amongst yourselves for there is a certain degree of humor in the reality of how you are progressing. We are inviting each of you experiencers to feel proud of who you are, individually. Many of you are yearning to know us, and so you have, as much as we are choosing to know you. When you expand your consciousness collectively, you can join in the brotherhood universally.

The National Aeronautic and Space Administration has not created this contact. All of you have, and this is why we celebrate your July Fourth Independence Day, for you are coming to terms with your own power in creating your collective future. Many of you are noticing that your governments will not figure out the solutions to your societal problems. They may not lead you into a peaceful future. This is the grand day of independence when your grassroots movement declares and recognizes that you will do it yourselves, for you have grown tired and weary of waiting and trusting for your so-called leaders to take you there. You are all understanding finally that they really may have no intention of doing so, and probably wouldn't know how to even if they did. You are individually coming into contact with your own understanding that your collective independence lies in the sense of unity amongst those who know in their hearts that there is another way. There is cause for great celebration, for as you tap into this awareness and understanding of your own potential in manifesting your future, with the help of your cosmic neighbors, you can get yourselves there.

The Fourth of July fireworks symbolize your ongoing celebration of the understanding that your future can be created by you and that you can and will overcome the tyranny of groups who seem to be leading your globe down the path toward your environmental demise. Now you are awakening to the ideas that as individuals you will hold hands and gain strength in your numbers, from a grassroots undertaking, you can begin to make the changes necessary to lead your civilization to a grander experience.

We know you are capable of this, for others before you have done just that and you have the memory in your cells of victory in overcoming oppression and tyranny from selfishly motivated groups intent on furthering their own purposes even when it means the decimation of your environment and the suffering of your impoverished.

The number four in numerology symbolizes the foundation, the structure upon which is laid the groundwork for an immense undertaking. Your July Fourth, Independence Day in the United States, brings truth with this understanding that you are laying the groundwork upon which you will rise free from the oppression of special interest groups intent on their own control. Yet the lot of you are creating something new. It has already started. You have already begun. You will slowly cease looking to one or two individuals as having the ability to transform your planet, because now, even your presidential elections, and the turn-out involved, demonstrate to you that you quit. You quit that belief system; you have quit fantasizing that transformation will be possible within the old framework, and you have begun to understand that an entirely new paradigm will be necessary. This can, and should, excite you, for the leaders of tomorrow will be from among your ranks. They will live what they teach. They will have an understanding grounded in spiritual ideas, and this will be important to you. These qualifications will mark the man or woman of wisdom, not what school was attended or how much affluence enabled a candidate to proceed so far. The foundation that you are laying, symbolized by the number four, is widespread throughout the globe, no matter the language that is spoken.

Extraterrestrial contact symbolizes, to a huge degree, the understanding that your world is not the same and will not continue down the same destructive path. No longer will you tolerate the mass destruction and the killing of each other. So celebrate in your recognition that you are awakening, that you are building the steps for your tomorrow, for your children, and for your children's children. Your willingness to think outside of the box and to consider the seemingly impossible marks you as a pioneer, and pioneers will change your future.

But there are still so many people who cannot believe that extraterrestrial contact is possible.

Where you are in your spiritual growth will depend upon your readiness to consider ideas that involve moving beyond your own egocentricity in reference to accepting other species in other places.

The egoic mind likes to feel superior. It wants you to feel split off from everyone else and to feel justified in having no union with others. You can conquer that type of thinking by first noticing it and then letting it drop off like so much extra baggage. Then you can begin to feel part of the all.

The reason why this is important is because you *are* part of the all, and as you recognize who you are, everything about you changes and evolves—not only personally, but collectively, for we have heard your voices asking why life must feel so full of struggle.

As you begin to notice your true self, you will train your mind to perceive differently how outcomes are established. It is a priceless gift, to finally come home and know that whatever outcome you would like established is yours simply for the creating. This seems so simple, but we are talking about many hundreds of years, in some cases thousands of years, in which your cells have a different experience of outcome. Your very cellular makeup holds tremendous memory of victimization and life with perpetual struggles, and so to convince your very being that this does not have to be the case can sometimes be a challenge. Of course your true self knows what is so, but the true self is joined by the lower energy bodies who argue constantly that life is a struggle, that no one can be trusted, and that paranormal phenomena cannot be part of everyday life.

We hope to touch in you a cellular memory just by your reading this communication. We have a mission in that we hope to remind some part of you, which does remember the idea, of your connection to other beings in the galaxy. Thank heaven for this contact, literally, for you have brought this to yourself through your consciousness and others, and this is just a first step. Have some patience and trust that there are more steps yet to come.

In the next ten years there is remarkable opportunity for expanded consciousness in all of you, and it would be a wonderful thing indeed for you to experience more tangible events proving our existence. But you must be ready on a few different levels, and that is what we are addressing.

Many of you, upon reading this, will exclaim, "I knew it. I have known it all along. I have felt the presence of these beings before." And you would be right. There is no container that holds one or two life-forms in the universe. There is an unlimited amount of neighborhoods out there going on forever and ever, so many groups of neighborhoods that it is difficult for you to even consider just us, let alone others, which is why we are starting with this relationship. But this does not mean that you can't retrieve your mind every once in a while and have it consider for a moment what is yet to come in your expansion.

There have been times in your history when you were on the verge of joining the universal family. There was a time on your planet before your textbooks recorded the goings-on that you did not quite make it because you destroyed yourself first. And so in some cases we are starting where we left off then. This is why there's so much attention on your people at this time.

There are some similarities now with that past fork in the road.

We are holding the vision for you to go this way, rather than that way. Sometimes all you need is the encouragement of a loving friend who holds the idea and helps you to touch your own confidence. We are that loving friend. We know you can do it. We know you may not want to repeat another go-round in your evolution where you keep getting to this place of near-expansion, of a blossoming of your culture and your masses, and then snuff yourselves out just prior to the big momentous leap.

Sift through your memory in meditation, and you may remember that this is how it happened. Build yourself a bridge to a new tomorrow by holding the confidence in someone else and this way you hold the confidence in yourself. As you do unto another, you shall do unto yourself. Give somebody else encouragement, just as we give it to you.

Just for the moment, picture yourself encased in a craft that allows you to travel at great distances at the speed of light, and, because of your awareness to all things universal, imagine that you have been able to create this experience in your reality. As you look forth into the solar system, you navigate precisely to the destination of your choice, and that may be a neighboring planet or star system where you have been invited for a picnic. Why not? Crazier things have happened. Do you have any idea how much progress your species has made technologically in the past hundred years alone? Do you realize that from the perspective of your ancestors, what is going on now would have seemed as absurd then as this idea that we are suggesting seems right now? You already have the basics of flight, and with a few tweaks to your physics, you will have the craft that can take you there.

When we suggest this type of afternoon in space, we do so because you think that this is fantasy, but it isn't. There will be a time when individuals and small groups of people can undertake these endeavors together. They do not have to be funded by governments, and so all the power of such an undertaking does not need to stay with the government. As you develop your relationship with your neighbors, we can trade "recipes," ideas of science and ideas of technology.

But what can we trade, given your superior technology?

What you offer is the opportunity for us to love you, to mentor you home. In this way we get to be angels.

How exciting it would be for some of you to have a relationship with us in which we show you schematics of just how these ideas can be applied, and for what purposes you can use them.

Most important, these ideas must begin in your thoughts. Through your books, movies, television shows and such, you have a scant glimpse of what that might look like, but notice that right now the underlying idea of much of that work is where groups are battling groups. We are suggesting that you leave this whole paradigm behind, and rather, picture yourself moving into the role of the unlimited, universal human, but doing so peacefully and spiritually. You don't need to take your warring mentality into your expressions of art and into your future. That is what we would ask you to notice. As you have ideas and fantasies about such a future, leave behind the old paradigm where one neighbor is battling another neighbor over a plot of land, or control of real estate, or over a special device, or over a planet or galaxy.

There is another way. There is the way of the peaceful universal human. Whenever you catch yourself thinking in those old terms, in which you assume that there must be anger and battling and spilled blood, recognize that this is purely habit. It is hard for you to imagine life without conflict somewhere nearby. In this, we challenge you screen writers, novelists, and playwrights. There is a different kind of conflict with which you can imbue your writings. For a change, create an antagonist that is not a neighbor. Create antagonists that are one's own mind and doubts, or one's own past, or one's own belief system. Break out of the old Hollywood story line which insists that the antagonist has to be the bad guy over there doing it to the good guy over here.

Welcome to new opportunities. There are so many in the arts, to create new ideas. There are so many new ideas just waiting to burst forth as your mind expands and allows your self to be led and mentored by those spiritual beings who have gone before you. You do not need to reinvent the wheel in every aspect.

Solitude helps quiet the mind, and through a quiet mind, more communication is possible from other realms. If you are wondering how you can take part in this process too, put your phone on hold, take it off the hook, barricade yourself from the worldly noise for the afternoon, and sit and invite us, and other realms, into your life. Healers, artists of all kinds, music writers to storywriters, this is your opportunity for healing. Do you want to take your culture some-place? Take your culture on a ride to see how your near future can look. Show them, through your creative genius, and have them ponder what that might look like, keeping the violence out of it. Find privately funded venture capitalists who won't insist that so many people have to be beheaded for the project to have merit. You can help your society to develop a taste for a different kind of media. The media can still be the same, but the flavor will be different. It is not necessary for hordes and hordes of people to crave, and to rush to see, movies that cost millions and millions of dollars to make, even if it tells an historical tale based on fact. Why would they, when there are so many other stories to tell? Stories of hope, of unlimited human potential, of star systems awaiting your arrival, of other beings in the universe, wanting you to reach out and be touched. Listen to other "regular" people who have incredible stories to tell, but no one to tell them to. Many among you have visited other realms, and you know of what we speak.

It is time now to offer a different kind of product. See your purpose, then, as an artist, in having a mission from God to help take your culture to your future as that universal human. It is not simply about entertaining for its own sake, because the barbarian of your mind will gravitate toward violence even as the other part of you resists. Why would you expose yourself to violence, even if it's "factual" or "historical" violence, when you can expose yourself to ideas that excite the soul and stir the deepest part of your passions?

Book publishers are in this group, because there is a responsibility also to allow your global tribe to be exposed to ideas that not many publishing companies presently want to publish. When you begin to shun stories of violence and anger and instead offer visionary products, then you are taking responsibility for helping to carve out a different avenue for your viewers and readers. That avenue could spark the imagination of your children, your teens, adults, and seniors into co-creating more experiences and communications from the myriad beings who are waiting to know you. There are time travelers, angels, spirit guides, and other physical beings such as us who, upon your invitation, will gladly make themselves known to you.

But some people would say that the only kind of "meeting"
that is acceptable to them are those where an otherworldly

being arrives in an "appropriate" manner, standing on the front stoop for all to see.

This insistence is precisely what shuts you off from experiencing more miracles. When you are open to Divinity expressing herself in the way that she knows best how to do at that particular time, then, and only then, do you have the welcome mat out. Sometimes your greatest dreams arrive clothed in garments that you do not recognize initially, and you cast them away saying, "That's not what I want." But the wise person knows to be on the lookout and on the alert because Divinity can come calling as expressed through many different aspects and avenues. When you insist that Spirit or inspiration must come one way, you have turned off twelve other ways in which the soul of the universe is attempting to help you create your dream.

You are the way-showers, the show-ers of the way home. That way home leads you directly into a family of beings, a family of which you are a part, and as you transition from your cultural understanding of who we are into a different cultural perspective, you will begin to see changes in the media. As long as many of you are calling us, we won't stay away. We are not foreigners. In some ways we are outcasts from your heart because society has labeled others off of your planet as negative. It is a prejudice, and you may want to start seeing it as that.

As you delve and dabble into the higher realms, there will be more evidence of our presence, and things will just work out. You will challenge yourself constantly to evolve, to spread love, to have nonjudgmental acceptance of others and to get yourself onto your path, no matter how difficult that may seem. No longer will you be able to tolerate exasperating work conditions because you will understand that you are creating it all—so just create something different.

Imagine this headline: "This news just in. Extraterrestrials spotted two miles from the coast on a sunny, balmy day as beachgoers glanced above." One day, that announcement could be in your papers, and we don't mean your tabloids. The slow integration into your consciousness of our existence has begun full force. You are on the threshold, just because of your interest, and are in the front row just as the curtains open. For your faith, you will be rewarded because the mysteries of the universe are there for your discovery. How will you create a way to integrate our existence within your life? It is not as far away as you might think.

Beyond the stars, there are groups who wait patiently for your choice. However, no matter what you choose, you will still choose life; one just may be a more direct route than the other. So do not fear that you will never get there because you absolutely will.

I was wondering how often you visit this planet and if you could tell us about some of your propulsion systems and how you travel. Do you travel faster than the speed of light?

We will not penetrate a portal to another realm, dimension, or location without first having it approved by all of our higher authority. But once approved, we can visit where we want at will. There is a magnetized energy field that permeates the universe, and we simply find a way to utilize these energy fields that are naturally occurring, similar to how your magnets pull certain alloys to themselves. So rather than being pushed or thrust from one quadrant to another, we are being pulled. We simply allow the full force of the pull to snap us like a stretched rubber band to itself. In this way, we both ride the current and also allow naturally occurring moving energy fields to bring us to where we choose to go. This is a simplified explanation of course, but what is worth noting is our ability to utilize naturally occurring phenomena and energy fields, to fuse with them rather than finding solutions for travel outside of naturally occurring phenomena. Does this make sense to you?

Well, yes to Bob, no to Lisette, but at what speed is this carried out?

At a speed consistent with the speed of thought, which is, in some cases, instantaneous, and in other cases, more deliberate based on "obstructions" from outside impulses. The speed at which we travel is a speed that you have difficulty comprehending, because you surmise that there is a distance of time between departure and arrival. However, we simply open a door and there is a rush of energy particles, which is sometimes experienced viscerally by humans who have participated in our "travel." It is more consistent to describe our travel as a process in which you make a decision. That would be more accurate because the thought propels the decision to arrive. This is why we say that it is as instantaneous as a thought. Once made, the choice to relocate is hastened or lengthened according to a number of variables. When we transport one group of beings, there may be a more instantaneous system of departure and arrival, depending on the density of the being who is in our midst. We may adjust this schedule to suit comfort levels. Moving along the river of energy particles can be both exhilarating and surprising to those beings who do not recall that experience from other incarnations, or from life on the other side.

Imagine traversing, in a small aircraft, the Grand Canyon on your planet, where heat rises from the floor of the canyon, it producing an effect on the small aircraft felt as turbulence. Now imagine, rather than streams of warm air that "collide" with a small plane and cause an "impact," very fast moving energy beams. Simply step into the energy beam and you can be pulled across time and space with the snap of a rubber band.

Also, you are asking one group. We do not speak for the entire universe. We commit to a certain "visitation schedule," if you will, based on an ever-changing, ever-expanding idea from you as to who we are. What we have done in the past may not be what we do in the future. Our "visitation schedule" is dictated by how all of you are opening to the idea of other beings from other realms. This is why we continue to remind you that we do not act selfishly with our own agenda here. We are ever-present and ever-vigilant to honor your— and we mean all of your—invitation and ability to open to our presence. We invite certain sightings at certain times as the energetic pattern of a certain locale invites us to do so. This may be surprising because there is a quality to unconsciousness which still believes that effects are outside of your control, but this is not the case. We work very much in concert with your highest idea, and that changes depending on where all of you are culturally and in an emotional, spiritual, and mental way. When we visit there, there is a strong pull for contact in some cases. Certain locations make this contact more promising because there is a group idea that it is possible—and so it is. Just as there are locations on your planet in which individuals claim that they are more prone to sightings than in other places. This is what you call a self-fulfilling prophecy because the more open you are spiritually in one location to receiving news from us (when we mean news we mean evidence of our existence), the more you create that.

Contact with extraterrestrials works no differently from the way that you create anything else. In addition, there are certain vibrational differences with respect to the frequency of certain places on your planet. This does not mean that we cannot go anywhere and everywhere. What it means is that there are certain locations in which the populace is more open to such events occurring, and therefore they do.

So which came first, your contact that appears to raise the vibration, or the vibration attracting your contact?

The answer to this seeming puzzle is in your idea that one must come before the other, when simultaneous occurrence is more the rule than the exception. We arrive because we are invited, and we are invited because we have arrived. It is not a timeline thing as in, "this first and this second," although our very explanation previously appears to contradict this, but we are attempting to explain ideas that you will understand. There are those of you who have placed yourselves in certain locations, and have made those decisions to be aware of us, far preceding your birth. Some of you have made these decisions to be in these areas and participate in contact or partake in observations of craft long before you were born. This reminds you of the grandiose unfolding of what is occurring. This implies that it is not about accidents. There is a grander plan, although, within the grand plan there is ability for momentary spontaneity for a decision to awaken and a willingness to participate with us, which can be made at any moment. Thus, a whole new set of events and experiences begins to unfold. So the best answer is that it is both. Some events seem to make others possible, and also, some events occur with the seeming precision of simultaneity.

There has been a lot of written material about the Roswell, New Mexico, accident in 1947. Were you involved in that accident and was there a crash?

Yes, there was a crash but this was not an accident, any more than any other accident is an accident. Speaking from the highest place, that event allowed a new level of discussion and debate among you and allowed others of you to make decisions about secreting documents and events. Some of you decided to subjugate your own knowledge of these events or to have your silence "bought." All of these actions were simply parts you have decided to play as part of the further unfolding of the consideration of other species.

As far as our specific involvement is concerned, this was a sister colony, so this did not involve us specifically, but you might wish to consider that such events are a gift. When your most enlightened masters have come to your planet throughout the ages, they have chosen circumstances and life events which would best suit their souls' idea of who they were, how they wished to unfold their own soul plan, and this was in conjunction with the soul plan of all others with whom that soul came in contact. Jesus' experience with the Romans was not an accident, but constructed by those souls to allow certain experience. In the same way, given this same universal principle, spiritual law states that all experience is created by self at some level. That incident too was created by all of the souls involved. There is no word *accident* in the dictionary of the divine. Of course, we understand the context of your question, but we are looking now at scenes behind your normal veil of observation. We are looking through the veil, which normally blocks you, as you begin to consider that there is a lot more going on than what you are currently looking at in front of you.

Certain souls are practicing courage, or are experiencing a lack of freedom of speech. Certain souls choose to experience conflicts in which the decision to take orders from the military conflicted with their ideas of how information should be disseminated when really "owned" by everyone. These events occur at intervals, which allow your species to integrate information in a certain fashion that allows internalization and an ability to consider certain phenomenon. Your own individual and cultural reaction to that "rumor" is a personal and cultural decision. This is why it is so difficult for us to tell you what will happen next because there could be fifteen thousand versions of what would happen next, based on your immediate decision about how you behold an event such as that.

Heroes are born from those events. Leaders and others are bought off. Soul stirrings are triggered and all of it allows for an opportunity for you over here in this geographic location to consider us while simultaneously, over there in that location in England, for instance, we will have another event with a crop circle. And over here in Buffalo, New York, a woman is claiming to have had an encounter experience;

and over there in The Czech Republic, there are remnants in the trees from a craft. Do you see? There is an orchestration of events, opportunities all, for reactions to spur and encourage further action on your part. How you proceed with that is what free will is all about.

Were there actually bodies recovered by our government? Were beings killed in that crash?

The beings who partook in that experience did so as a result of their soul plan and the soul plan of those who encountered them. Those physical beings ended a particular physical manifestation. Others who knew them do not partake of rituals of so-called death as you do. Yes, those bodies were changed like a suit of clothes and left there for your observation.

We know of few instances in which there is more interest and sense of benevolence than that particular mission because, like Jesus allowing a certain use of the physical body despite momentary discomfort, there was a much higher plan in the offing.

CHAPTER 7

Magic and Miracles

*Things have gotten really strange since the ETs have shown up.
It's been over a decade since that first night in my bedroom when
a windy cyclone blew my hair into knots, and blinding runway
lights seemed to cause my corneas to sizzle, and it felt as though
crackling and zapping had stung my skin into beef jerky. After that,
one of the first things to change, besides my attitude, was my sudden and surprising ability to see in a clairvoyant way and to hear
in a clairaudient way.*

*The images and sounds were at times seemingly mundane, like
the time I was driving and a voice and an image appeared, instruct-
ing me of a better alternate route than the one I had been considering. At other times, deeply meaningful or personal messages
come to me, like the time just weeks prior to my wedding day to
my then-second husband when I was startled to hear that my wonderful new fiancé and I would actually have "little time together."*

*Aside from garden-variety clairaudience and clairvoyance, the
hard truth is that all manner of other mysterious and unexplainable phenomena happens on a somewhat regular basis, whether it's
a bizarre light source emerging from a bush on a remote hiking*

*trail, or a raven flying within inches of my car window, "telling"
me to hit the brakes rather than proceed into the intersection.*

*Once, an old man, who I suppose was a spirit of some type,
appeared at my bedside holding my future book in his hand, ten
years prior to it being published. He said he was from the "future,"
and showed me how the pages of the book were yellow and worn
as though they were a hundred years old. To add to my perplexity
at seeing him, there was a young redheaded girl accompanying
him, whom I instantly recognized as me as an adolescent. It was
downright unnerving to gaze upon myself, minus the wrinkles, sitting before me, and I chuckled because I'd forgotten about all the
freckles I used to have. Before I could comment, they both van-
ished. Another time I awoke to a message about someone named
Arthur Buckley.*

*"Who's Arthur Buckley?" I said aloud into the otherwise quiet
of the bedroom.*

No response.

*"What do I need to know about Arthur Buckley?" I repeated,
familiar with their irritating habit of waking me up with some
interesting tidbit or the other, and then getting all tight-lipped as
soon as they get my attention.*

*My dog, Jessy, squinted up at me from a deep sleep, grumbled
once, then went back to sleep.*

*"Okay, fine," I said to my pillow as I settled back down to
sleep.*

*The next morning I trotted off to the bookstore and asked if
there was anything published by one Arthur Buckley. After some
digging by the clerk, I was handed his paperback book. Apparently
Buckley, who died many years ago, was a well-known magician of
his time, specializing in sleight of hand, particularly card tricks.
Back at home, with his book in hand, I broached the subject again.*

What does Arthur Buckley have to do with me?

There is a universal idea that one can transcend the seeming limits
of space and time so that magic no longer is trickery or simply sleight
of hand, but in fact, blossoms in a state of transformed reality.

Magic and Miracles

Arthur Buckley began and embodied a profession as a magician in which the movement of the hands through card tricks and other maneuvers seemed to bring life to magic. He, his spirit, encourages you, and others like you, for you in many ways are also bridging these two seemingly diametric realities: reality and magic in which the magician used to be one who creates illusion through trickery. To bridge our two worlds seems like magic. To many, this work brings up questions. To some, it may not seem real. To others, it seems incredible, and in some ways you are developing the artistry of the magician, not to create illusion, but rather to attract attention to where the illusion truly exists, which is your seeming reality. And this is the key, where you introduce the idea that what seems impossible is actually quite real, hence, real magic.

Arthur Buckley's early work fostered an elementary practice of working with illusion, and this is what you are shattering as you confront the myth that extraterrestrials are not real and that they have not yet had contact with humans. You are helping to shatter the illusion of your culture that insists that multidimensional beings cannot communicate with you, that extraterrestrial beings, who flit from planet to planet in crafts, could not be talking to humans.

As have others before you, you are bridging a gap in understanding for your people. The same characteristic is shared by your readers and the audience at the magic show. On the one hand, they are enjoying the entertainment of the magician, and on the other hand, they are seeking to know if it was an illusion, or if there was some ability on the part of the performer that allowed him to defy reality. The expert performer of magic seduces the audience into questioning if the magician has been able to tap into some cosmic frequency that allows him to maneuver around otherwise "normal" limitations of time and space that most of you take for granted. There is a similar quality to your culture with this phenomenon. With the magic act, the magician's assistant can float in the air, rabbits disappear, and regular household items take on qualities that defy logic. All of this tweaks the cellular memory within your species that such things are indeed possible when you step within the "magic" of multidimensional phenomena.

Unconsciously, your species has a desperate need to believe that such magic is possible because at some level you understand that unexplained divine phenomena may be the only way out of your quandary, and culturally, you secretly hold out hope that such "magic" can save you from your spiritual unconsciousness. As you observe the magic you wonder if it is a demonstration of the ability to tap into the invisible fabric of the divine, which can shatter the illusion of time and space. The magician's act inspires you to recall a latent memory of a time when you remembered that miracles are possible, and therefore all things are possible. You have thought that magic simply provides entertainment. In fact, it brings a cup of hope to a thirsty soul, allowing you to dabble and reminisce about the true limitless nature of your universe.

Houdini represented to many the yearning of the soul to tap into the fabric of pure potentiality. At some level you recognize that such artistry in "magic" also permeates paranormal phenomena. There seems to be a quality to phenomena similar to magic. In some ways, you perceive it as the same ball of wax. In this way, you embody qualities of the magician, like Houdini, for you make magic practical through the demonstration of your communications with extraterrestrials. You take seemingly magical ideas and make them real.

There are several guides who work with you, some Native American shamans, and this most interesting aspect of spirit guidance through Arthur Buckley touches your broadening understanding of what it is that the master magician provides: not more illusion, but rather, manifestation of that which seems to be contrary to your laws of science.

There are those who will minimize and trivialize this work as simply a cheap card trick. Bless this assessment and those who provide this feedback, for they speak from their own experience, and that is their experience of you and this work. Others will have a different experience. Become not burdened by critics of this process, for you know in your heart and your soul what you are experiencing.

Real magic embodies the cellular memory that creative beings can wave a magic baton and create from thin air, that, from the perspective of divine creation, you can hold up the black hat and pull out, from nothing, something. And so the magician's black hat and baton symbolize your cellular memory, which is precisely who you are becoming. All of you are magicians, because from thin air, can you produce the life of your dreams and the white rabbit, which symbolizes pure creation.

Right now you are as children seated in the front row of a glorious magic show with eyes wide open, mesmerized by the magician's presentation. To a lesser degree you are represented by the cynic who says, "Bah, this is just a magic show and a cheap carnival act at that." We speak of your culture's perspective of an awakened experience, in which seeming magic becomes interwoven throughout all of your affairs as you move into your next grand experience.

But the cynic is softening, for you are beginning to recognize that your ongoing cynicism is getting you nowhere but sadder. Eventually the scrooge notices that this perspective does not serve self, and so now you are returning to the wonder of the perspective of children beholding once again the memory of the childhood spent observing the wondrous magician's act, but this time, allowing for the possibility that "magic"—or miracles—runs throughout every aspect of Divinity. Be then as children with childlike wonder in your willingness to consider that it is time now to demonstrate how possible it is for magic to become part of your daily experience.

With this new perspective, you will find relief from your despair that life is an ongoing series of deadening events. Allow your higher self to demonstrate what is possible when miracles become part of your everyday experience. In this way will you tap into the higher dimensions and begin witnessing the magic act playing out throughout the universe. It is a glorious demonstration indeed. Step right up, and don't miss what is next in store for you.

Well, that raises a question. What is in store for humankind? Will we wipe ourselves out or can we reconfigure our shortcomings through something such as cloning, for example?

Your world is attempting to produce a higher functioning physical being through genetic cloning when, were you to put your resources and attention on producing a higher functioning physical being as a result of *consciousness*, you would get much further. The reason is that you can only go so far with manipulating genetics while you are, simultaneously, spiritually asleep.

It is a good sign, in some respects, that globally you are looking at and considering the idea of a more unlimited human vessel, one free of disease and one physically enhanced. What is positive is that you are all looking to the idea that there is more, so much more, of which you are capable physically. Yet, in many ways, you are going about it in a limited way, for you are developing this from the mindset of a species that looks to solve its problems from the same thinking that has created them. Instead, solve your problems physically from a grander awareness.

When you awaken spiritually, you will begin to change and heal your physical being. When you awaken your group consciousness, you will begin to notice that by unifying the aspects of your mind, body, and spirit, you are absolutely impacting your physical, emotional, and mental bodies. Although you can genetically manipulate and enhance certain physical vessels, you can only get so far, inasmuch as this does not address the status of your biological home in which this "perfected" physical vessel will be living. Again, your attention and finances are misplaced. What has been beneficial is how this has allowed for global group discussion that in turn has unleashed the desire to evolve to a more expanded physical species. But you are looking to make changes within the context of the symptoms, instead of the source of the problem. When you awaken and find ways to spend money and put your attention on those ways that will most benefit this awakening, then your enhancements, physical, spiritual, and intellectual, will be long-lasting and not limited to one or two vessels; but rather the whole globe will experience a lifting up of vibrational energy, and full healing will ensue.

To give you an example, what you are attempting genetically is akin to having a stable where you are wishing to produce a faster, sleeker, more highly functioning "model" of racehorse through your scientific manipulations. Then, you do produce this impressive steed, only to release it on the racetrack, where it trips and falls in the mire on the track, for the mire is seeping up from the polluted waters beneath. This perfected stallion still cannot master the course, for the course itself has not been improved or enhanced. All of your tinkering produces that which must still be relegated to a planetary consciousness and environment, which is seeking to make changes on a level that does not address where changes might be most beneficial and long-lasting.

It is another way to avoid noticing the areas where attention is most needed. You are once again diverting yourselves from noticing where the simplest and most easily remedied changes could be made with the most lasting impact. If you spend millions with these experimentations, you avoid noticing where else you could spend your dollars. You could instead find a way to stop the depletion of your trees, which are helping maintain the delicate balance of your planet's oxygenation. You might care for your homeless, who are huddled in bus stations to keep warm. Your children—your sons and daughters—they cry, for they have not had a real meal in weeks.

If you worked in a greenhouse to genetically produce the most beautiful red rose, and then you took those seeds and threw them in a desert and expected them to thrive, you would create an analogy to your present dilemma, for you are focusing on the symptom and not the cause. Fertilize instead the soil of your consciousness. Bring the "pH" up to a level that allows comprehension of the acts you are undertaking, and the choices that your governments make. These choices are not suited for your survival, nor are those choices representative of an empathic culture. When you find a way to create a new and improved red rose and then cast it into the barren wasteland, you will find that you wonder why it does not grow the way it did in the greenhouse. Such focus diverts your attention from healing the wasteland first, and from noticing how it once was lush. So, instead, put your resources and your attention on this question, and then the seeds that represent your physical vessel will, of necessity, awaken also because now the physical being will be directed by an awakened spirituality. In this case, all decisions, and therefore actions, become different. Then the environment is different, as will be your whole society, and so the experience of the physical being is different.

But how do we awaken the world?

Start by simply noticing that you are asleep and what you are doing while you are sleeping. Continue to increase your own awareness and find ways to bring world attention to what you all are actively doing that will contribute to your ongoing hopelessness and your impending destruction, should you continue as you are. Those of you in the media, whether employed by radio stations, newspapers, or television shows, when you feel that your highest ideas are censored because they are too far reaching, begin to hold hands with others in your field and together boycott the invisible thwarting of your awakening. Join hands with your seeming "competitors"—now one talk show host joins with another talk show host, one reporter with another, one anchorperson with another, and all of you together find strength in your union, so that the conglomerates, who seem to own the media through which you work, become unable to stop the tide of your collective interest. From New York to Los Angeles, let television, film, and radio personalities begin to work together like a labor union, but this will be a spiritual union of your culture, where you represent a grassroots uprising and a refusal to be silenced through censorship of "higher" reporting. Bring world attention to those examples that are most blatant and threatening, begin to put pressure on the establishment, and do not further allow your multinational corporations to control the media by continuing to ignore global issues.

You have wondered how you can make a difference and this is how you can do it. Motivation toward consciousness can be hastened when you are able to look squarely at your impending "doom," should you continue down a path of your own destruction. There is great responsibility when you have achieved celebrity and have media attention. Join forces with others of your stature, and you can focus significant world attention on those subjects that desperately need you to champion them. True, as individuals, it may be difficult to overcome censure, but together you can. Begin to understand the reason you have called celebrity to you, and recognize how imperative it is for you to join with others and find ways to shine the light of day on the darkest of your society's practices that most undermine life.

From the perspective of an evolved society, were one to attempt to rebuild a culture, an ecosystem and a planet, cloning the bald eagle to enable more to proliferate is a use of cloning that makes sense. But there is a big difference between turning this technology loose to children in the laboratory and confidently bestowing such responsibility on spiritually enlightened adults. Humans who are not spiritually awakened are like children loose in a laboratory, for your antics cannot address the highest spiritual morals, which have a hard time being discussed above the din of special interest groups who do not place planetary health as primary. When such groups are fueling the cause with their dollars from the sidelines, they will take you to the same arena where they have already taken you. Using such embryo technology to restock your animal life that is on the brink of extinction is one thing, but even here, the group performing this feat might better comprehend the issues involved when conducted from a perspective of full awareness and enlightenment. For this reason, this technology in the hands of a pubescent, egocentric population is more likely to create havoc than healing.

Generally, the problem is that you don't perceive of yourselves as spiritually unconscious—or as children, in the context of spiritual evolution—and therefore you don't see the challenge in what you are considering. Some of you do, but the special interest groups who wish to utilize this technology are the very groups who may be the most unconscious.

An awakened society conducts its affairs in a certain way. Your society, for the most part, conducts its affairs in a way that does not characterize an awakened society. Therefore, to develop technology that requires enlightenment to best utilize its benefits suggests that, no, you are not properly spiritually prepared to manage this technology, for you have not demonstrated that you are. The very fact that you perceive of using this technology to potentially create a more enhanced being, in the context of a polluted and dying environment, should provide an example of the degree to which you have the cart before the horse. Spiritual enlightenment is not born in a test tube, and you are so focused on superficiality that you have placed undue emphasis on an area that seems to provide tangible results to your dilemma. But this is an illusion, for without creating from a standpoint of an awakened society, collectively you are presently not driven by wisdom but by superficiality. In an effort to improve yourselves, you are attempting to sidestep the notion that greed and power often underlie and motivate the development and use of such technologies. When altruism and the ability to be motivated by the highest ideas of the group underlie your technologies, then and only then can you proceed with the motivation to find avenues for its highest use. At that time, when your affairs are no longer dictated by the greed and power-hungry motivations of individuals and companies, then could you use these and other technologies to enhance your species and your environment. Ironically, enlightened beings would then understand that, through consciousness, changes can be made to the physical being purely through intentional creation. This would not seem to be a mystery, for you could then make changes and adaptations as quickly and effectively as you are thinking you can do with a petri dish or test tube. The fact that you do not recognize this is proof that you are asleep and you are attempting to make changes and improve your situation with only a partial understanding.

Enlightenment allows for an understanding of true unlimitlessness and pure potentiality. Evolved groups can make tremendous changes in areas that, prior to enlightenment, were considered impossible to transform. As you begin to address issues of longevity and life without disease and illness, you have yet to understand that through individual and group consciousness, these changes, and more, can be made. It is only your present group consciousness that dictates your belief that the human being must age after a certain number of years, and for most all of you, the body then does so. Your present science dictates that it must, and so it does. A different outcome can be arrived at through an awakening, but to attempt to make such changes in the laboratory, filled with individuals who can be more asleep than awake, again focuses you on issues of your intellect rather than focusing you on how you can broaden your spiritual awakening, planet-wide.

Develop and demonstrate first an ability to create a loving, compassionate, and accepting culture. Beings imbued with such characteristics place their emphasis on different areas than you do. From this consciousness can you achieve much of what you hoped to create through cloning. In this case, and only this way, will you achieve lasting results. Transformation will be found through simplicity, not complexity. Symbolically, you are attempting to create the biologically perfect spotted owl, but then you plan to release it into an environment where you are still dumping your sewage into your waters. Creating a more enhanced human being while others of you are torturing each other on the other side of the globe is incongruous. Instead, build a foundation for a spiritual awakening, and from that base, flower your understanding, motivated by love and compassion for all. From this understanding will you step into your new technologies and skills with a greater ability to heal your planet.

Address cultures that subjugate certain members—women, or members of certain religions—and heal that rift. Notice where children are dying of thirst and starvation and have not the basics for survival. Place your global attention there. Place the expertise, education, and brilliance of your scientists, and figure out a solution for these dilemmas. Come out of the laboratory and go back to the plains and deserts of Africa, and address their dying and suffering masses there. Take off your white lab coats, and instead don the white robe of Divinity and bring forth not your test tube, but your cup of water and offer it to the thirsty. In this way, will you change your world. In this way, will you heal your planet. Allow yourselves the behaviors of a sensitive, compassionate culture that does not ignore any individuals or groups who suffer while you are playing chemistry in the back room. Instead, focus your financial backing and world attention on your global issues such as starvation, deforestation, and global warming. Where there are brilliant physicists, bring them to the starving people and start with your most basic dilemmas. Attend to your simplest yet most devastating problems and do not allow your intellects to waver from this mission, for you only postpone the inevitable. Eventually you will have to notice the waters rising due to global warming. You will be forced to notice that you are making decisions about how you furnish your house as motivated by tastes for beautiful wood, rather than allowing your trees to stand. Transformation will be found through simplicity, rather than complexity.

Cloning is simply an attempt to right a flailing system through manipulating the symptoms of that flailing system. Until you notice the greater environmental unease in which you are placing your newly genetically produced offspring, you will perpetuate your digression. Again, it is an example of the intellect avoiding the greater challenge before you. Consciousness produces genetically superior offspring. Consciousness maintains a genetically superior vessel. Enlightenment transforms all aspects of humanity. When you tinker with the symptoms, you simply continue finding a way to avoid what is really necessary to "fix" things, and end up congratulating yourselves on the marvels of science while ignoring how that same scientific community might be more impactfully creating change.

A genetically perfect rose raised in the greenhouse then transplanted to the desert will not thrive. A garden of roses transplanted to a wasteland will not change the wasteland. When you transform the barren plains, the loveliest and most perfect flowers will spring up on their own.

But there are those who say that aliens are doing this, that extraterrestrials are breeding with humans to create a fetus that is half-human and half-"alien."

This misconception has arisen, in part, as a result of experiencers who have met their young offspring as part of their encounters, and they have noticed that there appears to be a physical resemblance to both our species and yours. Certain physical characteristics of our species do become incorporated into these young offspring, due to the nature of the complex transformation that they undergo as part of the transition from your Earth to their new home. When you ask to begin to unravel some of the mysteries of contact between our species, you imply that, at some level, you can handle the answer.

There is no need to mix with your species and to produce a hybrid of sorts, although we are not suggesting that this has never occurred in the history of your planet. Behind the veil of mystery lies a relatively simple explanation. Sometimes those explanations are so simple that you may find yourself wanting for a more complex explanation. There is nothing complex about the nature of the universe, although perhaps the most complex ideas are ones that suggest two seeming contradictions in one placeholder. Imagine a time when our families meet in togetherness. We are as associated as one family is to another, for we are one brethren amongst many. Fear not our different appearance. Come to a new understanding of who we are. We ask that you allow us this forum and give us an opportunity to speak to your heart. When we come together like this, it is a sacred moment, for this has been written for a long, long time. Don't underestimate the soul of the universe. She would have us get along, would she not? Come now to a place where you can behold us in your thoughts and not shrink away, not as a UFO phenomenon, but as an ordinary occurrence that you may come to know your neighbor, who is, perhaps, farther away then you may understand. But our distance does not separate us. Our hearts and our souls are intrinsically linked.

The most controversial aspect of encounter phenomenon is, as experiencers have reported, seeing jar-like containers where human fetuses are developing, suspended in a liquid. This, many claim, is proof that we are heinous, unemotional scientists bent on furthering our species through the use of your reproductive abilities. Women report that they are pregnant, and then, mysteriously, their fetuses disappear. This claim of our retrieving reproductive material is at the heart of the idea that we are in the throes of recapturing our dying species through use of your females' reproductive organs. Let us speak on these ideas.

Magic and Miracles

When humankind decided to shift to a chemical producing planet, as evidenced by the powerful lobbying by your large chemical companies, you put into enactment a dangerous shift in the direction of your evolution, through the pollution of your waters and planet as a whole. You have set up the slow disenfranchisement of your own reproductive abilities, although there is no doubt that you are experiencing a population explosion. That new population, in many cases, has been contaminated by certain chemical reactions, which often affect your biological integrity. Although at times very subtle, by and large a course has been set, in which your species' reproductive cells produce an altered embryo. This does not mean that there is no hope for your species. Pointing out what is so can be tolerated by the psychologically and spiritually sophisticated soul.

We have indeed protected a sampling of your embryonic pool. As victimizing as this may seem, this has been an outcome that was agreed upon, with you, should your species in fact unconsciously move in the direction that it has moved. In other words, there was some possibility that your environmental decisions would be based on the bottom line of big business. If this possibility had been noticed by the souls before a particular incarnation, it was agreed that there would be a plan set up for counterbalancing this possibility. It was important to you, after the experience of Atlantis, to save some of your seed, rather than be wiped out entirely as you were once before. It was important to many of you to protect a certain number of your offspring in order to ensure the survival of your species, but also to use as a comparative model in looking at your physiological countenance, which is devolving through repeated exposure to pollution.

It is not written in stone that your beautiful planet is finished, nor are we suggesting that there is not hope. We are only explaining that possibilities had been noted in your evolution, and annihilation was one of those possibilities, although there are several types of ways one may annihilate another. With the repeated exposure to pollutants, the body physically responds through a compromised immune system. The mechanics of how we have retrieved your embryos, your fetuses, have been worked out after mountains of discussions and agreements as to the best way, and least traumatizing way, that this program could be enacted. You may object to the idea that a fetus is raised inside of an inanimate object, and yet we dare note that you presently grow children in a womb, in an environment in which there are emotional stress, physical pollutants, lack of health, and impoverishment.

We have initiated an adoption program, much like you have established on your own planet, where those who demonstrate their inability to care for their own offspring have those offspring placed elsewhere, in an environment that is best suited for the development of that being. But in your case, your entire species is demonstrating its inability to care for its offspring *on a long-term basis*. As a result, some of you agreed to participate, while in a state embodied by your highest consciousness, in a program that would entrust a certain number of the young of your species to our care, in the event that the planet becomes uninhabitable. Rest assured that these young ones of your species thrive in adopted homes, and they are placed only where the host species is enlightened and would necessarily refrain from prejudices to dissimilar species, unlike the behavior that you often exhibit. This way have human children been adopted through our programs, whereby we can ensure the development of your species, despite potential threats to your lineage. These programs in no way supercede your own souls' agreement and participation. We have not set this up alone. This program is a collaborative effort between certain of you and us, although admittedly you may not remember this agreement.

As you might imagine, there can be many significant differences in atmospheric and other conditions between your neighborhood and ours, which would entail an adaptation by the child, engendering a more suitable physical countenance, which is made possible in this transition to a different plane of existence. As a result, through some processes, procedures, and techniques, young human children do take on certain physical characteristics of the host family. There are numerous causes and reasons for this shift in the physical appearance and biological makeup. The shift is not harmful to these offspring and creates a higher functioning physical body, and at times the outward characteristics may be adjusted as a result of inner changes and adjustments.

This explains some of the reasons why a difference in physical appearance can happen to these special children. It is nothing to fear. They are not harmed. But just as your own children may have a different outward countenance while attending one school versus another, shortened hair and a particular uniform at a private school, or a different physical appearance more suitable to a different geographical location, so too these children of the universe often take on different physical characteristics, depending upon where they are placed. There is no need for alarm. As we said, there is no harm done. Remember, as we discussed, those precious souls have called those experiences to themselves. They are not victims of us. This subject has been seen as so taboo that there is tremendous resistance by most of you to objectively listening to the facts when it comes to this phenomenon. The single most empowering way to initiate change is to first notice where there might be denial and to consider where the light of truth shines.

Then do many experiencers actually have children living somewhere else, raised by extraterrestrials?

Yes. There are offspring of many of you, and those offspring themselves have chosen, through decisions made long before they incarnated, where their interest in soul development lay. When you get away from the idea that one's birthplace and birth circumstances are random, you begin to unlock the mysteries of the universe. So much trust is possible when you recognize to what degree we are involved with you. We have raised your offspring and we are currently mentoring several of you, individually as well as collectively. Between the realms of existence lie infinite possibilities. The idea that we partner the raising of children with you is a beautiful connection and can be a heartwarming thought as this connection to us begins to take hold. What is so interesting is that through tolerance, we can know and understand the soul of each other.

There is an idea that there is something evil that has been undertaken when one, through one's awakened spiritual, technological, and intellectual enlightenment, proactively produces effects on the human body that render it more functional than would have been possible without such intervention.

But you said previously that humans shouldn't manipulate the human body to achieve a higher functioning one through cloning, but now you state that extraterrestrials tinker with the human body. This seems to be a blatant contradiction.

Your culture has made certain allowances for particular members of your medical profession to open up the human body when it's deemed necessary, and you call it "surgery." Your culture agrees and allows this after these members of your society have received ample training to do so. Therefore, kindergarten teachers are not supervising brain surgery on their students, because they lack the necessary training. Should they receive that training, then you would gladly grant them permission to do so. This, you agree, makes sense. You have no objection to this "standard," which recognizes a "skill set" in one individual but not in another.

We are suggesting that your collective *spiritual* "training," which would make you proficient to cope with, supervise, and direct a cloning program of which you speak, has hardly even begun. And more important, the very fact that you don't notice your lack of spiritual "training," nor think that it is necessary to create the gains that you seek, is further evidence of your naiveté. Heading into these projects with this degree of naiveté is foolhardy, given the results you say you are wishing to achieve.

We have observed you to be on a downward spiral collectively with respect to increased numbers of seeming mysterious cancers and unexplained maladies. Often caused by environmental factors, and spiritual unconsciousness, these maladies and maladjustments in the human physical condition at times can be impacted by simply removing the physical being from your wasteland.

This may seem like a harsh term to describe your beautiful planet, but we say that with emphasis to get your attention. Your nest you call home is genetically polluted and impacted daily by big business, whose chief concern is often that which shows on a profit and loss statement. The fact that such shortsightedness has not only been allowed to flourish, but has been encouraged by your governments, speaks for the lack of awakening in general on your planet. As you begin to feel strength in your awakened voice, you will join hands together and find a way to enact legislation which prevents multinational conglomerates from destroying your home, even as they deposit their profits into their bank accounts, which sit atop this endangered home. As we, and others, in the greater area of your universal quadrant have noticed the possibilities of outcomes, one of them allows for the extinction of your species. This is not necessarily a probability—at least it wasn't, fifty years ago—but it is a possibility. Such steps were taken then to ensure that there was a record of your physical species.

When we look at your beautiful planet and how certain elements of it are dissolving, such as the ozone layer and soil content, we continue to take seriously those projects that instill and ensure the survivability of your species. You may protest that your species is best suited to your own planet, and we would wholeheartedly agree. And yet, would you stand by blindly and watch a people on your own planet threaten others of you to such a degree that there was question as to whether or not the children of the threatened group would make it to maturity? Certainly, there are currently groups of you who thwart the happy development of your women and children, and most of the planet stands by helplessly, unsure as to how to respond and react.

We put into place years ago, through your agreement with us, a plan that would ensure that your genetic code is established scientifically, should any catastrophe befall the masses of you.

In this way, your lineage will survive intact, although, admittedly, not on your own planet. It is ironic that you adopt this practice with certain animals, and you call this ecology and environmental protection. Consider it as one of our altruistic projects, where we exercise great empathy in our research with your young, where we monitor their development closely. Over all, they are resoundingly healthy, spiritually, physically, and mentally. They are not birthed through the normal gestation, as you have surmised through fragments in your memory. They often develop in simulated wombs and are then adopted into programs where sufficient love is provided. Relocation is then directed, and much love and encouragement are provided to these young ones. These children are seen as a great gift and remind us of our own heritage. We, too, destroyed ourselves more than once. In this way you give us a constant reminder of where a species can go when left to its intellectual pursuits alone. Despite our candid discussion of this, there will be many of you who will find this idea abhorrent, and yet, if you truly grasp the delicate way in which the fate of your species may hang in the balance, you, like us, would refer to this program as altruistic. Never doubt our love for humankind. Now you see how it is that we are all in this together.

CHAPTER 8

Money and Manifestation

During the last four months, I've flown in and out of my local airport almost a dozen times. Each trip, I have taken the same airline, and so I have had reason to visit the same terminal each time.

On the first trip, I saw him sitting alone with a worn bag that contained his belongings at his feet. Because it was biting cold and snowy outside, no doubt he sought refuge from the cold, and had found a nook where he could sleep, at least for a few hours. As I settled in waiting for the boarding announcement, I felt my heart ache as I looked at this homeless soul, who was attempting to sleep in an upright position, so as not to call attention to himself. Minutes later, he was chased off by a security guard, just as I began considering how I might help.

Over the next several months, I continued to see him, and I would invariably hand him a twenty-dollar bill, which he would accept shyly, but never utter a word. It was then that I noticed that he was a woman, about my own mother's age, dressed like a man. I looked in my wallet wondering how much cash I could spare.

I couldn't stop thinking about her for the rest of my trip, again pondering how it is that our society still cannot seem to address such pressing issues.

How can we as individuals help all those in need, and still have enough to care for our own families? Worldwide, there are so many people and projects that need our financial, and other, help. There are starving children, abused animals, endangered species, and decimated environments. It all seems so daunting.

Begin by envisioning a world in which everyone's needs are met and where peace and tranquility reign. This is where you must start because right now, you can hardly imagine it, let alone achieve it. It takes *training* to exercise the visionary muscle. Don't think that it doesn't. Every last one of you on the planet would be well served to begin exercising this visionary muscle, for this is where you will take back your hope for a new tomorrow. Right now, you are limited by a sense of being overwhelmed as to how things can possibly change, how a planet can change, how a political system can change, how a culture can wake up. It is only your lack of vision that keeps you confined to your box of hopelessness, or at least indifference, which is really hopelessness disguised. So do not trivialize our message to you as being about encouraging you to overextend yourselves. It is a matter of beginning to practice the principles of which you keep speaking, of which you all keep reading, on which you all keep lecturing.

It is time to come away from the intellectualizing of these ideas. Who better to heal a world than someone who begins showing how it is being done precisely in his own home environment? What type of grandiose thinking will it take to replenish your rain forests? What type of unlimited visioning will be required to cleanse your oceans and restore them to azure blue? What degree of forgiveness and appreciation for each other would be required to join the tribe of you in love to cease the fighting and enable you to heal your planetary home? Along the spectrum, it would be at the maximum end, not the minimum end, we can assure you.

Only your limited thinking prevents you from enacting the idea that you can do all of those things. Do start with your own life. Do make applicable these ideas personally. When the mind and intellect object that we are out of touch with reality, remember your oceans, for they are calling you. Remember your white tigers and remember your sea life, for they all whisper your name. Remember that we are suggesting that you begin now in the training ground of your own backyard. Create for yourselves a life of your dreams, so that you will confidently join hands with others who have done so too and create the *planet* of your dreams. You are the leaders of tomorrow morning. These leaders will not be dictated to by the intellect. The intellect can minimize, can shut down, and can intellectualize all the joyous spirit right out of the most grandiose scheme. This is what we confront in you for you have declared a deep longing to be part of the New World. That New World requires you to create her. Look to spirit within as the New Creator. Like the universe, there are no limits.

But how do we reach those limitless goals with our planet? Nothing ever seems to change.

We notice that you're afraid to dream big, yet degrees of grandeur have no range of difficulty when served up by the universe. This is one of the greatest myths of humankind, that one thing is more attainable than another thing, when there is no difference, from a purely causational perspective. When the soul holds an impassioned idea of an outcome, all events in the universe conspire to support that outcome, whether supporting you in buying a home or in buying back your planet from those who seem to own it. In this light, your comment is missing something. You forget—you all forget—that it is not necessary to know the precise mechanics that the universe might lay at your fingertips to support the vision. This is the point of the teaching. The intellect demands that the details be known. The mind demands that the pieces of the puzzle be in sight and observable. When you decide in the heart and soul of you for an outcome, that is when you surrender to the universe and allow the pieces to be pulled in from wherever necessary to support that vision.

How does a species such as ours return our lives to ones of bliss, clean up the lakes and rivers at the same time, and feed and house the impoverished?

We are inviting you to cease creating from where you are most comfortable. We are inviting you to instead let go of the need to *understand* how something would be created. Do you understand how the planets float in the universe? Do you understand the mechanics of how the millions of miraculous details in the functioning of your physical body can all take place? You wonder how it is that one person can create one thing and another person creates another thing. A person does not buy a million-dollar house because she has a million dollars, although that appears to be the case. Behind the scenes is another story, and this is what we are asking you to observe. Behind the scenes of that story is that in some manner, that home was envisioned. That lifestyle was envisioned prior to the availability of funds. And then the funds manifested, and then the house was purchased.

But do not think that we are advocating wasting your natural resources. We are only asking you to notice that you can practice transforming the finances and health of your life, to prepare you for transforming the finances and health of your globe.

The same principle, by the way, can be applied to your query as to how you can feed your masses. The knowing of that event is the place to start. The knowing and the holding of that vision and the seeing of that outcome is the first place to begin. The mechanics of "how" is what Divinity is up to. You do not have to know the details of "how"; in fact, your preoccupation with such details is what keeps you forever in the planning stages and never in the manifestation stage. This is the mediocrity from which you are yearning to expand. When you all definitively decide that you've had enough of toxins in your waters and starving children—when you've truly made that decision—the mechanics of how that change can occur will arrive on your doorstep. We do not refer to your life as mediocre, but rather the hamster wheel repetition of frustrated desires. We are simply addressing what you say you would like to practice creating. And so let's take it one step at a time. In the example of the million-dollar house, you have a certain idea as to what type of house, what type of dwelling—the best version and vision of a home for you. When you can joyously picture yourself living in that home *now*—or that planetary home—then you shall trigger the universe in assisting you to manifest that. The continued and ongoing erroneous assumption is that it is created the other way around, that you will believe it's possible when it happens.

There are countless "miracles" that can take place to support your abundant ideas. If you hold in your heart and soul that you would like to fly to Rome, and you viscerally feel and know yourself there, you feel the joy of seeing and experiencing the history of St. Michael's Cathedral of that location, you cannot help but create this precise outcome.

When you can smell the olive oil in the Italian restaurant of your fantasy, notice how quickly your trip to Rome is created. There are one hundred, times one hundred, times one hundred ways that this trip could be manifested. This seems like a ridiculously simple teaching. Many of you seem to know about it; you read about it, but very few of you practice it beyond and outside of your normal comfort level.

So go forth, and let's see how you play on the Monopoly board of your life and please think not that this is simply about material acquisition. It is about manifesting your desires individually so that you can confidently take the hand of your brethren and say, "I'm getting the hang of this. I know how we can do this thing called 'changing our experience,' so follow me, and let's do it together."

Creating Miracles

Miracles, in and of themselves, are not considered out of the ordinary to your space brethren as you call them, for we are in touch with our abilities of manifestation. In this way, seemingly impossible outcomes are called miracles, and yet when you begin to see pure potentiality as the blank slate on which you can create your fondest desires, you will then have a more functional understanding of creation and of how creation occurs. Through your passion will you grow to create joyously in a conscious manner.

Now you can drop your assumptions, for your next course dictates a perspective shift in which you challenge the current and prevailing thought system which says, "That is not possible because . . ." or, "That is improbable for this reason . . . " Are you thinking that you will wait to create grandly until the time when all of you become good at this at the same time? You may have to show your brothers and sisters how it's done. Whether in your board rooms or your marketing meetings, this is where you have an opportunity to model in which you say, "Follow me and I will show you by my example how to create from scratch." You say that you too want the opportunity of practicing creating magnificently? You say that you want the opportunity to be a leader, and yet new ideas are constantly thwarted?

Keep at it anyway. Invite them, your comrades: "Follow me, and

I will take you there. Follow me, and I will show you how I deal with my doubts when they arise. Watch me and I will model *through my behavior* a belief that all things are possible, that we do not need to defer to what has been done and tested previously."

Create a new mantra. Notice that you *can* create on a blank slate. In fact, you must. If you are to do it differently, you must. You know what your thinking has created for you thus far, for your balance sheet is stretched—the balance sheet of your natural resources is stretched. Those of you in a position to lead, then lead, but lead by your example, and not merely by your words. Lead with the passion of your heart and your soul. Through your example, invite others to notice your willingness to risk, for to stay the same ensures that your situation may be the same in another year. Do you want an opportunity to change the landscape of your corporations? Do you want to make a dent in your routine? This is your opportunity. Start with your own corporate family. It is not browbeating. Re-contextualize in your own mind what it is that you are up to. Notice that you are stuffing nothing down anybody's throat. You are in a position of management and leadership, you and others have placed yourselves there, and for your own souls' purpose, you shall, if courageous, step confidently into this more dynamic role. If others were comfortable stepping out far from the culturally predominant ideas, they would have done so, would they not have? We will repeat this. Were your colleagues comfortable in envisioning a new paradigm, they would be doing so. So stop waiting for consensus with respect to healing the world from your current political leaders. Step in to your magnificent ideas when they are imbued with love and concern for all.

Now we suggest that you see the master in yourself. But remember that the master is motivated by the highest love for brethren and universal healing. This does not mean that personal abundance through such a path is impossible. It means that many of you have confused your own personal agendas with that of the highest ideas which best serve you all.

Those who developed the ideas for the telegraph, or the airplane, or a pollution-free planet, have sponsored, and will sponsor, ideas that were considered impossible or beyond laughable. We cannot overemphasize this idea, although so many of your books reiterate and remind you over and over that the most courageous and limitless thinkers are ridiculed and often shunned. Yes, of course, you don't see it as it is occurring within your nine-to-five jobs, or your own daily disqualification of others' visionary ideas, but you can look back on it and notice how ridiculous new ideas were to those hearing new ideas—of flight, for example.

You visionaries, when you have your expansive ideas, do not need to argue them. It is not a matter of angry confrontation. The nuance, the difference inside, is what you see and feel in your heart; notice what you feel is possible. If Divinity is calling to you, and this is your personal project that your soul has brought to you, do not let others dampen your enthusiasm. The universe is counting on you. If you cannot find a sympathetic ear, then go elsewhere until you find one. But to withdraw from Divinity's voice would not be your highest idea for yourself. Notice that you are not necessarily even seeking agreement, you are only asking for the luxury of allowing a risk in presenting new ideas. To allow risk within the context of sameness is what leadership is all about. Somebody there must be willing to go to the uncomfortable place where there are fewer who share the vision than there are those who applaud it.

There is a palpable vibration that emits from the individual soul who steps out confidently, knowing that one person can change the world; that one person can have a huge impact on the way the world perceives a phenomenon. Be that one person.

We are your future: a state of enlightenment where all of the gifts and benefits of an evolved society await you. This is your carrot. Do it for the sake of your children. Be brave and courageous for the sake of your children's children. Take on the visage of a confident, visionary role where the idea of risk is not refuted by the mind, but new ideas are articulated despite the "risk."

It would seem that it is now necessary for all of you to create something different from what you have already created. You know where you will be in your near future if you stay the same, making the same decisions, based on the same criteria. Should you choose a more evolved path, the universe will conspire to get you the help you need to follow it.

That's easy for you to say. You probably don't pump gas for a living, given the expense of that spacecraft you fly. What does your culture use for money?

Money and Manifestation

The basis of legal tender presumes that all are in agreement that a certain one thing will be that which is used to facilitate the bartering of goods and services. It is based on a general agreement. This general agreement makes possible widespread acceptance and use of this medium of barter.

In our culture we do not require an element, such as rock, paper, or scissors, to be used as an instrument of bartering. We garner those items of need through a system of providing for each other in a way that enables all to have what is necessary. There is a story you tell in which you catch a glimpse of hell and see people starving despite the fact that everyone is sitting around a giant bowl of soup, since the spoons are too long to enable one to feed oneself. Then you visit heaven and see the same size group of people with the same spoons and the same soup, yet all are well nourished, since they have figured out that by feeding each other, they all can become nourished.

This story symbolizes how we provide and receive goods and services. We readily provide that which another needs, and they provide for us, since we have deeply internalized the understanding that when another flourishes, so does self. There is not the bickering and haggling necessary for jockeying for positions of ownership of pieces of rock and soil, which you call real estate. We do not attempt to slice up into arbitrary cubicles and boundaries our living quarters. We have discovered that when we engage in our most blissful activity and proceed from the perspective that we are all members within the same close-knit family, we naturally provide to self and others, knowing that others are doing the same for us. There is a perfect synchronicity involved, and all are well nourished, well cared for, and have everything required for a happy existence.

This paradigm is so vastly different from what you experience that you probably cannot begin to imagine what it might be like or how one could possibly proceed without survival conditions, in which one competes with another for the spoils. You can begin to imagine it if you simply pretend that you are part of the fictitious Swiss Family Robinson, deserted on a remote island with a few beloved friends and family members. Would you then grow your vegetables in the soil and ask your sister to pay you for a turnip? In this example, it seems ridiculous doesn't it? For some of you would grow turnips, and others would gather papayas, others of you might gather fish, and others might fix the tree house. You might, at the end of the day, join together in ceremony and celebration and share what you had, all bringing a different contribution based on your skills, your idea of blissful "work," and your artistic nature. Now if you can imagine this scenario, and surely you can, then simply expand on that idea, imagining that you now live in a global village where all of you behold those in the village as members of your own divine family, which, by the way, you are. You seem to be able to imagine this with a small group, but have difficulty imagining feeling this way about thousands or millions of others.

There would be pervasive harmony, for it could be said that you would even tend to notice and act upon your perceived understanding of another's need before you would notice and act upon your own, and others would be doing the same for you. This blending of love throughout your community is what is meant by creating heaven on Earth, or heaven where you are, for certainly there are other embodiments in physical existences on planets other than Earth.

The degree of peace and serenity that permeates such a culture as we describe might seem farfetched and lofty from where you are at the moment. But you would be surprised at how quickly you would move to those ideals, for they are what make up the higher part of you, despite your observations of your planetary existence right now. You know this to be true because when members of your community have suffered an ordeal through catastrophic earthquake or flood, hurricane or fire, you have witnessed yourself and others pulling together quite selflessly, and some of you have even risked your lives without a moment's hesitation. You and others have demonstrated an ability to be quick to determine and make manifest specifically what is needed and required by another at that moment. There are stories of complete strangers giving their lives to another simply out of a momentary decision. This is your nature, despite what you experience of yourself and others. So when you feel that it seems impossible to move your experience to resemble that of a community that we have described, do not be fooled, for you are not beasts waiting to evolve. You are divine beings, merely asleep. This is quite a shift in your understanding, which is why we ask you to not only begin to change your perception of self, but also to change your perception of your neighbor, for as you understand yourself to be thus, you can allow yourself to identify another as such. In this way will you grow quickly, spiritually, for you demonstrate your awakened understanding.

There is no toiling in our communities such as what you experience. We gleefully pursue our pleasure for its own sake. Each of us, too, has determined in what direction we are interested in proceeding, be it providing mentorship to a neighboring community such as yours or helping to restore a damaged planet, or helping create a star. There are different levels of practicing creation. You, too, can practice understanding that you can create your own experience. As you become expert at this, you can move on to other embodiments, in which you perfect this further and practice making the very things that God makes because you are part of God and therefore embody those traits that God enjoys. A group of you may join together and create an ecological environment on a planet, choosing the flora and creating flowers, much as your children in grade school are taken out back by their kindergarten teacher to practice growing peas in the soil. They plant the seeds, and the teacher takes them through an understanding of how plants are nurtured and how they grow. We do that too, but on a much grander scale, in that we might go to a planet like a blank slate and inhabit her. How is that for a field trip? How is that for a thesis or dissertation? Our schooling is not composed of slapping the pages of a term paper together and turning them in to a teacher for a grade. We demonstrate our excellence in understanding our divine heritage by creating.

And then, when the seeker understands and has recouped full memory of that divine ability, we do not label that as blasphemy. To have awakened fully and to recall that in order to be one, in order to be part of the divine whole, then Divinity must necessarily be able to be expressed consciously and powerfully through each part of that whole. If Divinity is miraculous and we are all part of Divinity, then the attributes of miracles are of a miraculous nature, including the attributes of each divine being. That would include, from your perspective, the ability to partake in such things as the creation of environmental homes elsewhere. You don't balk at the idea of creating something in your backyard. You don't recognize that you are creative beings playing outside on your little plot—which is precisely what we are doing on a grander scale—but in fact, you are.

We operate in unison with other beings and creatures and animals. There are many varieties, and we don't pretend that they don't exist, and we don't pretend that others who know of them or who have witnessed their existence are crazy. And we don't relegate our most colorful memories of what is so to children's fantasies. We may have gardens of flowers with the most delicate beings the size of a thimble and butterflies with wings as large as your dog in colors resembling a vivid stained glass window. If this sounds delightful, imagine the kindergarten class where you send your precious five-year-old. You want for your child to be exposed to colors and experiences outside in nature. You want him to be exposed to the wonders of nature and of the universe. We don't limit our culture to those times when we are five, and then require that we must move on to the tedium of the form-ative years. Our lives embody the gleeful kindergarten class on a grand scale with colors and music, animals, and the hands of our family, bliss-fully engaged in their favorite activities, all perfectly synchronized and blended to provide for another, just as another provides for us.

When you have trouble understanding how such an arrangement could be facilitated, remember the state of your environment before you muddled her up. You are in awe in your science class as you note the utter perfection of your environment, for one species provides what another needs and the circle of life seems brilliant beyond any one person's ability to have orchestrated it. Your plant and animal life are so perfectly in unison. What more do you think God could have created for a village of universal beings, than what she has provided there on Earth like a brilliantly woven fabric of intricate design? The intricacies are staggering when you stop to consider how your Moth-er Nature seems to orchestrate life-forms there, but as you consider what is possible in this realm, magnify that and imagine what the uni-verse has in store for an awakening universal being. This synchronis-tically woven fabric made manifest throughout the universe is available to all of you in your future.

Left to its own devices, have you ever seen your planet banging into the sun? This symmetry of the cosmos, and the way that it seems to be able to function and operate without the help of humankind's mathematicians and physicists, leaves the ego helpless to understand how it can all happen without its help. This same divine brilliance runs consistent throughout enlightened communities in the cosmos. And so it is not so far-fetched, if your planet can spin and rotate on its own, to imagine that communities exist that have returned to their divine inheritance and that have stepped into this divine flow, and it all simply works. The pieces of the puzzle fit together beautifully. How is that possible? Who knew which piece was needed where?

Who lay the borders and the corners of the puzzle? It is all just there, unfolding perfectly. These are the qualities of Divinity.

So, if your stars have been created and your sun warms your planet, and the oceans ebb and flow without a little man sitting in a clock tower pushing buttons to make this happen, then surely you can imagine a community of beings who live together harmoniously because they have tapped into the same divine essence that allows such magnificence to reign supreme throughout the galaxy. When you balk at the ideas we suggest that we embody, simply go observe one of your sunsets and notice the oranges and the pinks and wonder how those got there. How did those clouds get there? How do the colors hang there in that sunset, splashed in the sky at just the right moment when you needed to see them? Who has orchestrated the drops of rain on the prairie grasses? If this orchestration is possible, what think you is possible, and what could work through living beings as well?

To be able to trust in the practical application of harmonious community living, we understand, has not been part of your present reality. You can see perfection in God's creatures, or in the sky, or in the waterfall, but you have not yet remembered that this perfection also runs deeply through all of you, which is why you will soon remember that you too embody this magnificence. Then will you confidently begin to imagine and create universal villages where you cohabitate peacefully without a nagging doubt that it's possible. You will have tapped into how it is that you are part of it, rather than resisting that you are.

How does the chicken know to sit on her egg? Who told her how long she must sit on the egg for it to hatch? When you ask, "How does an enlightened being know the best thing to do, the best work upon which to embark?" We answer by asking you, "How does the chicken know she shall sit on her egg?" She is not complicated, or confused by a timetable that has her scurrying on freeways to collect green pieces of paper that she turns around with and scurries back on the freeway to give to somebody else. She is simply in touch with a deep knowing, and carries that out without a moment's hesitation. This divine connection is to where you are returning. You can learn much from your backyard hen.

It is the egoic mind that insists that sophisticated complexity is necessary for fulfillment. The egoic mind creates all manner of complication, drama, and untold gnashing of teeth in order to justify its existence. But enlightened societies are beautifully simple, just as your fantasy of Swiss Family Robinson on a paradisiacal island is also divinely simple. This does not imply that simplicity must be without technology, for certainly we would consider our existence to be beautifully simple, and yet we still enjoy superior technology. So we are not suggesting that in order to be evolved, you must be satisfied drinking from coconuts from morning until sunset. Many of you can relate to this as you scurry to and fro with your hectic schedules, alarm clocks, and frequent flyer miles, that there is a part of you that yearns for more hours in the day spent at your leisure, simply being who you long to be. This is our reminder that part of awakening means allowing the self to return to this life. The irony is not lost on most of you who have discovered that the more hours you work, and the greater your income, the less time you are spending in blissful pursuit of your highest ideals: time with loved ones, adventures to parts of your globe that you always wanted to see; the ability to move to a part of your planet where you have always wanted to live; the ability to cast off professionals, politicians, or educators with whom you consult, who no longer suit your ideas of who you are. At some point you will come to terms with how chaotic and unsatisfying your life has become. When you find that you perceive it as difficult to step into the life of your dreams, it gives you pause because you recognize that there is something out of sync with a life spent simply meeting obligations.

We are happy to send a reminder that your futures can hold less of this routine, for you will reach a point when you will no longer be willing to sacrifice the quality of your life for expectations of either others or your egoic mind. Then, all of you will shift, and it will be a blessed day indeed.

CHAPTER 9

Crop Circles and Other Contact

Last year I had a group on Thursday evenings where I invited others to get together with me to discuss their own encounter experiences, and how those experiences have changed their lives. One night, a German family of four, a mother, father, and their two teenage sons, arrived. They seemed "normal" enough, and listened as the group grew silent after hearing one woman cry softly about her ongoing shame about feeling that she was losing her mind after seeing "little people" dance in her guest house in the wee hours of the evening. She had also had encounter experiences. After glancing at her husband and then her sons, the German woman ventured forth with her own story.

"We have a home in Germany, and years ago we had some extraordinary UFO encounters. Some time after those encounters, while in the backyard, we saw gnomes who had come out onto the grass, but who live in the trees." Her sons and her husband nodded in agreement, seemingly thankful that someone in their family had finally spoken up about it.

"They're tiny little people," one of the boys continued with a strong accent, "but they exist. We have seen them, and they're very

shy." *The four of them stopped speaking, having tested the waters of belief from those of us sitting next to them.*

Theirs is not an unusual story. Something amazing happens when humans come into contact with otherworldly phenomena, particularly when they have encounter experiences. From personal experience, as well as after hearing from many others whose lives have changed drastically after their own encounters, it seems to me that there's more "paranormal" life going on around us than most of us are aware of. But more important, what we are beginning to understand is that it is not "paranormal" at all, but rather, naturally occurring events, and beings will come into our awareness, once we let go of our insistence that such things are only fantasy. We can accept that on our planet, right now, live beings who are half our own height, and we call them dwarfs or "little people." Why is it so hard to believe that there are also beings who are again half, or any other fraction, the size of them?

It had never really occurred to me to ask the ETs if they knew of any gnomes who were on Earth, until the afternoon that Bob asked the extraterrestrials this next question.

Can you tell us about crop circles and how they're made? Why are they there?

Our expression is made manifest through nature, for she doesn't protest, as you do, when we bestow evidence of ourselves.

Why do you refer to nature, life, and Divinity as "she"? I thought such things weren't relegated to one specific gender.

They aren't. That's why we have chosen a word that contains both genders—she—although you don't usually use it that way. "He" is contained in the word "she." Thus are both genders represented as one.

Nature gladly opens her door to us and creates with us in these artistic undertakings. When the Bible speaks of the lion lying down with the lamb, it speaks of a time when consciousness is such that full harmony is achieved between all of the universe's creations. Was it your thinking that you are separate from nature's bounty? Suppose we were to tell you that these living plants of which the crop circles are part co-create this lovely art for you through their transforming energetic particles into an altered state? But these crops are not victims of us, any more than experiencers are. There is a co-creation of the soul, the plants and greenery upon your beautiful planet, too, have a soul, and they create with us in this magnificent announcement that there is much, much more going on than punching a time clock and paying the bills.

Imagine the voice of Mother Earth participating with our consciousness through her children, that which grows from her bosom. We hold hands together and make manifest communications that, although seemingly quite complex, celebrate and announce the highest possibilities. These designs, which you call "crop circles" represent great markings from your collective heritage, those that would stir the soul at a very deep level upon contemplation. That heritage precedes your life there, and the soul of the green plants and yellow plants join in unison with the wake-up call. As you may surmise, nature has a vested interest in your waking up.

You have so disconnected from the life around you that you barely even notice the soul of the animals, let alone the soul of the plants, and as startling as this might seem, these crops are communicating to you. Be willing to allow your mind to settle for a moment while you contemplate what other wonders may be in store for you. It is almost inconceivable that these marvels are in your backyard and yet have drawn such little attention. Those things that draw applause and fantastic reactions are those things most transient to you. And yet, right at your side, are the plants making music in their very midst, from their very being. And hardly any of you are given pause. We say this not to scold you but to draw back to the earlier question as to how it is that we have not yet landed there. Were more of you ready for the awe-inspiring possibilities in your very backyard, on Earth and galactically, the denial would have broken away somewhat on a grander scale. There would be masses of you transporting your children to these locations to ponder the marvels that have been offered to you thus far. How many of you have shown your children these marvels? Perhaps you now better understand the workings of the mind and how the status quo is so more easily continued.

These are the marvels that are already there, without benefiting from your collective observation and discussion. How have you all responded so far? Do you think it would be any different if we landed right now? Can you imagine a field trip of children, standing there with adults allowing for a discussion in magic and the remarkable nature of life in the universe? And to not even discuss the possibility of cultural denial, and what that might mean, when raising your children passes on that very cultural denial.

Thousands upon thousands travel many miles to see ball games and such fascinations and yet evidence of such a grand demonstration goes virtually undiscussed and unnoticed. The Renoir, the Picasso, lay in your fields, beautiful reminders of heavenly intervention and co-creation. Bring no judgment to others who sleep, for allow this example to show each of you where you too sleep. Stonehenge reminds the soul of what was and what could be. Awaken the others and make a referral there.

The plants sing a vibration so unique during these episodes of transmutation that even your own people can detect these changes with your crude instruments. The molecular changes are so significant, and signify such magnificent possibilities, that it is a marvel that more of you have not used this alone to awaken.

It is an honor to participate in the awakening of humankind, and here is evidence of how Mother Earth herself has timed her involvement perfectly. Fear not that transformation is occurring. If your stalks of wheat perform such wizardry, what think you that your souls are up to? The clouds above you shape shift as well. Look up someday when you are grieving, and you will hear and see the angels in the clouds or a form that appears that speaks right to your heart. The stalks below and the clouds above, all in harmony. Kneel before the curtain opening and the players step forth so beautifully dressed and costumed, enough to dazzle any observer. But first you must put yourself in a place of observation and transition from a place of massive scurrying. This scurrying to and fro makes observing almost impossible. When more of you begin to notice the designs of the galaxies in your very soil, we have more surprises.

Some farmers have long suspected that the very plants seem to coalesce. There does not appear to be any sign of destruction. Like music notes coming forth from an instrument, the waves of electrical vibrations emit from nature's seedlings. Teach your children about the magnificence of potentiality. This is what we suggest, for this is the reason for our art. We embody potentiality in you. This is where you are heading. When you beckon understanding to you, it shall be received. As you ask for these understandings from the depths of your soul, you shall understand. We know who asks. To those we do come.

The tall sunflower knows of a time when it is best to re-seed. And so your species can call to itself a time when it re-seeds a new wave of thought. The spring of your new thoughts is upon you. The crop circles do just that, potentially. The forms can circle the thoughts, leading you back inward to yourself. Even a young child can surmise the significance of these events. Circle back to a time of great wonder, like in your science fiction, in which anything is possible. Circle back in your thoughts to a time in which it is no longer threatening to perceive of a magical world, where there are others who live close by, not as a threat, but as your brothers and sisters. We believe in possibilities. We invite you to notice them as well. It's about time. The soul of the world symbolically drums its fingers on the table, awaiting your readiness.

May I ask a question?

Certainly.

It would be of immense interest to those who study crop circles to know how they are accomplished technologically. Can you speak on that?

We have spoken on that. You do not understand that response, we understand.

You have already explained that?

We and the living plants commune. Is that too simple?

So it's not done from a craft through technological means such as energy beams of some sort?

When you sit down to eat a meal, there are numerous functions going on at one time. Technology may have been used to prepare the meal, and physical prowess may be required to move around the kitchen and to eventually end up seated at the table, and digestion is involved. So too, with this process, it is not purely technology, it is not purely communication. There is even digestion, if you will. Allow this metaphor: Digest the idea of multi-phenomena. The term *multi-phenomena* means that the mind protests that it must be one thing or the other, and yet when we engage with the soul of the universe, technology is never used alone. It's not necessary, except when thwarting the collective souls' desire, which is what you do. And so you have a situation, very simplistically described here, as entailing multi-phenomena, at least phenomena to your way of thinking. True miracles engage a mixture of variables. We cannot describe this as a process in which a button is pushed and out pops a result. Not only is this too simplistic, but it is not accurate. And so there is a partnership here, which is the miracle. Do you not see this? The partnering of living organisms with other living organisms is the simple miracle. You have assumed that we have pushed a button and impacted your plants in some way, because you cannot imagine co-creating with the plants. Your species would do well to notice our example in this. This partnering enables such miracles to take place and so your mind can only draw from the examples in your culture.

"Crop circles" can be more correctly likened to music that is created by an orchestra of us. The players from several different realms come together to produce a wondrous symphony, a display that tackles the mind of the scientist. If we told you that the elves and the faeries and the plants themselves had something to do with this, that we play the trombone and the blades of grass are plucking at the violin, then you would have a better understanding of how such things come to be. It is not produced in a factory. It is not the product of a cookie-cutter. Multi-phenomena are created from multiple dimensions. You ask this question from a very linear perspective. And we attempt to answer and not, as you say, to blow your mind by suggesting that there is so much more orchestrated in this very example then you could ever possibly grasp. Know only that this must be the case since your cultural denial about this phenomenon is so complete. That is your hint that something magnificent must be taking place. Does this answer satisfy you?

Not entirely.

What is your protest?

Well, it sounds kind of patronizing to say that you won't tell us how it happens because we couldn't understand it, so what is the purpose of doing it if we can't understand it?

You misunderstand the way in which you can't understand.

Then please enlighten me.

If we say to you, "We pick up our galactic walkie-talkies and punch the 'call' button and speak to the crops and say, 'Tonight at 2:00 A.M. please conduct yourselves this way,' and then the gnomes come out from the tree trunks, and the faeries with silver wings fly to the spot, and together we make music this way in the plants," do you understand that?

Like the trumpeter in a great symphony, we herald the beginning of a new stage of life for you, which the "crop circles" are announcing. They are a communication to you, much like this is a communication to you. You are all heading toward a life in which you no longer have a belief that you are all alone on that planet. Certainly, many of you have surmised that there are others, but now you will meet us, and others.

You have dismissed this type of communication as not being an example of having met us, yet when you speak on the telephone and meet someone for the first time telephonically, you have nonetheless had an introduction. For the most part, your global culture dismisses crop circles as evidence of communication. You can deal with your own "miracles" of technology when it comes to evolving means of communication. Even those of you who do not speak the same language may have a conference call in which a translator helps you bridge the gap between the differences in your languages. So, too, do your hearing-impaired even utilize devices and instruments to be able to use the telephone. In this case, crop circles symbolize a bridge between the differences in energy and distance. And to dismiss it as not real is fine, but we are still here, ready to meet you. As more and more of you can accept these types of communications, and more that will be developed soon, the more you are all readying yourselves for quantum leaps in the ability to accept our, and others', outstretched hands in friendship.

The idea that you are the sole inhabitor of your quadrant just doesn't make sense. And as we are invited by those of you who are capable of these types of meetings, we will step up to the plate ourselves, as you say, and represent the many of us out in these realms who wish to be part of the re-introduction of the universal species.

Consider if you were aware, through your technological abilities, of a particular tribe on an isolated island that had no knowledge of any other tribes on your planet, and because you have developed certain video capabilities, you had determined from your satellites perhaps, that such a species inhabited that island. And because you were able to understand and hear conversations among them, you understand their thinking processes. You would understand completely that they are utterly isolated from the knowing of the vastness of others in their close proximity. And to us, we are in your close proximity. Although you would wish to introduce yourselves to these tribespeople, you would take care not to simply arrive because your love for them would be so great, and in their belief that they be alone, they would be considerably jarred were you to simply show up. Since your color may be different, and perhaps you might have a different number of limbs, or a different number of eyes, or hair in a different location on the body or none at all, you understand that your appearance, and your presence, would be, and could be, so jarring that you would take it slow. You would introduce yourselves first to those whom you deem ready to be introduced to you. This is the same for us. We find our inroads to those souls like yourselves, who are available emotionally, physically, and spiritually.

Do you have a question?

What information would you want to convey in the early chapters of this book or on our website?

There is a group already poised to participate with this information. Those souls have readied themselves to know us more deeply for their own purposes. So your teammates are already in place. They await you. This phenomenon is no different from any other phenomenon. With reference to what particular subject is important to introduce early on, the main theme has already been touched upon, which is that we are your neighborly friend standing poised to greet you in friendship and to speak with others through their questions to us through you. For many it will ring true. For many it may not. But there are enough for whom it will, in fact, ring true. The relief for many to have another idea represented—that a meeting between us does not need to be coined an "abduction"—will be so profound. The conflict that this creates in the human psyche would be akin to contextualizing for your children as they go off to school that the procedures that go on there are part of random kidnappings and that they are not in control, that they may be harmed, and that they may be surgically operated upon to their detriment. That type of message would have a tremendous impact. Many of you have had contact and the culture contextualizes these experiences as your having been kidnapped by the use of the word, *abduction*. There is a residual effect upon the personality, and this is what you are unraveling with this book as you begin to explore this myth and allow for another idea about it. The relief can be quite profound, as other experiencers are introduced to the idea that not only may they not have been "abducted" but, in fact, they are actively taking part in the grand visitation between two species, and their very participation smacks of a certain spiritual readiness. When you think about this universally, it is a tremendous historical moment. We refer to it as a moment because it is, no matter how slow the passing of decades seems to you. It is a moment when one considers your current place in your evolution.

This is not only a profound opportunity for the both of you, Lisette and Bob, it is a profound opportunity in a time line of humanity. Think about this. You and others like you have brought yourselves to this time with tremendously courageous ideas and strong countenances, as you step into these uncharted territories. Despite skepticism and ridicule, gleefully step forth anyway, and you will join the merry men and women, all of you experiencers, who will show and demonstrate to others that this is not a ridiculous blabbering of new-age freaks. You set a trend in motion, you and your readers, all. This is what we would say. Welcome to this moment in time.

Do you have any idea of how many experiencers there are on the planet?

As we have said, we are not the only group who has been called forth and calls forth the experience between each of us. There are other groups, and if you are looking for a number, we can help you understand this way: Within your population on the planet, there are certain cultural pockets and tribes, depending on the background of the souls who have invited these types of communications and visitations, and because we are not the sole visitor, we represent just one species. An approximation of those of you who have experienced communications, whether this communication is one of face-to-face contact and experiences, or a derivative thereof, would be twenty percent of the population. Of that twenty percent, some of you have had, and will have, quite a process to pass through, in which you deal with the reality of those experiences.

All of it is part of the phenomena of the human personality coping with events and feelings associated with your culture's insistence that those experiences are absurd and impossible. This is a noble process that the soul undertakes. From your perspective, you may only mildly understand the gravity of this, but from where we are, we have a tremendous appreciation for the magnitude of this type of transition, for the resistance is at its strongest just before the seltzer bottle bursts open. This is why, just when it seems as though there are inroads being made, certain conservative elements seem to then have such a stranglehold that it seems that ideas that would be considered to be on the fringes will always be considered to be on the fringes. But it is impossible to stop what is in motion.

That twenty percent represents a mighty and formidable voice. It is not a random twenty percent, as the souls of you do nothing "randomly." And this does not even include those of you who say you have had no contact. You, Bob, are an example. You might consider that you have not had contact, but then what do you call this?

Twenty percent is a huge amount of people, maybe a billion people. It doesn't seem conceivable that it could be that many.

Why doesn't it seem conceivable?

It's such a huge number of people.

In relation to the cultural stigma or understanding?

No, in relation to the ability to have experiences in terms of crafts, or bringing people aboard crafts, it just seems like a tremendous number.

126

This number is not represented by every one of those having on-craft, face-to-face encounter experiences.

This includes other communication or sightings?

Whichever name you'd like to give it, there has been evidence given to a number of you that includes a significant encounter of the soul wherein that soul, that human, has had an awakened moment, which cannot be refuted at some level, as to direct experience that extraterrestrial life exists.

Some individuals have had significant face-to-face encounter experiences but have memory repression. Others have had sightings or dream experiences, which would seem to be less dramatic or less intense types of contacts, or meditative experiences which can be more impactful to the individual since there is memory, given the awareness and readiness of that particular soul. So, simply because one has had a direct encounter experience does not necessarily mean that that person is anywhere near ready to embrace, psychologically, emotionally, and spiritually, that experience, which is what you are about—which is what this project is up to.

As you awaken those memories in others who may have latent, fragmented memories, you are awakening a sleeping twenty percent. So awaken that group of people to what they themselves have experienced. Now you understand the power and dynamic nature of this undertaking. You potentially bring quite a powerful healing when you enable and allow this sleeping group to not only awaken to their own experiences and to begin to heal whatever residual impact they have had, but to join hands with that one voice: that percentage of people around the globe saying, "I too, know my neighbor," a cross section of the global population, from farmers to professors, from physicians to housewives, children, and teenagers, all who will no longer be quieted by a culture which denies those experiences. You are part of this awakening. You are part of this nudging. You are their brothers and sisters saying, "We believe you. Strengthen yourselves emotionally, strengthen yourselves physiologically and spiritually, because as you do, you help us all to ready for more contact."

Approximately what numbers have had actual experiences like the ones Lisette has had?

Are you referring to on board a craft, or having been invited to another location off of your planet in which you encounter other-worldly beings in the physical, is that what you are referring to?

Yes.

This would be approximately four to five percent of that number, forty or fifty million people.

And then of that number, how many are aware of those experiences, aware and are not denying them?

Then you again more than halve that number, which is about twenty to twenty-five million people.

It's still a huge number of people.

Yes. Would you like to know them?

Yes, I guess I would. Is this all in preparation for the larger contact later?

Naturally.

Are you referring to the idea of a universal village?

Yes, of course, that is why we say that this is such a spectacular time. It is difficult for you to have the appreciation because you are so close to the woods. It is difficult for you to understand the magnificence of this moment, which is why you ask us, intellectually, why there are so many otherworldly species observing you at the moment. This is an historical time for all of us, not just for humans, because your knowing us changes all of our experience.

One of Lisette's questions involves how you are able to take her physically through walls or float her through space.

The floating through space, as Lisette experienced when she was being transported, is not much different from the manner in which your aircraft float through space, although there are some differences, but notice how one seems so preposterous and the other so plausible. So in your belief system, an airplane can float, but a human cannot. Given your own types of arguments, a Boeing jet aircraft weighs significantly more, and yet you now as a culture accept that this is possible, but many of those who lived during a time that predated that first experience of flying thought it ridiculous to suggest that steel screwed together in a certain shape could make its way off the ground without strings.

For the body, which has a soulful countenance and is enlivened by significant energies, to be then elevated from a physical surface is not miraculous from our perspective. On a Saturday afternoon in the park, even your children's toys, inanimate objects, can get off the ground. It is just another symptom of the idea that there is such little recognition of who you are and of what you are capable. Were we to tell you that simply through your own electromagnetic field and your own energetic impulses can you activate such experiences for yourselves and others, you would readily dismiss it. When we direct our thoughts, in the case of this experience to which Lisette refers, in which she moved from one craft to another through levitation, so to speak, there is a combined electrical force field that is simply tapped into and cooperated with, rather than ignored, denied, and left unseen.

When we say that we communicate with your very growing plants through the creation of what you call crop circles, then when we say that we can communicate and cooperate with electrical impulses and the energy surrounding you, it is the same phenomenon, meaning, it is just about communing and eliciting that which is already there and making it part of our experience. We do not necessarily create something new; we simply have recontextualized our own understanding of what it is possible to play with. Even there, on your planet, a number of you—not a great number of you, but some—have heard stories of somebody having been levitated. It is not a parlor game. It is pure potentiality being expressed.

The moving particles that surround you carry a strong force field and when that force field is intentioned in a certain way, movement occurs, much like telekinesis.

As far as passing through seemingly solid objects, in some cases, not all, the experience occurs when, in fact, the physical body is in one location and the astral body passes through the wall, which is experienced this way because one recognizes the self as the true self and feels that the physical body has passed through the wall.

So it isn't the physical body passing through the wall?

These are two different questions in Lisette's case because they are two different experiences. The astral experience is as described, in which the astral body is passing through; however, the other experience can be described more easily. Rather than something passing through something else, it is better understood as demonstrated on the show, *Star Trek*, in which the molecules of the human body are transmutated, and they are "beamed up" through a change in the molecular structure. In that particular case, they would not necessarily refer to it as the body passing through a wall but rather as a change in structure of the physical, which is then made translucent and can then travel in any way that it needs to from point A to point B, because it has changed structure and that allows it to do so. Does that make sense?

Yes.

Physical matter is not as unchangeable as you might imagine. You can take a cup of water, freeze it, take it out of the freezer as a solid, put it in the microwave, and melt it in just a few minutes, and if you heat it long enough, it will become vapor, and then you can start the whole process over again. This does not inspire any of you with awe, and yet again, you think, "Ah, those laws of the universe do not apply to the human physical matter," but we would suggest that they do. It is only your understanding of what is, and is not, possible that prevents you from allowing that there are no limitations. You would think that the universe has allowed only the ice cube to enjoy these types of transformations, and yet how much more glorious are you then the cube of ice?

130

CHAPTER 10

Cover-Ups

Along the Oregon Trail of yesteryear, when brave families crossed the expanse of the country to reach fertile soil, farming opportunities, and hope for a better future for their children, the obstacles that they encountered were staggering. It was a daily occurrence for some mother to bury a child, and yet she stood up from the grave that she dug with her own hands and continued the journey. What was necessary was an incredible ability to get on with what was at hand; to be able to see the greater good coming from the loss of her child, and to remember, to always remember, that her future lay in front of her, not behind.

Experiencers and other UFO enthusiasts are also on an Oregon Trail of sorts, heading out to the new frontier, embracing ideas that the rest of the world hasn't caught on to yet. But unlike the families on the Oregon Trail, we sometimes get bogged down with the minutiae. We say we want to hear, to see, and to know extraterrestrials, but we have misplaced our emotional energy by proceeding, not toward that objective, but rather, in a never-ending cycle of blame toward those who we say are keeping us from those very experiences with ETs. Many believe that governmental cover-ups, which conceal knowledge of extraterrestrial activity and ongoing scientific discovery related to contact, are preventing our species from furthering individual contact and any benefits to our culture that could be derived from such contact.

But suppose that we really do create our own experience. Then what is to stop any of us from creating the relationships that we choose, even our relationships with otherworldly beings, and like our relationships with anyone else, they need not be shaped by or approved of by Uncle Sam or anyone else? It is only a belief that has us assuming that the government is somehow capable of doing something that we cannot, or worse, will prevent us from doing what we choose.

Certainly we have reason to be angry, but anger is unnecessary, for it only serves to distract us from recognizing that we can do it ourselves. It almost sounds ridiculous, but why have we spent so much energy attempting to wrest from agencies documentation of UFO encounters and cover-ups? Whatever information we think that the government or "black groups" are keeping from us, let's just get it ourselves, right from the source. Unless, of course, you believe that extraterrestrials only associate with governments and black groups.

Do you have a message for those tireless ambassadors who have worked for years, privately and publicly, in an attempt to force the government to come clean with what it knows?

We have heard your strong plea on behalf of your people regarding the dissemination of information from a few of you to the masses so that you can move in the direction that all of you are longing to move; however, as much as we applaud your efforts to imbue all of you with the power to gain access to this information, we would like to suggest another way to achieve the same thing. This suggestion comes through at a time when there is significant doubt about the nature of face-to-face contacts between extraterrestrials and humans among you. Even among those who are testifying at your committees, there are those who have a difficult time comprehending that "average" people around the planet are already having communications on a regular basis with enlightened beings from elsewhere.

Consider that the information that you are seeking can be made available to one hundred, and one thousand, and ten thousand of you around your globe, and that this information is *already* in the public domain. Yet what is needed is a vehicle by which to provide information to be made available to the appropriate sources. When you and your group can accept the fact that others on your planet, as we speak, are actively engaged in face-to-face encounters with evolved extraterrestrials, you will be able to understand the wisdom of our suggestion. But please notice that even individuals among all of you have certain doubts about such contact being possible. What would it mean to you if we told you that the information that you are seeking is more easily gained from simply accessing it from those who are already communing with us? This may take some "enlightenment" on your own part, but you may begin to shift your own understanding toward a perspective that allows for a perfect unfolding of evolution, even with respect to these phenomena.

Individuals around your planet are already having significant and meaningful discussions and contacts with evolved beings. It can seem tremendously threatening to consider that you do not necessarily need another committee of suits and ties to coordinate interspecies communication. These communications are occurring already with average people and are represented by almost every group on your planet. Simply find a way to allow these citizens the dignity to step forward and for them to tell you the information that you are requesting, and you will have an avalanche of input, both technological and spiritual, which will enable you to immediately have access to all that you seek.

If you notice any hesitancy on your part at hearing these words, you will see how you too have your own doubts when it comes to these phenomena. Allow for a moment of contemplation, and consider that complex technological information can be submitted by others to your groups. Such information is already available, yet the sources of these contacts with us have no avenue through which to impart this information. This is not your fault, of course. It is a cultural and global shunning of this possibility, intellectually and spiritually, as it applies to the idea that we actually exist. There is considerable shame and embarrassment in admitting to having face-to-face encounters or communications with us, and therefore it leaves the experiencer no avenue by which to proceed, even if the information they have is compelling.

This is one of the purposes of this book, to find an avenue through which others may come forward. When this veil of denial is lifted, you will have all that you are seeking.

Do not be surprised that your military-industrial complex is not the sole heir to universal ideas. In fact, in some cases, they have less specific information than do others. We are beings from a galaxy far away. We have evolved, despite your understanding otherwise, and though it is obvious to what systems are in place, you do not need to worry that we have somehow missed that the majority of your species yearn for peaceful contact with us. As enlightened beings, we have come to mentor you if invited, and many of you individually have already extended this invitation, which is why we have already come to you. The challenge is to find a way to encourage these individuals to submit their communications in the fullest manner, and contribute to the healing of the planet. These are all the ideas that you have already expressed. When you doubt that this is possible, you limit your own understanding of the Divinity expressed through individuals around the world.

Believe in the greater abilities of the universe and notice that we too have found a way to penetrate systems in place that attempt to disallow our communications. But we have been invited and encouraged by many of your souls, and those relationships exist whether most of you choose to believe it or not. There are technically oriented experiencers who hold schematics in their hands, and yet have no source to whom to disseminate this information. Who would they call? To where shall they mail the schematics? But as you begin to understand that there are many of those who have contact with otherworldly beings, then you can begin to shift your focus, which in turn gives incredible recognition and empowerment to experiencers. When you empower others by agreeing to consider that humans are having contacts on an individual basis, then you give significant credence to these ideas, and more and more experiencers will step forward and say, "I too have seen them and heard them, and here is what they have provided us."

Suppose you could find a way to hear from others, not simply from laypeople, but from scientists as well, who have had musings in the middle of the night and have wondered from whence they have come, or from others who have seen us through face-to-face encounter experiences and have come back with a message and insights or a schematic? When you cease discounting these ideas, you will begin to see proof as evidenced by the submissions that will come forth. But first, look to see the difference in the emphasis. Note how, when a consciousness shifts, it creates in a different way. When a lot of you allow these types of experiences of your fellows, you will all benefit. But begin now to invite and encourage the impossible. Invite and encourage those who already have this kind of information. They may begin to step forward, even if they are anonymous, since there is significant concern for one's safety and reputation.

We assign you a great task when we suggest that you consider that your goal is closer than you may have imagined. Come now to where we are, and let us suggest how you may yet receive what you seek. Bless you for your concerns for humankind.

But what about the cover-up that is going on at Roswell, New Mexico?

Roswell is a conclave uniquely suited for evidential experience and was thus impacted by joint agreement long ago. Even those in the military there, as part of the unfolding of that drama, through free will, decided how to respond. Do not discard the impact of that incident simply because one group denounces it by denying it altogether. When a seed is in the soil being watered, before it emerges as an early sprout, there is something going on within the soil. There is a stirring of its soul plan, for the seed holds within it an understanding of the direction toward which it grows. It does not grow downward into the earth, although the roots do, but the plant begins its growth long before you see it sprout. This incident, Roswell, like others, has begun your culture's awakening to our presence long before you see evidence of us. The refuting and denial of these events by certain groups provide all of you an outward demonstration of what your own egos and minds go through on an hourly basis. Judge not, for within self are also aspects that deny and refute the voice of Divinity on a regular basis. Your most outspoken critics of the behavior of your government and your military would do well to notice where those aspects of unconsciousness run through one's own life. Awakening means lovingly observing where the unconsciousness lies within others *but also within self.* This peaceful non-judgment allows you to awaken yourself and others. But without this perspective, the master becomes as self-righteous and as indignant as the student.

Are there still bodies of these beings kept somewhere?

Yes, they are attempting to preserve these physical shells, and this secrecy serves a power base that feels more secure retaining information in secret from the masses. There is an idea that knowledge is power, and to hold the knowledge to a few keeps the power centralized. This is one of the reasons why there is contact with many others and counter-contact, because the actions of a few can forestall this understanding of our existence only so long. Do not be troubled by the actions of your most fearful, which by the way, describes your leaders who seem to have the most power. They are the most fearful among you. When you recognize this, then you will emerge with a different leadership.

It just seems so hopeless to make changes. It seems so difficult. Where do we start? Sometimes, it seems overwhelmingly discouraging.

Discouragement and feelings of hopelessness and powerlessness are feelings best suited to a mind and thought system that are overwhelmed by events that one seems to have no impact or control over. But this is not the case. It is just an illusion. There are so many more of YOU than there are of the few who attempt to make the decisions for all of you. You need only notice this and then you will change your experience. Your protests can be made in ways other than a full-blown bloody revolution on your doorsteps. You protest with your purchasing power, and with your ability to cause your brethren to make observations about the state of things. As even your current "spiritual leaders" put aside interest in furthering their own personal agendas, they can help to create unison among activists in a way that initiates concrete change, not simply discussions of change. For even in this arena, there can be lack of unison and cooperation. You are all practicing finding that one voice. You will get there.

Forgiving Cover-Ups or "Black Projects"

Notice that life is not a huge board game of good versus evil, but rather all of our experiences eventually evolve to our highest expression of self. In the meantime, what this means is that my expression might not be yours, and yours not another's, but at the highest level, we *are* all in agreement.

As we begin to notice that we all are sharing in the one-soul of the universe, then we put down our childhood toys, those toys being represented as a certain way of thinking, and we begin to notice that it is not we who are the enemy, *nor is it anyone else who is the enemy*. So as you wonder about a conspiracy, what you neglect to notice is that this, too, is part of someone's perceived highest path. Given that person's truth, it is their chosen path. And so we will not encourage you to feel further split off from anyone. This is not why you have called yourself to this communication, but rather to notice how it is that we have evolved to an enlightened state, and that we did not do so as a result of finding each other guilty.

What we are suggesting is that it does not matter who has hid what, or who has operated from what standpoint of fear. It only matters how you will proceed from this moment forward. Sometimes the drama of the struggle keeps us connected to a part of ourselves that is passionate and yet we don't notice that the way of peace is unconsciously avoided because we are addicted to what we call passion, but what is really negative drama. And so how would the sage advise you when you wonder about conspiracies among the military or certain government officials? How would the sage suggest that you proceed?

The master would call you to bring a heart full of forgiveness toward all of your brethren, no matter their employer, no matter their employment, no matter their motive. Perhaps this is a time to let go of the fury that many of you hold for your own government, and for your own systems that have seemed to prevent the awakening of the planet. But we ask you to notice where you too are blocked, not to shame you, but rather to have you notice where you too could be considered to be "guilty" in the same vein that you have judged another. This judging will not take you to the place where you all say that you want to go, even if "they" are the very ones that you say are causing your lack of planetary evolution.

Instead, consider how you might proceed in love and how you can create from here, the planet that you choose. Take along the others who would like to accompany you on this path and go forward with them with what you do have. Does it matter why a group of your species have colluded, if at all, with another group, another species inter-galactically? Does it matter who all of these players are? Does it really matter? The continual need to analyze and dissect the workings of this drama are keeping you tied to this drama. When you proceed from a clean spiritual slate, you are stating that you would like to embark on a different path. That path does not lead to the doorway of struggle and drama. It just does not.

At first glance it looks as though struggle and faultfinding is the only door, that it is the only way to get from here to there; but this is a faulty perception and one that does not allow you to notice the Divinity all around you. If you have noticed that it is hard to proceed in any way without the idea of Divinity at hand, you would be accurate. That is what the process of meditation calls to one. It is a reminder, at least once in the morning, to connect with the Divinity that is everywhere. There is grace in the so-called evilest plan because God is in the all of it. If this idea is hard to accept, then perhaps you may return to some of your spiritual works and books and re-read what the masters have asked of you. When we forgive one another, we also forgive the military. When we forgive one another, we also forgive those who perpetuate cover-ups.

But you are the ones who have pointed out the destruction caused by our special interest groups.

We readily agree. To notice something is the first stage in changing it. But you can still feel peace and camaraderie while you are doing the noticing, and then the changing. There is some myth that you have that you are still not the source of your next creation, that somebody else is preventing you from being at the source of your next creation. That is faulty thinking and does not serve you at all, for you have disempowered yourself in the myth and belief that you cannot have a life of your choice.

Gather your fellows together, other ones, and together remind yourselves that your future is your own. It does not have to belong to anybody else. But as long as you believe that it does, it will. Can you not see how much more empowering it would be to proceed with the perspective that allows for full potentiality in all of your undertakings? In this way do many, many other doors open to you because you are not insisting that the solution to your dilemma is only through one door. When you see Divinity in your fellow, you stop mistrusting, and you start considering their stories, and empathically you begin to consider another way to get to where you say you want to go.

But when you stay entrenched in your struggle with your fellows—whom of course you do not see as your fellow, but as your adversary—you keep in place the active struggling, and in that struggling you will not notice Divinity, or another option.

We have not come here to point out who is your enemy, and who is your friend. We are suggesting that all of us together—all species together—are part of the same universal heartbeat. When you lay down your sword and consider your other options, other options are created by this very consideration. Do not be seduced into believing the mind's argument that you must slay your enemy who is called agribusiness, or the military, or the government, or the far right, or the aliens, or the Israelis, or the Pakistanis, or the Southern Baptists, or the Al Queda, or "black" groups. When you lay down your sword, you lay down your life to begin a new path. Take yourselves collectively on this new path, for investment in having been wronged will not free you from the bondage that you feel. And by awakening to the saint within your enemy can you begin to shed the layers of armor that weigh you down. You can no longer resist these ideas, calling them too lofty to embrace, calling them too idealistic to adopt. For you keep asking collectively, "How do we get there; how do we move our planet and our species to a place of peace?" The answer is provided, and yet your mind and your ego say, "No. That way is too unrealistic. We need to find another of us *guilty* first."

The masters have never subscribed to this idea. When you love your enemies, you have no enemies. This does not mean to cease causing the world to notice where there is injustice. It merely means to adopt now a different stance and to spend some of that emotional, intellectual, and psychological energy on the path of considering the way of the peaceful being. The way of the peaceful being is a journey toward a different path.

When you find a way to glean the information that is already available to you, you begin to step on to the path of the peaceful being. And so when you ask, "What species in the universe dares to convene with our military?" we respond that it is not our interest in furthering your cause in finding yet another group to be guilty. You have enough to work with right there. Instead, we ask for you to notice where and how you can collude with all of the expressions of Divinity around you. Spend some of your emotional energy noticing those expressions of Divinity around you. Trust in the idea that there is the perfect outcome in all of this and that would include how each of you chooses to express your own Divinity.

Although you are at different places in your individual evolution, you have collectively decided to play this moment together, and so sing this concerto tapped into your highest idea of yourself and others. You can tell the tree by the fruit that it bears, and so, before you dismiss our words, notice that any less of a response would render our identities as less than evolved.

You have called us to yourselves for you have asked how to get from here to there. You have called us because we have made this stretch; we have made this leap; we have made this jump. In your highest consciousness, you know this about us, because you know who we are. When you catch yourself believing that you will heal your planet through anger, retaliation, vindictiveness, and self-righteousness, you have clearly demonstrated that you are missing the point. Surprise your brethren; surprise your enemies; heal yourself of your unconscious need to be right and notice a different path, which will get you the same results. You may have to open your heart though, to believe and to notice that there is in fact another path.

The world awaits your personal awakening so that you can help gather up the others and show them the way. Many of the best leaders are those who have demonstrated many certain behaviors that might be considered to be unevolved or unconscious, and then for that leader to awaken has considerable power, because all relate to the being who has once been asleep. That has been the path of each one of us. We have all been asleep or unconscious at one time or another, in degrees sometimes more than less, and so the spiritual master says, "Follow me. Let us heal our planet through forgiveness, love, empathy, and a willingness to try it a different way."

This is not suggesting that no one should hold anyone accountable. This is not suggesting that citizens should not confront an entrenched hold by the government on dissemination of the truth. It only means that this is one aspect toward the healing of your planet. You are ignoring the other paths.

Be here now. Believe that you have divine guidance and feel love upon you and then express that love to others around you. Send a prayer of forgiveness to those you have deemed to have hurt you and your planet. This will heal you as well as them and will allow you to take notice of how you have stopped yourself from spreading forgiveness all over the planet and leading others to this path. Be an example of love expressed. Be an example of the peaceful way-shower. Love entails a willingness to no longer need to be right, to no longer need to appoint blame, but rather to understand how all of us hold some of the blame.

From this point on, you can progress deep in the knowledge that at some level all of you are responsible for the cultural denial that is in place about anything at all. Were you to consider these ideas, you would unleash a creative potential unmatched to this date. Create from this perspective, and you will see results quickly because you are declaring that the master creates grandly through love, forgiveness, and pure creative intent. See this as your window of opportunity to move to the next step through your creative avenues and notice how else you might get what you are seeking.

CHAPTER 11

Love and Sex

There are particular challenges associated with paranormal phenomena and how it impacts and shapes personal relationships, particularly when only one of you in a couple is experiencing phenomena. Certainly, having one or both partners suddenly open to otherworldly events and images does not have to cause problems, providing that there is a high degree of motivation to honor each other's highest idea about things.

An experiencer appears to have a tendency to be able to more clearly receive input from other realms—including one's own higher self—and sometimes that direction conflicts with the "standards" set up in the relationship. Ideally, it would seem that it would be most beneficial to be in touch with the soul's desires; however, the challenge occurs when one's own blossoming understanding of self begins to conflict with one's partner's. While it would seem that what is one's highest good is also another's, we don't always perceive of circumstances and events that cause us pain or trouble to be necessarily beneficial; we don't perceive it, that is, until some time has passed.

During my first marriage, the ETs would wait to visit when my husband was away on business trips. When he returned, he could never figure out why I was so bleary-eyed from emotional exhaustion. He didn't understand, even though I tried to tell him, that I spent some of my nights in the bedroom closet, terrified for my safety, considering what was coming in through the roof to get me. Part of my trauma, then, was impacted by the very nature of my feeling that I needed to hide what was going on with me. During those years, I believe my soul was asking me to be honest, to announce my own experience of the world, despite others' reactions. Perhaps to some degree we are all working on this, forever practicing with getting in touch with what is our truth, and then loving self enough to honor that truth, no matter the fallout.

My second marriage seemed doomed by the fact that, apparently, my higher self had only intended for it to be a short-term marriage. Looking back, I realize that due to my own fears and shortcomings, I agreed with my fiancé that marriage seemed the only acceptable option. But upon hearing and seeing the images of a message to me that suggested that our union was best kept to a short period, rather than marriage, "otherworldly" input again produced a challenge. Unlike my first marriage, this time I was brutally honest about all that I was seeing, hearing, and experiencing, for this partner invited such a degree of honesty; however, he didn't agree with my conclusion. As it turned out, the marriage ended two years later.

There are particular challenges associated with integrating encounter experiences and related phenomena into everyday life, particularly when only one member of the couple is experiencing it. And in fact, this was the very theme of my Thursday night group meetings. However, despite the sometimes prickly challenges, I do feel that such phenomena can enhance love, not cause one's partner to run screaming from the house.

Do evolved beings experience love as humans do?

There is an idea among you that an enlightened being comes along once in a while and lives on a mountaintop in isolation. This is one of your misconceptions, when you consider that there are entire cultures of beings that are enlightened and live together in harmony. Perhaps it is hard for you to imagine, since you find it so difficult to get along with one another on an individual level. We are here to tell you that we are from such a group, a group of evolved beings who live and work and play together quite harmoniously.

Our life together looks different from yours in many ways, and yet there are also some similarities. We, too, love to love. We partner as you do in one way, in that we often choose to partner with one being at a time, although there is no shame in exploring love in any of its shapes and forms with another. We do not punish our beloved for wishing to explore anything in any way. We do not have a personal reaction to another's yearning. We understand that motivation is an individual dynamic, and we do not personalize another's yearning for anything as personal rejection.

We are a group here speaking to you, and so although the channel hears us as one voice, this voice speaks for a group of us. When you begin to imagine, through your books and your television shows and your media, what a world filled with evolved beings would be like, then you will begin to more integrate these thoughts and ideas into your consciousness, and then it will not be so difficult to imagine life as part of an enlightened society.

If you recognize that you are creating from your thoughts, and that you spend very little of your thoughts on life as it might look in an evolved civilization, then you might not be surprised that you do not experience this yet. There have been some books that have described life as it might look in a highly enlightened culture. More will follow to ignite your imagination and your creativity, so that you can begin to envision this and then move in this direction in your thoughts, and eventually in your experience. Some of your intentional communities have attempted to adopt these ideas in a group living environment.

When we love, we don't have a worry as to the timeframe of that relationship. Our incarnation as an enlightened being is thousands of years, not less than one hundred and even at that, at least a third of it in declining health like your incarnation. Our life pursuit is enjoyed in myriad different ways, depending on the interest of the soul. As you can imagine, we have long since given up the idea that work and play are two different things. Our work is our play and our play is our work. And there is no sense of agony about how we fill our days, because we allow ourselves to trust in ourselves and in another, to pursue the interests of our heart and soul. You can imagine how this might positively impact a love relationship inasmuch as we are not depressed, exhausted, and internalizing anger about the daily circumstances of our life. We also make practical these ideas for all members of our group, including the oldest of us and the youngest, and so there is not one group deciding for another.

In this way have we eradicated depression and mental illness, for we are not split from our true selves. We have incorporated our true selves as part of our own identity. This, although seemingly simplistic, is a grand accomplishment and departure from your way of life, since almost everything that you are, in many cases, is as a result of anything *but* who you might choose to be at a soul level. We do not make decisions based on status, as our status is self-chosen. In other words, we are so clear as to the workings of the soul that we do not attempt to be who we are not, nor do we project that teaching and insist that our young, or our partners, or our elders spend their time or be in any way different from who they are as described by their own highest agenda. Far from creating anarchy, we have created peace and great joy amongst our culture.

Awakening means no longer living in a way that can be considered to be numb. We are very in touch with what is true for us about something, and we create from pure joy that way. We were not always like this, which is why we so strongly relate to where you are right now.

We develop our own creative interests, and those change over time. In most cases, since our life spans are much greater than yours, we do not need to exchange bodies and exchange soul purposes. We blend one into another because we can. Your life span is considerably shortened for a variety of reasons and we find it ironic that most of your short life is spent under the dictates of another authority, whether it is your parents, or your schools, or your culture, or government. It is no wonder there is so much sadness, depression, and anger. It is interesting how radical the idea is that when one is allowed to pursue one's highest idea and in turn allows another, society seems to magically fix itself. When one is as motivated to allow another's bliss as one's own, there is little conflict, because our training from the youngest of age is to allow the soul to hear itself. This way one does not spend a lifetime living outside of his own interests.

In order to transition to this type of culture, it is necessary to be fully in touch with the idea that the soul is the highest authority. Only then can you possibly enact a way of life in which you entrust another, no matter the age, with deciding and creating on her own. This does not mean that help is not provided, but that help is not dictated by the helper; it is dictated by the one who is requesting the help.

As far as love goes, we have long given up the idea that another belongs to us; in fact, in some cases we come from the opposite idea: that we belong to another. In other words, we look to how we can serve another, knowing that the more of service we are, the better we all function. In your society, you term this as co-dependency and dysfunction, sometimes confusing when one is clearly coming from love with projecting one's own needs onto another. A certain clarity is required, and yet we have no need to fix anyone else; we simply enjoy the idea of helping another to be blissful.

When we have taken the emphasis off our own pursuits in relation to minimizing another's, we have discovered that we have more bliss than ever. By simply being, with no thought of lording power over another or gaining a title that brings us special privilege, we enjoy a different style of closeness with each other. We develop our close friendships and family ties, not as a result of how one agrees with us, but rather as a result of an ever-increasing awareness that we are all deeply bonded. We may have a partner with whom we reside, and yet there is not a possessive quality that often permeates your own relationships.

Our children also come to us out of a union of love, and there is considerable discussion and involvement from many before an offspring is created. The society itself sees the child as its own and is part of these discussions because, in truth, it does take a village to raise a child, when one considers that the experience of love models love, and then will be embodied by the child. And so producing a child is not considered a right of an individual or a couple, but rather it is, on many levels, a group undertaking, since the group feels so much responsibility for each child's welfare. In this way, there are no spontaneous births for emotional or financial reasons, but rather it is as thought out as many of you might think out and discuss the plans for the building of your houses. And only the most qualified, as deemed by the group, are gifted with the opportunity to genetically produce an offspring. By the same token, that couple does not view their offspring as their property. And so they do not impart their own dysfunction on those offspring,

Love and Sex

since the fact that they have been gifted with the opportunity to be parents means that they often are the wisest among us. Even within enlightenment, there are degrees of wisdom.

When two of us come together to create a child, we do so through a process that is, in some ways, similar to your own, but we do not need to share bodily secretions. There is a ceremony between the couple in which there is ritual and the coming together, but we create from a more conscious place, and so the process is not a biological undertaking of sperm and ovum. In your culture, this process is not dependent upon enlightenment. In ours, it is. The couple produce an offspring based on a conjoined celebration, much like your own, except that we do not have accidents, and only the highest level of creating lovingly produces an offspring.

Our sexual encounters are less about physical sensations than they are about a great blending of our body, mind, and spirit. Without all of these, reproduction is impossible. We would have it no other way. The physical pleasure is an outpouring from our state of emotional and spiritual bliss. This way is the child created, but developed in vitro and through a system that might seem to you to be disconnected from our bodies, but in fact allows for the understanding that each child is a "product" of the culture rather than of one or two people. In some cases, you might label this as "test-tube babies," who are in the tubes longer than yours are, but it is a far different outcome, in that, although we do not proceed with the process of gestation individually, gestation occurs, but it occurs to the delight and participation of the entire group. This is one of our huge differences. This way there is great community love and support for each offspring and again, we cannot overemphasize how each child is not "owned" by one or two, but is an extension of the entire community.

Since we have great experience, having destroyed ourselves a couple of times through our own evolutionary processes, we have a clear understanding of which ideas produce the best outcome. We have noticed that the fullest expression of love, respect, and freedom produces the best outcome for our offspring. This takes a certain degree of enlightenment to carry out. We have long since addressed our own ego and emotional issues, and we tend to not project those unresolved issues onto our offspring. In addition, through this type of upbringing, our young exhibit wisdom at a very early age, because they are encouraged to do so.

147

At the heart of this encouragement is how we assist in any way possible the young soul in identifying the desires of *its* soul, not of anyone else's. We have learned from experience that when the soul is denied its highest expression, all members of the group suffer. For this reason, our culture does not produce angry and depressed children and adolescents, who, either earlier or later, turn to "deviant" behavior. And so we all have a vested interest in providing opportunities for each soul to find full expression. As a result, we do not experience outcomes of anger, such as crime or disease. We left those behind a long time ago, although the memory is kept alive as to what type of life that produces, as a result of our observations of you. This is another way that you also provide us with a gift. Through our observations of you, we can remember our own past and how such actions and behaviors produce certain types of societies.

We do not say this in a haughty manner because we fully understand that you too are on your path of evolution, so this is not a judgment at all; this is only observing what is so. We have been on the same path as you. Our culture has experienced crime, sadness, torture, and annihilation in every conceivable way, and so we speak from personal experience when we say that we have come to notice what produces glory and what does not.

How do you sexually procreate? I don't seem to be able to hear you. I was asking how it is that your species is able to procreate?

You are having trouble accessing certain information because you have preconceived ideas about particular questions and where our response is different from your idea, our voice and your mind clash, and nothing happens, which is okay; simply notice the clashing and let it go. You experience this as a stalemate of sorts, which touches some of your earlier issues of ability and whether you will have sufficient skills to continue this process. Actually, you can use that noticing as an indicator of when your mind is engaged; simply take the steps necessary to disengage the mind, as you are doing right now.

Regarding the question of our sexual organs and how we procreate, let's try it again, shall we? We too have male and female genders. We do link physically in a union of love, but the linking does not entail the male's genitals engaged with the female's reproductive organs.

How this "semen" generates an offspring is somewhat complex, but we can explain it this way. Through an exchange of what might be termed high voltage energy between the couple, there is produced an electromagnetic surge. That surge—our version of semen—along with the union of spiritual connection, emotional connection, and through this physical exchange of energy, creates an offspring by this energy, much like the energy that shoots forth the torpedo from the submarine, although this analogy we use with humor.

There is a physical manifestation from the linking of energies. This physical residue (energetic "semen") as a result of magnetic and electrochemical combinations, result in a chemical reaction. That chemical reaction produces an embryo. There is physical pleasure in this exchange, and that resultant matter created from this surge in energy is the early stages of the embryo. This matter is then placed in an in vitro environment, where it establishes a link to the collective and there thrives for a period of time until it has developed sufficiently.

The reason we no longer have genitals is because we evolved to the point where we chose to create our offspring from a more unified union of body, mind, and spirit, not simply from the body alone, although even in the cases of physical intercourse, there can be the connection in love; yet over time, we chose to create in a different way. This difference is a result of all manner of eons of sexual dysfunction and lopsided physical emphasis. When we grew to the point where we decided to establish a new basis for creating our young, we chose to put into place a co-creation by two beings via their spiritual connection, their emotional and mental union, and the electrical charge that they create as a result of their physical energies. These physical energies are made possible through their spiritual and emotional connection, so all three are interdependently connected.

Our young do not nurse as do yours. They, too, as do we, nourish themselves from light energy. As mentioned previously, our eyes provide an avenue for nutritional absorption, as does our skin. We have established a strong connection with our young, and the entire community rejoices in the upbringing of the child. We do not have population explosion problems nor do we have more young than those for whom we can adequately provide love and encouragement. We do not perceive this as limiting, or restrictive, because we have experienced first-hand living within a population that cannot be adequately supported by the host planet. We, like you, develop strong bonds with one another, and where we once practiced tolerating one another, we now have hundreds of years together in partnering in which to create intimacy.

We enjoy relatively perfect health through a combination of applied techniques developed with an understanding of biochemistry and electromagnetic frequencies, but also, when there is lack of pollution, environmentally, emotionally, mentally, and spiritually, health is a natural outcome. Also, we created the idea that there is no need to limit the incarnation to 80, 90, or 100 years, but rather we have discovered that we are indeed at cause. These things can be decided upon by the soul, and when we decided to choose longevity, we noticed what created longevity. Sometimes one of us may have an altercation with our own physical being in which harmony is disrupted, and in those cases we do not cut out the organ, nor medicate the symptoms, but rather look immediately to the potential cause and heal it from that level.

Illness and disease are very rare although initiates, our youngest, for instance, do have opportunities to explore less-than-perfect health and to be caused to notice how they would choose to progress. Health is almost always chosen and the noticing of what causes and creates health is studied and embraced, rather than denied and ignored. We do not have conflicting voices from corporations and other vested interests, selling their ideas to physicians, educational programs, or others, as to what creates health, whether or not those ideas create health or not, and in fact often create disease rather than well-being. We are free to create a home environment whereby the residents are the custodians of their home environment. No vested interest would be allowed to create a stranglehold on any group of us, particularly our young.

Very few of you experience yourselves fully. Were you to integrate and heal the parts of you that are split off and separate from your consciousness, you would be so much more alive that you would scarcely know what to feel joy about next. Do you have a question?

How does one recover those split-off parts of self?

Precisely the opposite way that most of you are currently dealing with those disowned parts of you. Presently, most of you have a difficult time beholding those parts, and so there are feelings of guilt, denial, shame, anger, upset, and regret. When those feelings are present, you are beholding self. And so the key is to gently and lovingly hold that part of self in non-judgment and just be willing to look there. By looking there, be able to notice it first without guilt or shame, and then to lovingly be willing to surrender to it. The word "surrender" is sometimes difficult for you to understand because it connotes ideas that you must just accept it and never attempt to change it; but in fact, when you surrender, you are just allowing what is to be for the moment.

The greatest courage, first of all, comes into play when you become willing to notice the split off parts of self. Most of you notice those in others and not in yourself. Particularly around issues of sexuality, or issues of intimacy, you will notice it in another, but not in yourself. Love and relationships can heal when, rather than using those aspects of each other to make each other wrong, you lovingly help hold those aspects of each other to mutually heal them together. Usually, just the opposite occurs after spending some time in relationship, as two people are clearly observant of another's unhealed aspects, and then it is pointed out in a way that becomes punishing. Obviously, not only is this not creating a healing, but it is also driving the unhealed aspect further into hiding.

Think of those unhealed aspects as frightened children, whom you are attempting to coax out of hiding into a safe embrace, assuring these parts that no harm will befall them. Currently, you are impatient and harsh with your own and others' unhealed aspects. Instead, begin to perceive of those unhealed aspects as lost children. You wouldn't think of attempting to shame and scold a lost child taken in off the street by demanding that she notice how messed up she is. As you re-contextualize those aspects of self that are devastated, wounded, and unhealed, coax them out with love and safety. And then if they enter the space of observation, so that you can see all aspects, be tender, as tender as you would be with a wounded, lost child. There is a myth among many of you that says that somehow, when you point out an unhealed aspect in another, you can correct it by shaming or punishing the undesired behavior or characteristic, but that part of self will simply run further into hiding. In fact, this metaphor for other aspects of "self" is not too far off the literal meaning, inasmuch as previous incarnations are held cellularly. So to a huge degree, you literally have aspects of those selves along with you. You know that they're there, because there are residual feelings that come up from seemingly nowhere, and yet the presence of the feeling is the first step in noticing those aspects. When one is numb, as exhibited by depression, one has not yet gotten to the step of *feeling*; and so feel congratulatory if at least you are feeling something, even if that feeling is sadness; for you are not numb, you are feeling.

Those of you who don't feel anything will instead feel unconsciously, and may instead cope with those feelings through various artificial substances or modalities. Forgive yourself, and allow that one day you will feel ready to look at what hurts so much that you can't feel anything. This is the divine purpose for relationship, for together you can heal aspects that you may not have an opportunity to heal by yourself.

Sexuality between lovers of your species so often takes on the opposite feeling to the very reason you conjoin in the first place. As we have said before, over time, in some cases, there is greater opportunity for healing, for tenderness, for feelings of safety and for feelings of self-expression. But so often, the opposite is the case. Yet can you imagine that in our realm, we may experience one another for thousands of years? In your paradigm, seven years is the accepted turning point, which you call the "seven-year itch," in which sexuality between you often goes flat. For us, seven years is quicker than a blink of the eye; it is a second, given the length of our embodiment and our relationships.

> *There are so many different areas that we are working on. We want love, happiness, and perfect health, which reminds me, can you please give us the cure for cancer?*

The answer to that question is so simple it would be readily rejected, even by you.

> *Give it to me anyway.*

Consciousness cures cancer. Three words.

> *That sounds simplistic.*

That does not mean that this answer cannot be expounded upon, because certainly a more lengthy explanation might induce thought and reflection, and we would necessarily provide such explanation, yet do you see the dichotomy of asking seemingly complex questions and attempting to receive an answer at the level from which you are asking it?

Most people would ask for a chemical formula or a magic pill that would provide a cure rather than ask for consciousness.

And yet if the combined intellect, financial investment, and energetic output were thrust into this question from a standpoint of "How do we raise consciousness, both individually as well as collectively?" the puzzle would solve itself. And so in some ways, it is ironic that the consciousness from which the question is posed cannot hear the true answer. Yet many can, obviously, which is why many of you have had cancer, and have overcome it. Sometimes it appears that a modality has "cured" the cancer. Do you believe that a modality cures anything? Even vitamins "work" because you deeply believe that they will. Often times, of course, such a benchmark realization as a cancer diagnosis begins the soul's journey down a different path. Deep introspection and reflection ensue. Life changes are made. Different choices are considered for the first time, and lo and behold, a different outcome is experienced. There are biochemical and electromagnetic modalities that greatly enhance certain biological and biochemical functions, and yet even the pursuit of such treatments requires a certain consciousness beyond what the masses currently accept as primary. One may not necessarily find those treatments dispensed by physicians of conventional repute. The willingness to make a change in one's dietary habits can, although not always, be an indication of a greater degree of consciousness—as opposed to unconsciousness. This is obviously old news, but the cure for cancer is the cure for sleepwalking. Wake up, and you will be cured.

CHAPTER 12

Animals and Cattle Mutilations

For many years, just as an encounter experience would begin, all the telltale phenomena would erupt in my bedroom, as though someone had thrown a switch in some sound studio at Universal Studios. What would invariably happen next was that signature feeling of sleepiness, despite a whirlwind of activity occurring around me. One summer evening just as the lights, sounds, and vibrations began, I was able to glance at my young son sleeping in the bed nearby. We were living in a studio apartment at the time, and so I was able to look over at him just as the encounter began. He had been playing with his kitten, who was tugging playfully on his pajama sleeve, when, just seconds prior to my own repose, both he and the kitten fell instantly into what appeared to be a sound sleep. Having often been around animals as an encounter began, particularly dogs and cats, I have noticed that they too react with the same sleepy response and fall suddenly asleep.

One surprising "side effect" that has happened as a result of the encounters seems to be a pronounced ability to identify and relate to animals. Like many people, I have always felt a strong rapport with animals, particularly my own pets, but beyond that, at times, I would intermittently "hear" the animals' "thoughts"—at least that's the only way that I can describe it. One time I came across what appeared to be a stray dog, who was without a collar, and I was considering rescuing it so that it wouldn't get hit by a car, but instead, I suddenly "heard" the canine object, stating that he, in fact, had an owner and a home.

It does seem that encounter experiences open up the experiencer to all manner of profound abilities, although some of those abilities fade over time. Perhaps they are not really special abilities at all, but rather, exposure to initial phenomena simply returns us to our truest nature as members of the universal heartbeat. In any event, it seems that, as a result of exposing oneself to seemingly magical universal energies through encounter experiences, one more strongly reunites with a communion with the animals. I wondered how the Group experience and relate to the animal kingdom.

Do you have pets?

We do share our environment with other living beings, some of whom you would categorize as pets, but we do not have the myriad problems you have, associated with such others, primarily because we behold them differently. They are more in common with your idea about companions, except we see them as closer to ourselves than you do your pets. For instance, as we discussed previously, we behold them as having more of a quality of that of siblings, almost, in that they share our environment, and we are able to commune with them through telepathy. This began, by the way, as a result of our understanding that they are not beneath or below us, but rather they are also God's creatures. We, of course, do not kill them, nor do we eat them, nor do they kill or eat us. We co-exist harmoniously and they bring great pleasure through their diversity in appearance and characteristics.

It is difficult for you to comprehend just how magnificent Earth is, because of the extraordinary diversity of your plants and animals. One could spend one's entire life traveling your globe and appreciating God's wonders. We do this somewhat, although we don't limit ourselves to one planet. As anthropologists, we travel a great deal and appreciate God's diversity throughout the galaxy. But not all environments have the extraordinary diversity of your home.

Of course, the young always appreciate diverse peoples and creatures, and this is the case with our young as well. Some of our animals have characteristics that you would normally attribute only to one certain species and not another. For instance, your birds tend to fly and yet there are other kinds of animals who can also fly, or move through the air, but are not limited to needing wings to do so.

Between the planes of existence there are interdimensional travelers. Not all of these travelers are what you would consider to be beings, but may more closely resemble what you would call animals. There is, for example, a white furry creature that looks something like your llama, which flies between realms and delivers comfort and encouragement to certain beings that have a connection to this creature. The connections between each of you and certain animals or beings can be very personal, depending on where your lives have been, and what other creatures have been a part of those lives. Often, this ongoing contact and communication can occur between realms, during sleep, or between lives. This explains some of your rapport with different species even there on your planet. Some of you are drawn to, and collect, snakes. Others breed dogs, and others of you have a close rapport with horses. Others are bird watchers and others work in aquariums. Each soul draws to itself those species that embody characteristics that assist the soul in its development.

In addition, during that "time" that you spend on the other side between dimensions, there is much communication, cohabitation, and sometimes travel with myriad different beings, depending upon the interests of the soul. Some of you have great interests in animals, more so than others, and you can be certain that as you pass from one incarnation to the next, in that in-between life, there is much "time" spent (if you will allow the use of that word) relating to and working with the animal realm as well as the fairy realm. Again, this is an idea that your mass consciousness holds at bay, because were you to recognize the great degree of rapport that all beings have with one another, you would hardly be able to treat other beings, specifically your animals, as you do. In order to protect this denial, there is often times a resistance to looking more closely at this area, for you would not be able to tolerate your cattle or chickens' factory living conditions, or your own eating habits, if you were to recognize that energetically and soulfully, they are more your brothers and sisters than you know.

Most of your children have an immediate rapport through their imagination and stories of magical animals with special abilities. This is not a made-up fantasy world, but is the experience in the universe, and your youngest remember bonds from other lives with previous animal friends. At one time on your planet, it was your experience as well. There was a time when your animals were more closely attuned with you and could communicate with you. Some of you retain this ability even now. There was an agreement in your souls to return to that state of communion and that state exists similar to what it once was like on your planet, in some locations in the universe.

It is not an accident or coincidence that your young children are drawn to the small, furry, stuffed animal toys that are given so freely from adults to children. Something in the adult's soul remembers this connection as well and recalls how comforted and gleeful the relationships were between you and these beings. And so the giving of stuffed animal toys to children touches in you a longing, and a memory of the camaraderie that once was. So, although most adults have split off from the aspect of self that deeply resonates with this connection with the animal kingdom, you nonetheless allow an indulgence through your children, and thus have still found a way to stay connected with your own fondest memories and understandings.

There is a sadness within most of you at the recognition as to how you have moved so far from this natural camaraderie, love, and honoring to your current state in which one group holds the other group hostage, and enslaves that group—which is precisely what is occurring, as you have enslaved your animals and produce them now for food. A part of you does resonate to a feeling of profound sadness, as you retain a lingering memory of how it once was, and how far you have moved from that blessed connection.

But know that this is okay. You will heal this, too. Mother Earth embodies non-judgment at its fullest, for she too has a soul and patiently awaits the day when harmony is returned to her shores. She has observed a time when the species loved together and played together, and one did not hold dominion over the other through the form of production and killing. She, too, knows that in time, all will be healed.

Imagine an environment that is endowed with the color and diversity of your living beings without ever having a thought or need to exploit them, or their body parts, in any way, or to attempt to find entertainment through the killing of them for pleasure, when they are used as mere target practice. Think of this for a moment, and you will understand how far you have come from the state of your original relationship to these beings.

Imagine a time, when you are not so engrossed in your workaday world, in which you pursue the visceral pleasures of simply being alive, by enjoying all that is there for you to enjoy, yet imposing no destruction or exploitation on any of it. Imagine having created the time to simply enjoy the wonders of the baby elephant, instead of spending most of your lives doing everything but that. Instead of spending most of your time on freeways, you will recapture your quality of life. You will return to a time in which you find great pleasure, as you once did, by simply tracing the patterns of the zebra's coat beneath your fingertips (and the zebra will be happy for you to do so) to see if you can feel the difference between the texture of the differing colors. The zebra misses that touch, too.

There are places where there is a quality of life that you cannot imagine, in which no being holds another as inferior. There will be a time when you do not rush your children into adulthood, to move from the lazy meandering of the morning into a hurried life of competition and keeping up with the Joneses; in which your time is spent simply and blissfully enjoying one another and observing the delights around you.

There are places in the universe in which souls work with energies of all different species. There are beings and creatures so exquisite in detail. Picture a butterfly wing, so intricate in its design, the beauty so beyond any framed painting of your great masters, that the very wing of the butterfly is revered much as you revere a Picasso. How many of you have considered the butterfly wing as a Matisse? There are places that souls who have endured either great pain or suffering visit and inhabit. They go to such places during certain incarnations where healing energies are provided by certain species, what you might consider a healing retreat. This can also occur as part of your life between lives.

For instance, some of you have experienced the healing energies and delight of watching dolphins frolicking in the water, and for some of you, a healing might require spending some passage of time simply communing with these creatures. It is all up to you entirely. No one tells you where you must go. You discover this, as you pass from your physical vessel, when you realize you can feel like a kid in a candy store for you can create anything, in any environment that you choose. You are only limited by your imagination as to what is possible. And so how would you like to spend your time? We are using the context of "time," because you understand that word. But when you remember between lives how it is that you allow yourself full freedom to be in your bliss, if you can touch into more of that memory, you will tolerate less of the hectic devices of your creations. Who will start by saying, "I don't wish to keep up this frenzy."

The Fate of the Beloved Max

I have a pet potbelly pig that I adore, but he has so many health challenges, that I'm wondering if it's more humane to euthanize him now. But if he's going to end up as a soul in some pig who's in some factory, living a tortured life until he's slaughtered for bacon, then I don't know if that's any better— and then I'd just be hastening him to that end. What happens to animals when they die? What happens to their souls? Will Max incarnate as a pig again?

We can tell you that there is no suffering on the other side for your Max or other animals.

Well, I know there's no suffering on the other side. The question was, will he incarnate into a worse life than he's got now?

Your question does not allow for the grander mosaic of the unfolding of each soul—or the universe for that matter. You are worried for your beloved pet. But you have forgotten that even the souls of the animals are part of a grand design. You can no more "protect" them than you can "protect" your own child's soul from calling to itself what it would like to call to itself. You are the one who is making up what is considered "good" or "bad," and what is considered to be "suffering" or "bliss." For that matter, the "condition" you say that your pig endures right now with his health is better than some of the population of children and adults of your world. Your pet is better fed and better cared for than many humans in the world. And so, what is suffering? It is purely a made-up definition.

It is commendable to be compassionate and sensitive to the needs of others and to the needs of your pets, who in many cases are dependent on your kindness and compassion for their well-being. But hereto, even with your pet's physical condition, these circumstances have been set up this way by God—and by your pet—and so, do not feel that there is anything to be protected from in any future expression of your pet's soul.

Well, will he reincarnate into another pig, or to a horse, or what? Where will he go when he dies?

He will go to the place where all souls go, which is to turn to the one-soul, which is the light, and you will see him again, as you well know, when you too transcend this incarnation. You will see him in the blink of an eye.

I miss him already. I don't know why I have such a strong connection to my pets. But I love him.

He is such a gentle animal, and you nurtured him as a little piglet when he was mauled, and his youth was interwoven with your son's youth, for you raised both him and your son, on your beloved ranch, both of them, at a time when you were also so much in love with your land. It was a life that, at the time, you had hoped would continue forever. And so your little pet has had so much to do with your own son's upbringing, because you have made your pets so much a part of your family life. So your pet's well-being is very important to you. But as far as where he goes, you know where his body goes. You already know the answer to that question. The answer to the question of where his soul goes is that it does return to God, and God has a special place and a special rhythm and pattern and "program" for the animals. They do not have to return to this realm on this earth. They, too, can create different experiences in different dimensions and locations in the universe, depending on a host of different criteria.

Your pets are part of God's family. It is understandable how many of you have such strong connection to them, especially when they bring you such happiness and joy, and bring such joy and happiness to your children, who also seem to resonate with them so strongly.

The animals, as we have told you before, had been very deeply connected to you as a species at the time of Atlantis. They were not relegated to the "lower" status of food, as they are now in many cases. They were co-inhabitants of your environment, and you honored them in a way that celebrated their special form in the way that held their embodiment. You honored the gifts that they brought to your children and to your planet. You considered them to be like great contributions of art because they "light up" your planet and your environment. Imagine your globe without any animals, and you will understand the perspective that you had then, which was much more appreciative of them than you are now. For now, they are seen, in so many cases, as food value.

In your decision of whether or not to have a veterinarian euthanize your beloved pet because you wonder if he is suffering unnecessarily, we can tell you that you will know when it is the time to do this. Trust that you have the sensitivity to be in touch with his purpose and his mission as well as your own, and if that means staying with you for years to come, simply ask God for this guidance as in all things, and trust that the answer is there for you.

Cattle Mutilations

What do you have to do with livestock, with cattle and sheep? I saw them during my 1992 encounter. I saw cattle and sheep suspended in the air by nylon type cords. Is there any connection between these, and what's commonly referred to as "cattle mutilations"?

The cattle and sheep that you saw during your encounter were hanging there as a result of environmental studies on their deteriorating condition in a general sense. In other words, we have been categorizing the results of the changes in some of your animals' physiology. The animals that you saw were no longer alive, but through a process whereby they were no longer physically deteriorating, we were able

161

to continue studying the effects that your environment has had on them. This would include the food, and how it has been processed and grown and what, if any, effect that has had on them, as well as what effect has resulted on humans who in turn ingest those very animals.

We are anthropologists. We study cultures, and we are very interested in the social sciences. We are interested to know how your culture has impacted, and is being impacted, by certain stimuli. Sheep and cattle represent some of your dietary animal products, consumed and worn there, and we have been interested to know how the animals themselves are faring, as well as how humans are doing as a result of years and years of ingesting them. The reason that you saw them in the first place was because of your very participation in our laboratory and hospital. They were not harmed, and they experienced no suffering. We had removed them painlessly from pastures around the world, sometimes due to their impending or ensured illness or slaughter, or other times when they were well, but by mutual agreement with them. You may be surprised to hear that the animals, too, have souls and participate in their own evolution, just as you do. It is an honor to be able to have access to their physical forms, and those animals that have been well enough to allow us to study a healthy body have been returned unharmed, and in other cases, they simply agree to change vessels.

When you come to us and ask us details of such things as the so-called "cattle mutilations," we will answer the question, but we ask that you also notice that this is an opportunity for your mind to latch on to fear. This is an opportunity for you to forget that there is a divine perfection unfolding before you, that this is God's universe and that there are benevolent beings all around you. We tell you this because, just as so many of you find yourselves watching horror movies, listening to the morning news, which is almost the same thing, and reading the newspaper, which is filled with a litany of accounts, one after the other, a laundry list of "things that are going wrong," there is a tendency for you to unconsciously decide that you are in danger, that there is something to fear, or that there is something that is other than perfect.

The cattle mutilations are just that. They are animals that have been targeted by certain individuals or groups in the galaxy for their own purposes. In addition, there are also individuals and groups of humans who target animals for ritualistic purposes. Neither, by the way, suggests that somehow this universe is unsafe. You will ask for more details about this, just as the freeway driver passes the pile-up and cannot help but look at the wreckage, even if he knows that he might see blood, gore, or trauma having occurred to one or more people. And so, we will not indulge this tendency, although you will define it as curiosity. We answer the question just to clear up the mystery, although like the crop circles, you already seem to have the answer on the one hand, but it leaves you no further along necessarily in your acceptance of us on the other hand.

You are safe. There may have been crime a mere mile from you, or a block from you, but that does not necessarily mean that your world is unsafe, for even when you transition from your body, you have still been "safe." We ask that you notice the mind's insistence on qualifying the universe as an unsafe neighborhood and finding, and then latching onto, a shred of evidence to prove that outer space is barbaric. We remind you again of your hypocrisy when you place your own animals in fields and grow them quite purposefully to later take to slaughter, having subjected those same animals to the most horrendous living conditions, and then the most tortuous slaughtering conditions, and this you have labeled as okay. In some cases, their hide is partially removed before they are even dead. And then, if that's not enough, you put pieces of them in your mouth and eat them. And yet, this you don't see as barbaric or as evidence that YOU are unsafe to be around. This is the way of the mind, and yet the mind prefers to focus on a group or activity in the galaxy, which chooses to exhibit similar behavior—and this horrifies you. And so we will not dwell here, but rather, if you find it appalling, look to your own habits, your own culture, and your own practices and notice the same degree of barbarity.

We will not collude with you in finding fault with another species. This is an important teaching, for this is just one area in which you are so split off from your own behaviors, that you would dwell on another whose practices are somewhat similar, call those barbaric, but not notice your own hand in the cruelty to your animals.

We mean to offer you a different way of looking at certain phenomena. Although it may not seem like it, this is simply another way to say that ye who is without sin may cast the first stone. And our teaching here is offering you a way to notice that we invite you to choose other than judgment, and if you don't like the way animals are treated, including cattle, by others, then do what you can do to change your own behaviors around that.

> *But at least we don't go into another's home and steal someone else's life-forms.*

You don't? You have gone into the plant kingdom and the animal kingdom and to the depths of the oceans, and you have plundered and pillaged everything that you can get your hands on—and we say this without judgment. But you have made the statement, and we feel obliged to provide you an answer from a higher source.

CHAPTER 13

The New Human

You've heard of the proverbial shoemaker whose own kids don scruffy shoes, or the minister who's spouting family values while having an affair, or the federal government that demands honest tax returns and will punish you if you lie, but regularly eschews transparency in its own affairs and cover-ups. Just as soon as I get to judging others for being hypocritical or holding back some of the truth, or not walking their talk, I remember my own inability to make practical my advice when it comes to encounter phenomena and raising a child.

It's my feeling that it's time for encounter experiencers everywhere to stand up and be counted, to be brave and to start a cultural movement in which more and more of us admit to our experiences, so that we can start dismantling the shame and ridicule so associated with such honesty. But time and again, I struggle with how to speak my own truth, how to make that truth practical and not have it adversely affect my son.

Now I didn't just fall off the self-awareness turnip truck. I know all about how each of our souls calls to itself the perfect people and events who will best facilitate the soul's agenda, that there's really no such things as coincidences, etc., and that my son "chose" me as his mother. However, God help me, motherly instinct kicks in big time when it comes to my parenting. So although it's easy to see how inconsistent Thomas Jefferson was while he both penned the Declaration of Independence and owned hundreds of other humans as his slaves, I suppose I too have inherited my culture's presumption and bias about certain things. Nonetheless, it would seem that bravery of character is called for, but many times I still lack backbone and get all squishy and cautious about my truth when it applies to children. I'm constantly weighing the issues, forever checking social propriety as to how being truthful can be too much truth within certain settings.

When my publisher, Hampton Roads, first hosted my new book by displaying a few initial chapters on its www.hrpub.com website, I'm embarrassed to say that I actually told my son not to mention it to anybody at his school. I had this image of him shattering the tone in the computer room as his classmates popped up my website on their monitors. This kind of publicity I don't need, and I told him so. It was a breach of my newfound confidence, but I still didn't amend my direction. I suppose when all is said and done, I just don't want to face down any more raised eyebrows at parent-teacher conferences.

One morning in Los Angeles I appeared on my very first live radio interview. During the time that I was on the air, I silently prayed that no one I knew would recognize my voice or my name. I dreaded that my then-employer might suddenly tune into talk radio, or that my mother would be channel surfing. This interview was during a time when I was still conflicted about coming out of the closet.

Once when my son was in first grade, the teacher took me aside during the evening "open house" and showed me my son's most recent artwork. The other children had displayed sweet crayon pictures of horses and dragons, but my own child had produced a portrait of an "alien." He didn't get that from my stories. In fact, I was perfectly appropriate throughout his youth and did not indulge him with the details of my own encounters. But he himself has seen things and experienced things, and some of it, when he was very young, he wrote off as "nightmares," for he clearly wasn't *ready to face or embrace some of what he witnessed. In the example of his classroom, you'd think that his teacher would have shrugged off his portrait as so much tabloid-inspired musings, but not her. She wondered what was going on at home.*

So, like others before me, I try to model to my son to live his own truth, to march to the beat of his own drummer, and above all, to stand proud and venture forth with his own moral code—as long as that truth doesn't cause too much of a stir while he's still underage.

I have found that I believe that it's important to follow the lead of the child or teenager when it comes to discussing such phenomena. I haven't burdened my son with my own emotional issues or discussed the encounters with him as they occurred. But I do speak often of phenomena in general, how it might seem scary, but how it's not a bad thing. I would hope that he grew up with an understanding that being witness to extraordinary phenomena is not a curse but rather can be a blessing and a gift. I have attempted to address, in a general way, how important it is to feel free to come to terms with one's own paranormal, or other, experiences. But unless he specifically asks me about my own encounters, I have tended to wait for him to come of age before exposing him to my wild ride.

But sometimes I wonder how long it will be before discussion of paranormal phenomena is made part of grade school "show and tell." Certainly children everywhere are experiencing it, as are their parents. But for right now, for the most part, it's barely safe for children and others to mention such events in a counselor's office, let alone on the playground. It will be a glorious day indeed when our culture bursts forth from a spiritual renewal and is able to embrace all experience as part of everyday life.

> *How will the whole world awaken when it doesn't seem that everyone **wants** to awaken spiritually? Many people are still busy finding ways to destroy one another.*

There is a phenomenon that occurs during an evolutionary awakening, which by the way is what you are in the midst of. Many of you are poised to jump-start yourselves on the road to your own enlightenment and you will inspire others to do the same. Sometimes it does not feel that this is the case, because while many of you are still building bombs, others are seeking to awaken. Yet the awakened ones will carry the bomb builders toward mass awakening. You will sponsor them just as we are sponsoring you.

It is easy to feel discouraged only if you believe that at the heart of the matter is a robotic machine, when in fact the core of all of you is love and light. So do not doubt that you will ever evolve spiritually, or that your neighbors will evolve, even as they seem to go in the opposite direction. You will evolve. We have and so too will you.

When a species brings itself to the precipice of awakening, there is a group consciousness that asks questions and seeks answers. Certain books are brought to many of you for this purpose. Just at the right time, certain movies arrive. Although, as far as the total global population goes, it does not seem that the majority of you are purchasing or viewing enlightening books or movies. But you sponsors are buying the books. And you sponsors will carry the rest of you. It is not a chore. You have chosen for it to be this way, for your love of humanity, and your love of your present Earth home, has called this to you and you to it. This is your path. You cannot be that surprised to hear this.

Although we operate under the auspices of the Divine, so, too, do your angels, your spirit guides, and so, too, is God there for all of you. Even your questions of encounter experiences are not too difficult for God to answer, and God brings answers in so many different ways: through your dreams, meditations, through an article that you might read, or through a meeting with a trusted friend. The one-source—or God, if you prefer to use this name—will speak to you, to your heart. So fear not that your question will be unanswered. If you seek an answer, you will in fact receive one. This, by the way, is a universal law. If you intend it you can experience it. This holds true for creating the life that pleases you, as well as having a question answered that seems to elude you.

We deliver the news that "extraterrestrials" are part of the God source, and that perhaps is news. When a soul is ready for answers, for healing, and for understanding, the soul creates that healing. You will call to yourself all experience, all that is necessary to bring you to the next place in your development. Your memory may have been shrouded in forgetfulness or in denial, but as you call forth an unfettered line to the God source, you will bring to yourself all the tools necessary to create a healing for yourself. Look inside, for we do not wish to send a message that says, "We are the only source out here," for we tap into the same source that is available to you. All knowing is available to all souls, everywhere. This source is the same source that you are invited to access. So do not be misled into feeling that your quandary may yet be unsolved. You have it within you to bring healing and peace to yourself.

As you develop further understanding of how you have called to yourself encounter experiences or other phenomena, you will begin to play yet a bigger role in experiencing the awakened human. The awakened human becomes part of the universal family, although really, you have always been this; but now it will be part of your own understanding and after all, until you understand your magnificence, your experience may be limited.

Whenever an idea comes to you, you have been practicing recognizing that God and the Divine may have inspired this idea. This way, you develop an understanding that all of your questions have answers. All of your creativity can be expressed once you place yourself on that path and know in your heart and feel the satisfaction of expressing yourselves fully. That will be your next experience.

As encounter experiencers, you may have issues that have multi-layers of emotions, requiring you to heal issues that others are not presently dealing with. As you internalize your understanding that no experience—particularly paranormal phenomena—has been brought to your soul as an accident or coincidence, or as a random occurrence, you can begin to recognize just how grand your role is on this planet at this time.

Can you imagine looking back to a planet that was once so isolated that the inhabitants knew of no other beings other than themselves? This is your experience as a group on your globe. We can assure you that this experience will change. How can it possibly not? How can it not evolve along with everything else?

But suppose we destroy ourselves before that ever occurs?

Create with others a magnificent future, right now, and start with your own neighborhood, individually. Address homelessness and poverty as it exists in your own backyard. Start in your mind, proceed with your words, and embody peace in your actions. Then you will begin to understand that as you yourself awaken, this is how you can sponsor your housemate, you can sponsor your next-door neighbor, through your own idea that this is possible. Bring that leadership to a group that is thirsty to be met by a joyous, peaceful countenance. Notice who is attracted to you and your presence.

What values do enlightened beings admire and model to their young?

Values embodied and exhibited in pursuit of seemingly selfless dedication to the whole. We say seemingly, because at a certain level of awareness, one understands in a very real way that the status and health of the whole is the status and health of the individual, and vice versa.

At some point, it is true that one simply outgrows pursuing endeavors that fail to spiritually broaden the individual and the collective. How this plays itself out is determined by the degree of evolution of the individual and the culture. There are myriad examples of the opposite of this in your culture. For example, tireless dedication by individuals and groups toward areas that would produce the most significant healing often receive the least amount of attention and accolades, for in order to stay in denial and to remain split off from the areas that do need attention, it would be necessary to withhold the sponsorship of your society's appreciation, whether through financial rewards or media attention.

We will use this illustration: Where there is a deep wound on the physical being, there is a natural tendency to protect it with bandages and by avoiding physical activity that would cause further exposure to contact, which would in turn cause further pain. In this metaphor, that protectiveness can symbolize the deep wounds of your collective peoples and your culture. There are deep, tender wounds regarding your knowing of what you are doing to each other and your planetary home, all while you are busy chasing golf balls. These activities often mask hopelessness in an individual who does not recognize how one can possibly make a dent in the numbers of your elderly who are destitute, or the needs of your homeless, or the starvation of your children worldwide. And so the mind splits off through a protective mechanism and finds pursuit in entertainment and experiences that allow most effectively a deflection of noticing the wound, and thereby avoidance of feeling the pain and the oozing infection of that wound. This is further illustrated during wartime when the public is drawn to light comedies and story lines lacking depth, because the consciousness desperately seeks relief for its underlying angst. That relief is often found in simplistic activities lacking in deep spiritual reflection, in order to divert society's nagging conscience.

To illustrate, masses of your people are mesmerized by events that glorify where a ball bounces or rolls. This can be an indication of society's unconscious attempt to anesthetize a growing wound by so easily and readily finding mass appeal in the journey of a little green ball or large brown one. You then grant celebrity status to those who can bounce, bat, hit, or strike those balls the best.

This does not take away from the individual accomplishment of your professional athletes, but what it does symbolize is your global tendency to deny funds, attention, and reward often to the very individuals and groups who are making the greatest headway toward the healing of your globe. Instead you lavish your praise, attention, and wealth upon activities and obsessions that keep you diverted from your most pressing global wounds. This is a double-edged sword, to which many of your environmentalists can attest, because in the declaration of the wake-up call, there is a tendency for your society to not merely ignore, but to actually punish the messenger by channeling that unconscious rage at self and society—and to unconsciously project that anger at activists or others who remind you of your tendency at the moment to destroy yourselves and your home. These are the individuals who are most effectively making practical higher ideals and yet are most denied and rejected by society. Instead, you wake up to your morning paper, eager to read about and follow up on the goings-on of a bouncing ball. This is not to say that there is anything at all wrong with sports. We are only asking you to notice how much attention is placed on such things, *in relation to your global dilemmas.*

There is a societal counter-poise which balances the scales in the avoidance of noticing your wounds and those come in the framework and context of individuals and endeavors that might lack depth of meaning, and which do not trigger your deep remorse at the reality of your situation. This is not a hopeless scenario; it is simply where you are right now at the crossroad. There is naturally, before the awakening, a tendency to most vociferously seek the proverbial hole in the sand, as in the cartoon image of your ostrich that seeks to hide its head, symbolizing an unwillingness to hold within one's awareness the nature of your world. It is not a coincidence at this time that athletes' incomes reflect the most they have ever reflected, while simultaneously funds are diverted from your most urgent environmental and social projects. Many of you are willing to pay for the luxury of not feeling or being made aware of other people's situations and events which trigger feelings of desperate hopelessness and powerlessness. Hence, attendance at games where balls bounce, roll, are thrown, and are hit generate huge turnouts.

As the addict or alcoholic awakens to the behaviors that are decimating self, there can be a time just preceding that awakening in which the personality most desperately seeks the most shallow of pursuits. Often times just prior to awakening, the sleepwalking is at its most heightened state. The endeavors most celebrated by a culture that is desperately asleep will have a certain quality. Those qualities tend to have characteristics that initially allow you to most effectively continue the sleepwalking.

In the royal courts of old, outside the windows would be occurring a Sunday afternoon beheading, while inside the building would be conducted business as usual, for to look out the window would cause much discomfort as to the nature of the culture and one's own seeming lack of ability to intervene in such senselessness. There could be those playing marbles in the hall, happily chattering while their fellows were outside the wall being tortured. It is important to begin to identify and to notice the psychic pain that each of you hold as you see daily the further decimation of your planet and how you contribute individually and collectively to that despite your best intentions.

The more pain there is collectively, the more potential there is for avenues of entertainment to be encouraged through different means in order to allow some relief, by denying the degree of catastrophe that goes on within many different levels environmentally, socially, politically, physically, and spiritually.

This does not mean that enlightened beings do not engage in relaxing activities that involve hobby-like pursuits. But enlightened beings would first tend to a gaping gunshot wound, in their fellow or in themselves, before playing Ping-Pong. The wound would first be tended to, for gangrene awaits and to deny the wound by upping the stakes at the Ping-Pong table is purely a form of denial. So it is not wrong, nor is it "bad," it is simply an example of a culture that cannot, at this moment, seem to put societal attention on the wound, because to do so would strike alarm at the heart of humankind. To treat a wound as life threatening would first require that one notice it as such, and not pretend it's a light bruise. Enlightened beings would certainly pursue the delightful play of Ping-Pong, but *after* having facilitated the funds and attention to the wound in the same manner and degree to which those funds, awareness, and attention would be made available to the Ping-Pong match and its players. To do so the other way around is sleepwalking.

For the record, if you think there is joyful glee in the social interaction during such games now, imagine the widespread relief and joy with which your culture will pursue its social gatherings after the gaping wounds are attended to. As it stands, your financial and media decisions are placed disproportionately to benefit the Ping-Pong games.

Blessed be to your professional Ping-Pong players and others who use their position of championship to direct social awareness to this social dynamic. Use your notoriety toward world healing, and use it to direct the media to cover events that are pressing but are usually avoided, particularly those events that are not "popular" to champion.

> *It does seem that we as a culture do indeed assign "prestige" to certain suffering in comparison to other suffering. For example, as horrible as the terrorist attacks were in New York, it is an everyday occurrence worldwide for there to be children who are left as orphans, or for there to be families who cannot afford to bury a loved one, or for a child to be without health insurance, or for there to be thousands of deaths by starvation or violence.*

Yes, this is why it is so helpful to continue to show yourselves to yourselves, by showing the world what is happening with all of you at this moment, and why. Take to the areas of your planet where there is the most darkness—not with evil, for we don't contextualize it this way—but where the light of Divinity is the most dim. If you have notoriety, show your fellow what is happening as you all sleep. Bring attention to the areas on your globe that require the most healing. Be spokespeople for the products that embody the greatest potential for a paradigm shift. Endorse products which can change your world, but which have had virtually no media attention whatsoever, for these products threaten your multinational corporations.

This is a grand way to use celebrity. If the media cameras are following, find those areas and bring the cameras with you until you hear a roar of your citizenry that will not be quieted, for the role models of your culture will be spearheading your youth and small businesses toward a grass roots uprising. A grass roots awakening is available to your planet, led by any of you who can find a creative way to help celebrate those ideas, products, projects, and endeavors that confront entrenched norms that threaten your globe. If you are a being who is gifted with status and personality, use it wonderfully to bring attention to those practices that threaten your individual and collective survival. This way can you help motivate multinational corporations to begin making decisions based on the understanding that your population is holding them accountable, and will be watching their level of social responsibility.

This can only happen if there is a way to bring those practices out into the light of world observation. Here is a wonderful opportunity for individuals, in a position to do so, to gather together with other "healers" as you begin to encourage each other that you and other citizens can change the world. The boardrooms of your most insensitive conglomerates will begin to take notice, for there are more of you en masse with your purchaser voices than there are of them. Find each other and find gleefully creative ways to shine the spotlight of the camera on those individuals, groups, and organizations who are doing the most destruction to your environment and your culture, and who are most ignoring the social plight of others who suffer. This is not about punishment. It is about causing your culture to observe the reality of your situation right now and to awaken from your collective denial. The goal is not to bemoan how stupid you all are, but rather to simply announce, "Let's not do this anymore to ourselves."

You can awaken the voting masses that are feeling desperately voiceless and hopeless about engendering change. The avenues for creative genius in this area are countless and will help awaken glee within you as you pursue these because you will have awakened the healer and the intense guilt of each of you, cellularly, will be assuaged. Symbolically, you will each sob tears of relief as you take up the path, applauding yourselves for finally having tended to your wounds. You will forgive yourself, for your hatred is self-directed at your denial, because you know that the future of your children's planetary home is iffy. You know this and yet you feel hopeless to change it and helpless to do anything about it. Join hands through your creative endeavors, and those of you in positions of "power" through your individual celebrity or notoriety, this is your opportunity to bring your fellows to opportunities of healing. For this reason you may have brought your celebrity to yourself. Don't fall into further sleepiness and pursue the path of your culture's destruction, but rather hear the whisper of your soul, reminding you of why you have brought this opportunity to yourself at this very moment when your Mother Earth awaits your lead.

You said that there are actually very few "bad guys," both here on Earth and out there in the galaxy. The mind just automatically wants to know more about this. Just one criminal can do a lot of, well, evil or harm. You're saying not to worry about so-called evil, but simply to change it. But people want to know about the "bad" extraterrestrials. Tell us who they are, and the kind of "bad" that they do. We're not at your level of enlightenment, so how can we not worry about what they might do to us?

Blessed are those who come before a truth and attempt to consider for a moment how that truth would feel were they to adopt it as their own. We readily understand that you do in fact exist from a place of fear in many cases. But what you don't recognize is that you are getting ready for a leap in your evolution, and so we bring you these ideas so that you can hold them in the palm of your hand, just as you take this leap.

It is as though as you leap, you will have had the benefit of having already pondered some of these ideas. So when we suggest to you that should someone try to slay us for wanting to possess what we have, we would simply give them what they seek, from where you are right now, it seems as though this is an impossible ideology to adopt. And perhaps from where you are at this very second, it is. But let those who have ears to hear, listen. For we are passing along the great tidings that you are on the precipice, about ready to jump into your new future as a universal human. That universal being will not only know his and her neighbors, but you will begin to adopt some of these evolved ideas yourselves.

When Jesus went from home to home and from village to village, did he warn his countrymen of the "evils" of the Roman Empire? Or did he suggest that no fear was necessary, that the greatest gift one could bestow on oneself or another was that of loving acceptance? Change is not only possible within the context of "acceptance" but is more effective. Acceptance suggests that as you seek to make changes, you are not angry and spiteful, you simply decide to embark upon a different path. Do you see the difference in nuance? And yet you come to us, and you want us to warn you of a potential deviant. For what reason? So that you can then fill your thoughts with worry and name another enemy and call this very being into your reality? When and if it is important for your soul to have information, trust that you will call any information to you.

But the greater reason behind your question is one of a general tendency among you toward the idea that it is not safe at home or out there. Particularly, out there in the cosmos. How can you begin to adopt an idea that this is a peaceful, loving universe? Given your present mentality, what you have most to "fear," if anything, is your brethren right there next to you, and even they are not justified in having you fear them. Yet you look to the vastness of the universe and it doesn't feel safe, because you haven't yet included it in your definition of "home."

When you look beyond your normal way of thinking, you stretch your mind. This is what we are asking from you, yet you keep attempting to bring our conversation back to the level at which fear reigns. It would seem that you are attempting to have a conversation, but staying in the safety of your own ego-driven mentality. We are suggesting that the very nature of the fact that you are having this conversation suggests that you are becoming someone else—and that someone else is actually the real you. You are remembering who you are, and as you remember who you are, you will draw out some of these patterns of thinking that symbolize the fearful human. That fearful human is evolving. It is okay to decide to think in a different way. It is okay to catch yourself protesting, and stating, "But surely there is someone out there to fear. Tell us about him or her so that we may know what to expect," and yet such a question lacks the fundamental understanding that what you focus upon, you call to yourself.

There are so many ideas yet to discuss. There are so many avenues left to explore. Fearing that there is one group of bandits out there, and that you need to know more about them, comes back to your earlier assumption that you are not safe and that even if you were safe, your safety would only be temporary. We are inviting you to swap that type of thinking and to begin to adopt the idea that there is bountiful peace; peace reigns supreme. Avail yourself of that and move into that experience and choose it for yourself. The constant need to focus on the potential lack, and the potential pitfalls, the potential problems, the potential perpetrator, the potential criminal, is not the type of thinking embodied by the master. The master simply knows that all is well, no matter what. And armed with this peaceful countenance, then can you most effectively change those events and practices of your culture that don't suit your survival.

Is there no room for you to think this way? Is there no way for you to get beyond this concern? Can you at least recognize how the mind keeps you from celebrating what is, in an attempt to have you focus on "what-could-go-wrong"? The mind justifies this behavior by suggesting that it must be vigilant for you, otherwise harm will befall you, for by not being vigilant, you will certainly meet all of the potential pitfalls in life. But has this been true from your experience? Is it not enough to just know that out there, there is the all of it as symbolized by contrast between the mountain and the valley, the ocean and the desert, the tornado and the calm? And out of all the experiences and outcomes, you are attempting to practice the mechanics of choosing the outcome that you *prefer* while simultaneously, calmly, and lovingly noticing what is not working. The mind screams that this is not possible, that this is denial. If that is the case, then Jesus was in an awful lot of denial.

There are beings, just as there are humans, who will take advantage of those of you who invite such experience. The way to invite negative experience—and it is "negative" by your own definition—is to stay focused on that energy, and you will draw to yourself plenty of those types of experiences, for they share your energetic vibration. When you elevate your thoughts and come into alignment with your bliss, you are living the life of the master. Then, and only then, can you begin to understand what it is like to cease one's addiction to classifying and categorizing potential quicksand.

Superimpose a new idea of what is possible for the New Human.

The New Human is motivated by peace and ensures that for all members. The New Human is not limited to die at less than one hundred years old, nor is the New Human relegated to present-day cultural assumptions. The New Human travels not only to other continents unfettered, but travels off the planet, and may visit with other inhabitants of crafts, launched in the bay of the universe.

The New Human no longer expects to have certain biological transformations occur that are consistent with what you call "aging," and so these progressions of deterioration do not occur. You have assumed that because they do occur, then they must, but it is the other way around. They occur because you assume that they will.

The New Human begins revamping his whole understanding of what humanity can be. Disease and illness become a thing of the past, because as you align with some other ideas about how to exist, certain symptoms of limited consciousness drop away.

As the New Human begins to live longer than one hundred years or even thousands of years, you will begin to break the mold and stop programming yourselves to continue what you have been doing, as you have assumed is a biological imperative.

To take one small example, consider the topic of nutrition, as most of your "experts" have proselytized as to what nutrition is. You will no longer assume that certain foods are necessary for health. For as some of you drop these assumptions and hold in your thoughts a different idea of existing, it will prove to you what you cannot believe right now. If there are enlightened beings that do not ingest foods, but glean all of their sustenance and nourishment from light, it is also possible for the human species to develop to this stage of evolution. Surprisingly, it is not necessarily a huge biological adaptation that needs to take place, but simply an understanding that it can. Your entire culture is based on more assumption than you realize. You don't yet recognize how fully your assumptions play themselves out because you hold them as true. And your experiences follow your beliefs. Some of you do have a different experience that is contrary to your cultural understanding, and therefore you understand what is possible.

There are a few beings—human beings—on your planet who live solely on light. Do you think that they believe that they will die if they do not ingest food? If they had that belief, they would. When you argue that anorexics die after not eating, what do you assume their belief is at a very deep level? Deep down, they share the belief of most of you that certain foods and nutrients *are* required to sustain a healthful body and as they cease to take in those nutrients, their body follows the direction of their belief. We are not advocating that you cease eating. We are simply pointing out that your assumptions about everything, in every area, from physiology to the nature of the universe, set up what your experience becomes.

But eating is an avenue of social pleasure, too.

We have evolved beyond our need to gain pleasure from moving our mouths in a certain way around a certain substance, and doing so within a group of us. We no longer need this activity as social recreation or as a biological benefit. As a result, we seek other avenues of expression for enjoying ourselves, which has allowed us to create a different kind of life altogether.

We participate in the growing of the flowers and plants, purely through the enjoyment of doing so, seeing what colors come up. Our young experiment with the joys of harmoniously creating *with* the flowers, but we are not attempting to get something from them, any more than we are attempting to get something from each other. So you see, our love for the plants and animals has shifted as it has shifted for each other, and so will yours. When your paradigm shifts, you will stop exploiting each other and every living thing, and so your tastes will have evolved—literally.

Generally, a collective calls to itself a vehicle that brings the heralding of new ideas, when it deems that it is ready to be exposed to new ideas. Although you may not remember from an evolutionary perspective, we are right on time, as requested. We are bringing you a news bulletin and offering you ideas that you may have never considered before. You cannot even imagine what your planet would be like if none of you ate food for survival. You would grow your flowers and plants simply for the joy of growing. You would care for your animals, not to ultimately kill them, but to enjoy their being, and you would not breed and torture them in factories any longer. Your pollution would be greatly reduced with the ceasing of this practice alone. As your consciousness expands and you are able to hold these ideas as possible, you will have collectively triggered a new shift that begins now. Your awakening brings more possibilities to you.

So, although you may not run out and make radical changes, once you hear some ideas, you will never be the same. For you cannot return to complete sleepiness once you have been nudged awake, and you have seen or heard ideas that help you to permanently lose a degree of your unconsciousness.

CHAPTER 14

The New Revolution

*One night I awoke to the sensation of an out-of-body experi-
ence beginning full force. Prior to my encounters, nothing of the
sort had ever happened to me, at least that I was aware of, but
since the encounters, out-of-body experiences and episodes of
remote viewing have become more common. As usual, during this
particular experience, the normal crackling and popping occurred,
initiating a separation of what I suppose is my astral body from my
physical body. I really have little understanding of what or how
any of this stuff happens, from a scientific standpoint. I only know
that it does happen, and it all began after I started having
encounter experiences.*

*Oftentimes, I have "traveled" down white tunnels of energy,
much like those reported by survivors of near-death experiences. I
don't know where I'm going, and sometimes, I don't understand
what I've seen. One time, after a quick trip down some sort of tunnel, I came upon the most wondrous city of gold. It was indescrib-
ably intricate and beautiful, and I hovered above the city from my
vantage point, in my astral body.*

Another time, I came upon some odd-looking inhabitants who appeared to be about nine feet tall and otherwise resembled the Group in facial characteristics. They were also gray in color. Upon returning home to my bed, I was again frustrated by my limited memory, having retained mere fragments of images that still remain a mystery.

Although a full explanation is lacking, as every year passes, I am left with an ever-expanding appreciation for just how complex and diverse universal experience can be. Just imagine what awaits us all as we let go of our limited ideas about what is going on out there. Wouldn't it be fun to spend a lazy Sunday in another dimension?

Is Earth the most beautiful planet your group has ever seen? I'm sure that there are a whole lot of planets, but I can't imagine how many could be more diverse than this one.

There are several planets that emulate the bluest blues and the greenest greens of your planet, and some even have colors that yours does not. Picture, if you can, a place where you can not only see a rainbow, but you can actually touch it and taste it. Can you imagine such a thing? There exists just such a planet where one can celebrate the joys of the senses. It is a delight to behold and is like stepping into one your children's picture books and having it come alive with brilliance of color, taste, and sensation. These "rainbow centers" as they are called, are healing centers, due to their vibratory essence. As you might imagine, such an experience would be extraordinarily enlivening.

Tell me more.

There are animals that you would marvel at.

I would love to hear about animals. Please tell me about them.

Picture the softest bear cubs with fur as satiny as are the ears of your own yellow lab, and rather than these bear cubs being in a zoo or in the wilderness somewhere, these delightful creatures abound where children play. Our young do not need to resort to imagination in play with stuffed toy animals because they have the real thing. These creatures bring delight to children's play and imagination, and there are many kinds of these little creatures, which gravitate toward our young and of course, our young toward them. There are very strong vibrations of love coming from such encounters and playtime, sheer and utter joy and contentment. Most parents can picture such an event only in their wildest imagination. Think of looking to where your child plays and seeing her engaged in the most delightful play with other children, and these playtime animals also delight in playing and loving them. It's like a fantasy to you, isn't it?

Yes, how delightful. Instead of children starving on the streets of Calcutta, you describe them enjoying the most wondrous of existences.

Imagine a place where mothers meet to renew their bond with their children on benchmark intervals, much like your children's birthdays, when you might gather, except in this case events are arranged for families to spend special time together in which to celebrate their special reasons for incarnating. The young are able to review their experiences and celebrate those with the group and then imagine what else or what more that they would like to create for themselves. Of course they have long since understood and integrated the idea that creation begins with imagination, and imagination is key in discussions throughout childhood and beyond.

There is a planet that is home to those souls who yearn to experience the delights of what you observe to be that which is limited to the experience of animals on Earth. Have you ever stood watching the expanse of a hawk at wing, wheeling on the thermals, and wished that you could be there too, flying as free as a bird?

Like every day; I imagine that every day.

Yes, many of you do, and on this planet, you could experience that or the exhilaration of the speed, musculature, and strength of the horse galloping freely. You would be able to experience how that feels, to be able to run at great speeds, like the stallion upon the plains.

Wow.

Have you ever wondered what it would be like to swim in the bluest, warmest ocean of your dreams with bright fish and exquisite colors of coral and other sea life all around?

No doubt many scuba divers can attest to what that feels like.

Yes, but picture doing this without oxygen tanks strapped to your body, having no concern for how you will breathe under water. Why do you think that movies and cartoons of mermaids so appeal to your young? It is because internally, you hold the memory of all that is possible, and yearn to experience that again. To be able to taste the freedom of the eagle and to fly, to be at one with the ocean and to know its depths, to converse with the plains by feeling your strong legs fly across the dunes with the wind in your face, this is the soul's version of your Disneyland.

And I thought that Wild Country Safari was something.

Come with us, and we will take you on a journey and describe to you the wonders of the universe. From your planet, you might gaze up into the night sky and see the stars twinkling in the distance, but it does not feel personal to you. It does not feel as though your cousin Bertha is out there and that you share more characteristics than you don't. If you will but stand next time and look out into the vastness of the night and imagine that someone, somewhere, is doing the same from their end, then you will know how much it is that you both share. Suppose you could hop on a shuttle and visit Bertha for the evening. Would you? Children don't often venture out of their backyards at night. They stay close to home. If you asked them why, they might reply, "because we're not allowed to." But as a parent, if you invited them to venture out because it is safe beyond your doorstep, would they? You are like children, this way. For you are still frightened of what you might discover.

No, it's our limited technology that prevents our greater freedom.

Really? You are having a hard enough time getting along and accepting others of your kind when they are on the other side of your globe. If you could step onto a shuttle tonight, if we could make that available to you and you could head into the dark night to meet one of your neighbors far away, what fear would you bring? What prejudices would you have?

Some of you are already doing this to some degree, so do not think that this experience is 200 years away from you. Those humans who have left their home planet and have ventured forth beyond the safety of their living rooms have often traversed through incredible emotional processes. Every time Lisette left her bed, she wondered if she would ever again see her son, for the unknown can be so unnerving. But someone must be the frontrunner of universal experience. Those of you who have so chosen it, experience it.

> *I love the idea of expanding our collective experience to know our galactic neighbors. I just hope we don't need to leave Earth for other reasons. Just how close is this planet to the point of no return in supporting life through the depletion of its resources?*

You already are at the point where it does not sufficiently support life as evidenced by the demise of your animal species. How much more evidence do you need?

How much longer will you wait—you, and you, and you? How much longer will you forestall recognizing that the time for overturning your entrenched system has arrived? Be inspired by what has taken place before you with the colonization here in this country, and use it to model what you will do next with the uprising of your people and your ability to flourish forward into the universe. Your newly emerging "tea party" will celebrate its new way of conducting your affairs by demonstrating to the universe your newly recognized sense of self. You will have more help than you can imagine, for many simply await your dawning. You have always had this self inside, this enlightened soul, but now you are remembering and recognizing just who is there within you.

Are you stunned by this answer?

> *No, I just don't understand how our current leaders do not recognize where they are taking us. They are, after all, destroying their own planet as well.*

Yes, and that is the definition of being asleep, for they know not how they effect an impact on themselves and their own beloved. But the greater question is, those of you who *do* recognize where you are going, what more can you do? How much more powerfully can you organize? How much more effectively can you demonstrate and recreate something? This is the question that might be answered. For you who *are* awake and are doing the noticing, are the next leaders, don't you see this? You continually wait for your politicians to awaken, so that they can lead you to a healing, but if they were capable of this right now, they would have led you by now.

This is part of your denial of accepting full power and responsibility within self, because you keep waiting for others to do it for you. Again, you have in some ways parentified your so-called political leaders, because they are leading, but not where you would like to go. You have parentified them because you still see them as all-powerful, you still see them as the effective route to your glorious future. And so give this up. There is a certain amount of anger and emotion in letting go of this fantasy, because you will have to realize that no one else will do it for you. You must take the responsibility yourselves.

Ironically, it will require a shift in your thinking to start perceiving as ineffective the very people whom you presently perceive as powerful and effective. For the most part, they are asleep to grander spiritual and universal ideas. You must drop the notion that they embody the new voice, for they are as children in costumes, put there by other children in costumes. We use the analogy of children, for they have not put aside their childish pursuit of collecting the toys of seeming power.

You who notice, and you who have inside a deep stirring of your soul, a grief that won't go away from what you observe as happening around you, you are responsible, if you choose to take your fellows to a spiritual renewal.

Were you surprised in the 1960s, when there was such strong opposition to the hippie movement and the protests of that time, for that infectious idea of change is very, very powerful and can bring down systems of government where they don't work.

Be those starry-eyed young people once again. Come outside again with the same hopefulness. Many of you from that era have become so hopeless, in that it seems impossible, those ideals seem so ridiculous, but this is precisely the movement that will turn the tide and create the change. It is no accident that there are so many of you from that time now having reached a degree of maturity in which you can more powerfully organize. You have positions of authority. You have the wisdom to orchestrate demonstrations and change. You have the ability and confidence to model for your children that it is not okay, given where you say you would like to be in the next twenty years, to allow repression and dominion by a few over the lot of you.

Do you not feel grief when you take your children to a mountain lake and your child asks you, "Why has this water been allowed to become polluted?" or to the West Coast in Southern California where there are signs posted on the beach that say "No swimming today, levels of pollution are high"? To have to cause young children to understand why this has been allowed is numbing for you. You know it to be so, because it's difficult to explain how it is that so many millions of people have stood by and allowed your homeless to remain so, and your children to die of starvation, and your trees to be cut in the name of special interest groups, when other products are available, and where your oceans are so polluted you would become ill if you immersed yourselves in them. When you must keep your children out of your waters it is difficult to explain to them how and why it is that millions are impacted adversely by the choices of a few.

This is what you will change. The degree of relief that you will feel as you begin this shift will be enormous.

Put in place those processes and projects so that you will see in your lifetime significant changes, and you will not regret having passed this glorious opportunity to be part of your new revolution.

From the time of Revolutionary America, Thomas Jefferson and all those involved with the pursuits of the Founding Fathers, inspired people to believe that changes not only could be made but were in fact being made, ready or not. And that is what your next step is, right now.

The Second Generation

The Second Generation of human life on planet Earth has been foretold since the beginning of time. It is the grand awakening in which you will all partake. You are part of the awakening, but you have also been part of the plan from the beginning, "planning" your unawakened state, and then also planning your process of awakening, and then your awakened state. You have all wanted to experience this, those of you here present in these days. It is part of a grand theatre production. You all have your roles. You thought it fun to experience the deadening thud of unconsciousness year after year, thousands of years upon thousands of years; and now to plan your escape from unconsciousness is also the par for the course. We have all planned it this way, all of us who partake in any role with each other. It is hardly a waste of time, incarnating, living, and then experiencing the profound joy of waking up and beholding one's true Divinity within, when just moments before, one was asleep, caught in the almost deathlike grip of the comatose.

Come now, and take your place. You are just beginning to start the first act. Much preparation has gone on before now for millennia, but significantly now for the last thirty years. And now many await their participation in the production. Never before in all of humanity has there been the time of such portent, enlarging understanding as to who you are. This time shall be marked by an increase in your recognition of not only who you are within, but also you will begin to recognize who others are. This is beneficial, because as you remember on a deeper level who each player is in this life and others, you will tend to be more forgiving, more patient, and yet more forthright in following through with your idea of what you would like to accomplish this time around.

Before you awaken globally, you are awakening individually, noticing small things within yourself that are changing. Perhaps your diet is changing slowly. Perhaps you are less likely to create, or feel justified in continuing, your individual conflicts with family or co-workers. Perhaps you have given up the desperate chasing of material goals, or perhaps you have lessened your competitiveness with others and are satisfied in simply enjoying the breath of life and allowing others theirs.

Bestowing kindness on one another is the mark of the Second Generation of your species. This will be your prime motivation, not hoarding your ideas, your wealth, your name, or your reputation, but rather simply showing kindness where you can. Jesus chose his disciples from humble fishermen, as well as from the educated, because worldly status does not hold value with the divine as does one's decision to show kindness, express love for one another, and behold each of you as the enlightened beings that you are inside. The requisites for such behaviors are not found in titles, in academic degrees, or in bank accounts, but are found in simple desires of the heart. These are the qualities that are glorified by the universe: kindness, patience, helpfulness to one another, and an ability to cast not the first stone of judgment. Let the trumpets announce every act of your kind words. Let the violin soothe and accompany your thoughts and prayers and wishes to help another. For that is part of the plan, also, to reap what you have sown through reincarnation and yet to agree to help each other through those trials as this process is carried out.

You can live in a manner that allows for simple pleasures, return to a way of life symbolized by the garden of Eden, in which you lament not your inability to purchase more things, but instead gleefully simplify, helping where you can to raise the consciousness in your self-selected role as the Earth awakens.

We dare to ask you if there is anything more you might be, through your thoughts and your deeds, in order to bring about desired results that you have long ago agreed upon for this day and time and age. Do not be misled. Awakening is simpler than you have imagined, for you are awakening to love, not sorrow. You are awakening in the direction of Divinity. You do not have to close down further.

Humankind will come to an understanding of how life proceeds from here that is dictated by how you are conducting yourselves this very moment. This includes the next step that you might take with otherworldly entities such as ourselves—"extraterrestrials." Some of you have already had, and are having, ongoing daily contact, while others of you are wondering why you have not.

Why do you refer to it as the "Second Generation"? It implies that there are only two generations when there are hundreds of thousands of them, given how many years have passed since the beginning of humankind.

Yes, of course, literally, there have been more than two generations since the beginning of your species, but this is the time in which there will be so many significant changes that everything before this generation will be considered as the first and everything hence as the second. These will not only be intellectual changes, but physical, emotional, and of course, spiritual changes. All become unified as one. Your problems prior to this were when you sought to improve or change aspects of one body only, meaning of just one or two bodies of the emotional, physical, spiritual, or intellectual bodies, but now you are beginning to understand that an integrated human aligns all these aspects and raises them all to a higher vibration simultaneously.

You can liken the end of your dominating ruling party to that of the end of the Crown's dominion over the inhabitants of the new America. There are similarities with your democracy, today, although you do not wish to look at it this way. You have moved far from what you created after the colonization and all that was achieved through your Declaration of Independence. A slow but consistent chipping away of your freedoms has occurred, so that some of you would hardly recognize how far from the documents of your Founding Fathers you have come. When you agree to simply observe what is so, then can you be more willing and able to decide to make changes if you choose.

You in America are an example in many ways to the rest of your brothers and sisters on the globe. In your country, when the citizens stand by and allow coercion by the wealthy, corruption, and special interests to take power, it sets a powerful precedent and does not provide the shining example of your freedom and those rights that you enacted once before during the days of the revolution. Should you endeavor to conclude that there is much work to be done, should you conclude that you do not wish to leave a homeland where your children would be raised within a self-serving government, then make a collective decision to join forces together and stand by no longer.

The new millennium is encouraging an awakening on all levels. Your political arena is simply symbolic of how far you are removed from your own power base. But that can change, that can shift. When you doubt the ability of your people to create a whole planet that makes sense to you and your children, you allow the present system to remain unchanged. Doubt and seeming obstacles that take the form of "How on Earth can we make changes?" does not allow for possibilities to present themselves as to how specifically you can get from here to there. Those who have a firm arm over you would prefer that you stay in doubt. Some have a preference to keep the system as it is, unchallenged, and it can be so as long as you continue to feel hopeless about having millions and millions of people make changes on your own behalf.

Dismantling a system and replacing it with one that embodies spiritual ideas is less difficult than you think it is. It simply takes a concerted effort of like-minded and like-heartened individuals who decide that this is as far as it goes, and no further. Instead, you have allowed for it to go further and further toward the potential demise of all of you, and the only way you cope is to hold the hope that one day in the future you would all stand up for your freedoms. Well, that day is here now. Wait no longer.

Can we really do this? Can we really become an evolved society?

We are sending you an outpouring of love, for all things are possible, and this too can come to pass. We encourage you with the same love and hope as you might have when you look at your young children. There is delight in you as you behold them, and you are teared up at the sheer joy of them. This is the way we feel at this moment for you. It is because you and others don't realize the potentiality for your near future and how you can bridge your present to the most glorious evolution of yourselves. We hear and observe the stretching of your identity as that of the new universal being, each of you awakening and recognizing the ability to create anything.

You will begin to recognize that you are taking yourselves further and further down the road of pure creativity to a place of no limitations. Do you wish to live beyond ninety years? Then choose it, and intend it, and make it so, and involve all of the discussions relating to how this might happen. This is what you are doing, individually, and, more and more, collectively. From this state of "assume nothing," assume no limitations. Assume not your heredity in matters of these ideas—your heredity meaning what it seems is possible for humans to do and not to do. Thousands of you have met extraterrestrials. These ideas would have seemed like stark raving lunacy not too long ago.

There are planets upon which the inhabitants practice growing stars and creating living organisms like plants, just for practice, because evolved beings can do that. This is what you might say makes practical the Bible's Book of Genesis. This is integrated, soul-level creation. One is not proceeding from the intellect alone; one is proceeding through an integrated process, and when one proceeds this way and connects to that Divinity, one is guided. Fear not horrendous consequences. Trust in the divine to lead you home to each other and to your self.

As you break from the restraints of your confined mold of what is acceptable and unacceptable, when you come up against resistance within self, do yourself a favor and look there. This will reveal a blockage. No need to judge it. Simply notice it and love it and if you dare, discuss it and say, "Hmm, I notice this about myself, that this discussion induces my having some sensitivity around this or that." In this way you unravel blockages. The soul calls to itself all of experience including conversations, explorations through dialogues and experience. As a Universal Human, you are not limited to only one modality of healing. There is a brilliant plan that the soul utilizes to engender the sweeping out of the cobwebs and the achieving of the emotional clarity and healing that the soul is requesting of you. All the synchronicities that bring you to any particular experience, even this, has been called to you by you. Ponder that.

The state of affairs of your relationships with each other will improve decidedly as you allow your partner and yourself to spill out of your own box. Patients lie in hospital beds around the world confiding in the stranger in the bed next to them their deepest desires, their wildest dreams for the future, their deepest fears, because at a time of vulnerability, one is desperate to connect to another and to have the discussions of a lifetime. When you begin to bring that level of freedom to your relationships, you instill a unique, fertile ground for growth and healing, not to mention a tender emotional connection between two people.

Your soul wants to release the pressure from blockages and issues that you may not be consciously aware of. This phenomenon is much like a bottle of seltzer water with the top on, and there is a build-up, and through your soul bringing to you certain discussions and experiences, you have the opportunity to finally remove the cap. And when done, there seems to be an explosion of emotion. That explosion is your telltale sign that there has been a blockage, which is now moving past the bottleneck. Celebrate that feeling because you have finally called and brought to yourself a moment, an opportunity, to heal and release the blockage.

Such moments, opportunities, and celebrations of life have been called to you by you, snippets in time and an opportunity for a glorious expression of tender connections.

The New Revolution

Beyond your time and space, we evolved to a more natural resonance of a greater potential for a living species, which is to say that
we don't have the limitations that you do with respect to our physical being and the way that our emotions drive our experience. But we
still love deeply, we feel joy as you do, but we have endeavored to
heal our fears and fearful motivations, and we have decided to live
consciously. When one lives consciously, one does not behave for reasons unknown to self.

Charlottesville, Virginia, the home of Thomas Jefferson, is a place
that resonates with your country's revolutionary beginnings, and this
is a palpable locale in which to get in touch with the same memory
of awakening and making manifest again your New World. This is
important because from the intellect's standpoint, it seems so long
ago when these events took place, from the protesting at the Boston
Tea Party to your fledgling, emerging new government, in which the
powerful elite was overtaken by a grass roots group of inspired and
visionary leadership.

Go ahead and reenact this now. It is just that simple. It takes only
a memory of how you have done it before. At this time, your *globe*
will join in the "tea party" of the populace's endeavors to throw off
the tyranny of the power elite, which is often motivated by everything other than the interests and benefit of your whole collective.

Your new world can emerge in the same fashion with inspired
visionaries at the helm, tempting you to step out from under oppression and to be able to "worship" as you please without threat of punishment. But in this case, your expression of worship is your
announcement of "worshiping" the needs of all of you, not just a few
of you. Your new worship is holding important your environmental
and social issues that concern you, without having these concerns
minimized or trivialized. This trivialization on the part of big business, government, and those who have not yet internalized the plight
of your world's homeless and starving is your modern form of repression and threat of retribution as indicated by their response to
activism in all its forms.

There are some startling parallels right now between the time of
the American Revolution and now, inasmuch as now you endeavor to
express yourselves and to express your freedom of worship: your

The New Revolution

freedom to choose what is important to you, without having your lawmakers make choices based on what is important to those who have collected the most wealth. As you do so, notice those similarities; notice the courage and the commitment necessary in the days of Thomas Jefferson and John Adams, in which adults simply refused to be "parented" any longer by the Crown, and refused to tolerate any longer the ongoing repression and influence of a small group. They were willing to risk it all in order to make a New World, and a new way of living through a philosophy that honors freedom. You do not have freedom when you have no say in how your planet is treated. You have no freedom when you have seemingly no control over the decimation of your natural resources or the ignoring of your disenfranchised. We are not telling you something that you do not know, but notice where you yearn for freedom and where the movement can begin.

American Revolutionary politics allowed for a new voice to emerge. That new voice was as ridiculed then by those in the "office" of the Crown, as is the new-age voice now by the working elite and politicians. We see evidence in this through your media, newspapers, and reviews of work that is ongoing by your activists and spiritualists.

Coincidentally, Charlottesville, Virginia, is the home of Hampton Roads Publishing Company, which has as one of its neighbors Monticello, the home of Thomas Jefferson. So, it's intriguing that you mention the time of revolutionary America and how we are at that time of "revolution" again. The book, The Return of the Revolutionaries, *which Hampton Roads plans to publish in 2003, goes so far as to suggest that the very souls who embodied the visionaries of the Revolution have actually reincarnated and live among us today.*

The author, Walter Semkiw, M. D., not only identifies who these people are now, but compares their sketches from yester-year to their current photographs. His theory is that physical features, particularly facial architecture, personality traits, and even writing styles, are all actually retained from one lifetime to another, thus helping to establish a match in their identities. The physical similarities are truly uncanny and it's exciting to think that we can organize together again and make the changes that we all dream of. What you're saying, together with what Semkiw states in his book, implies so much. Are we really at that level of "history making" right now, poised to change the course of the future?

Even then, during the time of the creation of your new Declaration of Independence and the Constitution, your "Founding Fathers" suspected that what they were endeavoring would have far-reaching implications, and many of you, too, recognize that now, today, something is underway. Either you will continue as you are and face the consequences of that, or something will change. In this way, should you change and embark upon a path toward heightened awareness, you will imbue broader applications of spirituality in your day-to-day lives. From the perspective of your culture, it is even to be considered "revolutionary" simply to agree that your species is threatened. What could supercede this understanding as newsworthy? What could take precedence over this in the history books of your species?

Collectively, you are growing up. You will look back on this time and be proud of your participation, all of you, for no matter your role, you have relegated your soul here, now, and so whatever way you are playing, you are part of the revolution. Even during the revolution of 1776, there was much concerted effort behind the scenes. Each participant had a role. Even the housewives and the slaves, all were participating in what would be seen as the new awakening of your country. This way, too, you are all now embarking upon the new awakening of your *species*. What happened then could be considered "small potatoes" in comparison to what is now at hand. For what do you think you have prepared yourselves? Now you will take yourselves beyond a revolution embarked upon in one country, and globally, you will revolutionize your whole idea of what it means to be human.

Yes, you all are at the moment of your revolution in that you will no longer stay constant in your sleepiness. You are revolutionizing the idea that an awakening is not only necessary, but must occur if you choose to continue this paradigm of your species. Anyone who would like to participate, may do so. Even the sleepwalkers participate for they create the context for those of you who yearn to experience yourselves as a light and a voice in the din of forgetfulness and worldly noise.

Unfasten your seat belt. Stand up from the table of your assumptions. Put your seat in an upright position for now you are free to move about your galaxy. This is what your current revolution is spearheading, for an awakened human first takes back her home before going forth into the broader home of her universe. And like any good neighbor, we are there to help you through the transition.

CHAPTER 15

Video Conferencing

One weekend in Chicago, at the extravagant Book Expo, where publishers, authors, and related professionals in the book industry participate in a monolithic convention, Bob and I slouched in chairs at day's end, happy but exhausted. As the tingling began in my scalp, I grabbed the tape recorder and popped in a fresh cassette tape. Curiously, an image also began to form in front of me. Was it the cover of Time Magazine? *It had a red border around it. I couldn't make out the cover photograph, or the caption, but I was very interested to know what the image had to do with my impending communication.*

During previous communications, the subject of "video conferencing" had come up; not between clients and brokers on Wall Street, but between those on Main Street, USA and Anywhere In The Universe. But I was having difficulty with the concepts. What did they mean by "video conferencing?" Into what wall socket would we—or they—plug an apparatus? And further, what was needed electronically? A video monitor? Soundboard? A television? I handed the tape recorder to Bob so that he could monitor the recording process. After a quick test of the equipment and after recording the month, day, and year, Bob pushed the "record" button and a communication began to come through.

Admittedly, it reads like Greek to me, though from a scientific standpoint, it seems overly simplistic. And I can't even be certain that I've captured their communication precisely. But for fun, we've included it here, just to practice living on the edge and also, just in case it is accurate—and therefore possible—we thought you'd enjoy being part of our next adventure in our ongoing journey of talking to extraterrestrials.

When we say that we can connect to you through video conferencing, we mean that we can integrate with you via a method that allows a connection between our minds and yours. But that does not rule out the physical probability that will enable you to connect to us in a more tangible way, through your modes of electronics, utilizing a conductor. A conductor can be an experiencer, and that experiencer takes the energies from one realm to another, which is precisely what is occurring during channeling. Video conferencing our image and energies expressed through communications is no more sophisticated an idea than what is going on right now with this communication. If you think that it is, then you don't understand this process of communication. The word "channeling" has much assumptive quality to it. It is a common word in your language use, and many of you recognize the word at sight, but few of you grasp the complex modalities that are engaged, in order to bring us and others through to you. When it seems as though the next step is a huge one, it is only because you don't recognize the sophistication of what is going on right here.

When you look from a tall skyscraper to the street below and see the little cars that are the size of a pinprick, from that distance you do not have an understanding of the complexity of the fuel-injected engine, or how the fibers make up the carpet in the cars, because you are so far removed from the details. Although this process of communication might be right "next" to you, there is still a void in your understanding of what is involved. Were you to comprehend this more fully, you would readily embrace, as we do, the next program in our communication. You would not readily dismiss it; not that you are explicitly, but we recognize that, were you to make such an announcement, eyebrows would rise. Explain to others our wild idea, and invite them along on the journey.

The ability of one person or another to connect with us is best facilitated when certain variables are present, just as an Olympic swimmer brings certain variables to the physical body and to the personality. We have often encouraged you to announce that communication is available to everybody, which it is, and the reason for this sharp, strong connection with us here is because certain variables are present. And it is a worthy endeavor for all of us to pursue this line of communication in this way, for reasons of lineage, "past, present, and future."

Bob, your connection and contribution here is strong. What you represent is symbolized by a kind of electronic adapter. Bob's energies and presence facilitate the dynamics of these communications and more. His function is something like that of an adapter, and this is a simplistic explanation. Were you to attempt to fit a component into an appliance, the fit would require a bridge, and that bridge is that adapter and describes your function. In the work of traditional channeling, your role would be described as that of a "conductor." Your participation better facilitates all of the energies to make a connection on every level and to materialize, and consequently, it is a magical combination, the two of you and others, because the pieces of the puzzle are present. You wonder why we seem to encourage this combination. How can we not encourage such wonderful synergy?

Your joint energetic participation in the manner that you have set for yourselves through telephone conversations and constant communications is, to a high degree, the reason for its success thus far. The encouragement Bob offers is a piece of that, but Bob is capable of providing that encouragement precisely because he ideologically, deeply comprehends this material for many reasons. This is why you do not provide shallow encouragement as she once wondered, but rather, you provide encouragement based on a soulful understanding of what we are all choosing, and also of what is possible. So, for now, your participation is so vital and your strength is ever present, despite the miles between you. There is a very strong aura of your presence in all of this work, to which she will attest.

So, what does this suggest for video conferencing between humans and extraterrestrials?

Through some experimentation and playful abandonment through pure magnificent creation, you can proceed, *if you can imagine it.* The most playful of you would be required, because limited assumptions about what is, and is not, possible would hinder your progress.

But does someone need to invent some type of electronic device first to facilitate this?

The pattern of "technology" has already been established. The basic premise is there. Simply expand on the idea, and pretend that we are not where we are, that we are just a little ways away, and it will not seem so impossible. Ponder deeply what is going on during channeling and these communications, and notice the extraordinary similarities between video conferencing and such channeling/communications, particularly in this case, in which energies are being pulled from the unit of the cranium. One might say that with certain modifications here with Lisette, you as a "specimen" are quite suited to this function. Certain individuals have devices in their hearts to make them function better. As a result of such interventions, the patient is not more restricted, but less so, because science has found a way to prolong life.

In this way, there is more freedom here too, not less. Pacemaker recipients have decided that through placing a mechanism within them, they would be better suited and more able to live out the rest of their stated purpose. And so, too, Lisette has chosen a path that includes a mechanism that allows her to act as a conduit between our worlds. How this will play itself out, how it will proceed, how it will unfold, you will see. It is a marvelous day in the park, as when children leap for joy at the idea of a whole day before them without school, and some of these ideas bring to you the same carefree abandon as you marvel at the creative opportunities, at the soul level, to experience the wonder of all of us. The wonder *of* all of us is to wonder *at* all of us. We with you, and you with us. It is an extraordinary opportunity.

Humankind is so quick to leap to fear and judgment at the very notion of potential "manipulation" by extraterrestrials of the human species; and yet humans jump to help humans all the time in ways that are considered benevolent and evolutionary, and you don't label it as "manipulation." When you protest at our participation with you, it is your fear voicing its self-righteousness because the mind says, "Ah, the next step is manipulative control, and this is what we have known all along. The enemy is out there and is waiting to control us. I have suspected all along that the universe is unsafe."

How soon can we attempt this video communication?

You will be displeased with our answer. Time does not exist for us. Time is relative to you and your realm, but know this, that as you proceed, so shall you be; and so were we to say, "Things will occur in five years," what that can create is a mind that says, "Okay, in four years and two months we will begin thinking about this, and then in four years and nine months we will go to an electronics store and purchase some technical equipment." Do you see how the question of time is tricky for us to answer? The degree of your capability for creating something from nothing will answer your question. We can only encourage you to begin creating whatever you choose as soon as you would like to experience that in your reality. Some of you can perceive of an idea and experience it a short time later. Others take a little longer. The point here is to reconsider the idea of postponing creative endeavors. If your choice is to move in a direction, then move in that direction. Pull that experience out of the potential reality and pull it to you.

Who might be involved in developing this video conferencing process?

Please bear with us as we remind you that the procession of the creative process and the coordination of the smallest details require wondrous synchronicities, which simply fall into place with no more struggling than the lifting of a pencil. When you go forth with intention, anything is possible. The names of the players are already there in your palette. This answer applies to anything. As with all events, the players arrive according to their precise appointed timetable and it is no different here.

The same principles apply, whether you are intent on "inventing" video conferencing between us, or finding the perfect creative director and team for a publishing project such as this. It is no more complex than what you have already done. It is no more difficult than making it from one side of the street to another, from one side of town to another, from one side of the globe to another, from one end of the universe to another. All of it begins with intention. That is where miracles exist. The message in this book is that all things are possible, including the knowing of us. And the relationship between us is not limited to any one type of contact or communication, any more than the relationship between any of you is limited.

Of those of you who begin to ponder these ideas, including the idea of video conferencing with us, who has more of a possible experience of that outcome, you or one who has never given the idea a thought? The names of the players are the minutiae. The *decision* to create magnificently is the challenge. The decision requires trust and faith and intention and this would require a grand vision indeed.

There are those who insist that "the grays" are evil and manipulative, and they won't let go of that prejudice about you.

The Spanish Conquistadors rode rampant through the countryside, and at times pillaged their countrymen for lack of a better understanding that all diverse peoples are inherently free and inherently one. There are many among you who perceive of us as certain galactic conquistadors. In some ways, you are image consultants. It is not an easy job. You may be rebuffed at every turn in some quarters. It takes creative possibility thinking to change the image of a cultural hold on a certain idea. As image consultants, you are addressing a cultural presumption and naming it as what it is, which is prejudice. You are attempting, on our behalf, to shift an image from that of a conquistador and pillager to one of an enlightened, gentle species. This is a leap, at best, in many corners of your population, but a necessary first step in attempting to address and heal a level of fear that is prevalent there. For some of you, this belief is not even conscious. The slow introduction of us through these communications and video conferencing introduces the seeming conquistador, and at arm's length, allows a culture to begin to internalize the idea of our neighborliness. It is a gentle approach, slow to catch on at first, considering this from a global perspective and considering your present understanding of the numbers of you who read and purchase books, when relating to the population as a whole. But do not be concerned with numbers.

To each of you, notice your strategic location on the planet, notice your strategic birth circumstances, and notice to where you have brought yourselves, in order to play this delightful and fun-loving game. You will find the perfect way in which to carry out your role in this chess game. Simply enjoy the process, for this is a treat and one that you have called upon, and so enjoy your differing experiences on the path.

Teleconferencing and video conferencing both allow the connection of energetic frequencies to occur, one through a visual means and the other through an audio means. By utilizing the energetic participation of Lisette's transmitting abilities, you can connect to us through a process that enables you to receive a visual display of our vocal frequencies. The visual display will be one of our incoming vocal resonances. This is visual data, not simply audio. This is a first step of what we call video conferencing, because you can receive a visual cue from our communication. The facial image of us can be transmitted too, but first things first. The initial stage can be a visual readout and display of our frequencies being transmitted from our area to yours. When you put your energetic frequencies to a component that can read this, output is achieved, measured, and quantified.

Of course there are those who will refute this possibility and call it trickery, but those are not the ones who you are initially reaching. Where there is doubt and denial, there is sometimes "cement," and some people's ideas are cemented firmly in place until, of their choosing, they change. Do not concern yourself with these critics. Simply carry on and tarry not, for you do not know what thing leads to another. You do not see what early processes and procedures give birth and give rise to the next stage.

There is an audio component here as well, that links through to a visual display. They are connected. Differentiate between what you know, in your heart and soul, of what would be possible and what your mind refutes as ridiculous. Go with the soul. Let the mind alone. Let it refute and deny what it will, and carry forth your endeavors. We are of the notion that whatever it is you undertake with energetic fervor, you can achieve, and we are standing by to aid you in those processes. Be of the belief that nothing is out of your reach and nothing is impossible. Why should *this* be? Believe in the inner workings of faith and in the other participants in the cosmos, and know that Divinity will inspire you and us to create camaraderie between us. This can be considered to be one of the purposes of the universe.

If you would rather not contemplate this idea because it seems ridiculous and impossible, do not. There will be no retribution in any way. It does not take great scholars to understand that observable communication between us is possible. Have you not noticed that even some of your animal specialists and behaviorists have found a way to interpret the signals and the language of the gorilla?

> *You're referring to the amazing abilities of Koko the gorilla, who's been using sign language to communicate with humans since the 1970s.*

This has been documented, and a whole language has been distilled to enable one species to converse with another. Then what more would you say is possible between us? You and the gorilla are seemingly separated by a difference in your species and, in some ways, are part of different "worlds," are you not? One hundred years ago had it been suggested that communication between gorillas and humans would be occurring, what would have been the response? So consider this before you refute the potential and the possibilities of what we are suggesting between us.

If you develop anything, develop a broader acceptance of focusing on the joyous outcome, and not necessarily understanding the income. By *in-come* we mean the minutiae and the details surrounding the hows and whys of how something might work. Step up onto that path toward that direction and have faith and trust in all of your ability as a team to bring this into reality. If you are looking for the answer from the perspective of a perfect science, you will not find it, because you are *creating* this "perfect science" in your backyard and in your garage. You are *rewriting* the definition of what science is. So do not look to your textbooks to explain it to you. Look to the nature of the divine. Look to the nature of the universe. Look to the grandest idea possible and then you will know from where the technology comes.

A sequel can detail and describe the process by which you proceed with this. Document your journey, for you are not simply journaling a mechanical process, you are reminding your fellows how to go forth armed only with a wild idea. You do not need NASA to find us.

All that you have read, all that has been published on the subject of creating out of thin air, now you need read no further. Now you will demonstrate it. What do you think all those books have been leading you to?

There you go, with playful abandon. Bring in the playmates, the ones who find glee in such an undertaking, and step forward into these experiments, seeking not so specific guidance from us that you are left feeling incapable and dependent on us, but rather, know that we are here to guide you. We will help you along the way, but you too are a universal being. Make that demonstration, please. Tap into your own knowing, as you tap into us. We are with you and you with us, there in your habitat, connecting through the cosmos this wonderful display to others. Document your process and your findings, and don't be surprised when you look back on your humble beginnings in your "garage" and smile in amazement. Great endeavors have often started with just such wide-eyed naiveté, since you and your team are not jaded as to what you cannot do.

From this level of possibility thinking can your world's "current events" be changed forever.

CHAPTER 16

Where We Are Going from Here

A few weeks ago a good friend of mine was venting to me about her irritation with a relative of hers, whom she described as ridiculously frugal. She described her cousin to be frugal to the point of being dysfunctional. My friend went on to say how annoying it was to be around this cousin, and that she was somewhat befuddled by how hot her blood boiled whenever the two got together. "She drives me nuts just to be around her," my friend said in exasperation.

Now this got me to pondering things, because it is not the first time that I have noticed that the very characteristic someone is bemoaning describes them perfectly. In the case of my friend, I didn't have the heart to retort that she herself was a candidate for president of the Cheapskate Association and had recycled her yearly day planner for seven years straight, crossing out the days of the week to match whatever was current for that year. Despite her income, she was downright miserly, so to hear her complaining of someone else—and to not notice that she had the very same characteristic—was intriguing to me and really started me thinking about how what annoys us may have some relevance. In particu-

lar, I wondered how this dynamic might play itself out with respect to encounter phenomena.

I've been considering that perhaps what bugs me most about someone else is really my own identical character defect.

Those who most elicit your irritation and resentment often do best represent you—they embody the very characteristic you have, which you are being asked to notice, reflect upon, and thus heal. All souls everywhere have set it up this way. Those others whom you most vociferously judge and reject touch most closely to your own tender wound, your defensive recognition that you're beholding parts of yourself that you recognize at some level as most needing adjustment. When those characteristics show up in another to trigger this reaction in you, give thanks to that other, for they bring you the gift of self-examination. How else does a sleeping person awaken, but to be nudged from slumber by what you feel as irritation, judgment, criticism, and self-righteousness? Of course, much of the time you are not aware of the gift another brings you and instead you attempt to avoid those whom you say you dislike.

Then how do we reconcile this paradox, that we're avoiding those whom our souls are attracting?

The soul first attracts your likeness through another and then the mind supervises the repelling, for the soul has no enemies, but the intellect does. It is the intellect that keeps track on a ledger of those whom you deemed to have wronged you, whereas the highest part of you has no objection with anyone. And so the mind judges, condemns, finds foolish, finds fault with and resists, repels, recoils from, has contempt for, and does all this while the soul waits patiently and calls to itself yet another person, in another location, at another time, to once again trigger you until you notice the other in you. This way you address those disowned aspects of yourself, as you are ready to.

But certainly not all characteristics that we find distasteful in another reflect or mirror the same in us? Take, for example, the characteristics of an alcoholic married to a woman who objects to his drinking. If she doesn't drink at all herself, what would he be reflecting back to her?

For "irritating" characteristics to show up in one's life and thus trigger a response in judgment, criticism, resentment, or self-righteousness, means that something is up with the soul's agenda. Admittedly, these ideas are not for the squeamish, but if your life is working okay and you think you're ready for the spiritual big leagues, consider that the master is not irritated by anyone in any circumstance, and therefore can call to himself or herself all experience without judgment or feelings of superiority.

The soul often calls to itself, through friends, co-workers, tenants, employers, children, and neighbors, characteristics and attributes that are shared in common—but seem to be disguised in another. The specifics of how those characteristics and attributes are shared may not be identical. The woman in your example might ask herself in what area does she too manifest behaviors of addiction, of being out of control, or of manifesting a particular weakness. The introspective seeker will consider in what ways might she too exhibit indulgence with another substance, food, or sex, or perhaps she has an addiction to emotionally bullying others, or a predeliction for judging others. This is very personal work we are up to now with this message, and so stay with it. In your example, the soul asks why one would judge so harshly the alcoholic when one shares the same characteristic, but in varied detail. Conversely, those attributes you are moved to most love and admire in others, you often embody yourself, at least to some degree. So you see, just look to see who you are surrounded by—and of those, who is igniting a response in you—and you will know areas of your own spiritual growth that are asking to be addressed and healed.

> But what of a surly, bad-tempered businessman who is annoyed and perturbed by the antics of rambunctious adolescents nearby? Are you saying that these adolescents have characteristics in common with him?

When you are triggered by another to an angry or irritated reaction, annoyance, judgment, or jealousy, you may be beholding similar characteristics in yourself that need healing or you may have called to yourself characteristics that your higher self is asking you to develop, those that you don't currently exhibit. In the case of the businessman, his soul may be asking him to "lighten up," to find again joy, laughter, and hilarity as embodied by the young people around him. The more rigid he is, the more he will find himself triggered and/or surrounded by those who embody jovial abandon. In his case, the characteristics in another may even show up looking like irresponsibility, for his soul is asking that his rigid tendencies be relaxed and balanced with playfulness. This is why the habitually punctual end up marrying the chronically late. Opposites do attract for a wondrous, soulful reason.

Okay, but getting back to your example of the alcoholic triggering contempt in the teetotaler, surely an addiction to food is not as damaging to oneself or others as an addiction to alcohol. And so why would the soul put so much emphasis on healing that?

From a spiritual standpoint, who is to say which "preoccupation with meaningless" is "worse" than another? Whatever illusion your focus is trained upon prevents you from applying yourself more fully to the moment of now. Only the intellect, which is intent on avoiding how it too seeks refuge in the meaningless, would designate degrees of guilt to one's brethren for choosing an illusion different from one's own. Unconsciousness is unconsciousness, although we understand that you are responding through the eyes of your culture's laws and rules about such things. But we are speaking to you from the standpoint of reaching an awakened state, and from this perspective, there is no degree of guilt as doled out by your culture. In fact, the path that keeps you reasonably functional, yet still out of touch with your higher self, will ensure that you may be less likely to be motivated to heal, whereas the alcoholic or addict can more quickly "hit bottom" and therefore more quickly move toward awakening. Of course, at the highest level, nothing is meaningless, since all events and circumstances become part of the soul's grand unfolding. But we are speaking now of how you each condemn your brother.

At the very least, unhealed aspects—preoccupation of all sorts—cause joylessness. Who is to judge which preoccupation is "worse" than another? There are plenty of enraged, albeit sober and "clean" people, who spread anger and upset with lightning speed, and that ripple effect spreads unhappiness in all directions. So you may find a moody, enraged teetotaler who calls to herself some kind of relationship with the addict or alcoholic. Although your drunk drivers get more bad press, the soul of the world asks you to notice and heal any behavior or characteristic which prevents you from being your fullest and kindest, most compassionate, most loving self. So stop judging another's addiction when you have one yourself. Were you to deeply comprehend this, individual healing would quickly lead to what?

Global healing?

Yes, since these concepts can also apply globally, as one culture ceases judging another for "wrongdoing."

If a group attacks you and leaves the families of its victims homeless, grieving, or disenfranchised in some manner, it is your country's opportunity to ask if your own country has, or is currently, conducting itself in a manner which actively participates in or allows the same disenfranchisement of its own people, within its own boundaries and elsewhere. Who is to say which "attack" is more exploitive, menacing, and therefore lethal: a superpower's steady but covert disenfranchisement of other countries' natural resources and their peoples, to include the disenfranchisement of its own elderly and impoverished—or sudden, overt "attack" led by a few?

Some people would consider your suggestion impertinent, given our country's present circumstances in the war on terrorism.

Whether in your individual relationships or your cultural, ethnic, and global relationships, the intellect plays tricks, for it does not identify the other as yourself but insists that you have no connection and therefore nothing in common with that other's unhealed characteristics. And then you name this other your enemy and try to punish him. This is an illusion, for had you no connection, the other would not be part of your experience and would not be eliciting your explosive reaction. This holds true both individually and collectively. Just for a moment, let the intellect drop and consider this the very next time you judge your friend or relative, or take up arms and start a war. Both may be healed with the same adjustment in perspective.

It has been proclaimed that healing takes place when we love another, when we embrace that other, not when we find others guilty and kill them. One of the agendas of the soul is to find a way to have compassion for others who seem hopelessly different from oneself. So the souls of all of us have found a remarkable way to do just that, to have compassion for others who would seem to have nothing at all in common with ourselves. We are all part of a grand plan that provides a way for us to understand each other and to internalize the knowing that we are all one.

How can we internalize that we are all one? It seems like such a lofty idea to make practical.

By living more than one life simultaneously.

Do you mean at once? We're other people at the same time?

There is no such thing as "time" as you describe it, but yes, it is the grand irony. At any given moment, you are more than the "you" reading this right now. There are more of "you" on the planet sharing the same soul. These are the mechanics through which the soul comes to "understand" and have compassion for everyone. If you find that you cannot relate to someone, that you are judging them all over the place, you have basically made an announcement to the universe that you don't understand them, and therefore you need to walk in their shoes in order to understand them. *Literally.* Hence reincarnation. Hence embodiments that take turns being the all of it. And so even some of your politicians and military leaders who are currently leading the assault on Afghanistan are actually living concurrent embodiments in that very country, possibly even as part of the very network with whom they are at war.

This idea would not be considered very politically correct.

Notice how ironic it is that suggesting that you may have unhealed aspects and characteristics similar to that of your most hated enemy is considered politically incorrect. Yet in an evolved culture, the very mark of "politics"—leadership—embodies wisdom that conducts itself in a way that furthers peace.

*But we didn't start it. We've responded so that we can have
peace, not more violence.*

In the short term, this may seem to be the case, just as when you
physically strike out at a misbehaving child, and that child's errant
behavior appears to instantly be corrected. But enlightened cultures
would look beyond the seemingly immediate outcome and look to
the greater principles being modeled. If you want to model to your
children that physical violence does not solve things, then you would
not engage in those behaviors yourself. If you see yourself as the
wiser, then go forth with behaviors and actions that embody wisdom
and that produce the long-term goals that you say you are seeking.

Even Jesus said what you do to another you do to yourself. Now
we will help you to bring this teaching full circle: You have not understood this to be a literal truth. Those who most offend you are in fact
yourself, for you attract and react to those who most embody your
own characteristics.

And here is the interesting part: In your embodiment right now,
some of the emotions and fears from your concurrent embodiments
"bleed through" to your own, which is why you say that "one part"
of you wants this, when another "part of you" wants that. This you
describe as being conflicted because you are aware of the differing
aspects of self. You have not understood that your self might be
dozens of you—and often times you can feel those other "you"s having opinions about you, others whom you know or have judgments
about, and what you're up to. At times you can "feel" what their
opinion and objection is to whatever is at hand. Your job is to "meet"
the other aspects of yourself through others—through the vehicle of
being triggered by others—whether individually or globally—and feel
genuine compassion and understanding and non-judgment where you
once felt hatred.

This way do you integrate all the aspects of you and create *per-
manent* peace. For you step into your enemies' shoes and see it from
their perspective. From this standpoint is peacekeeping instilled. For
you can no longer see that other as the enemy because you "remember" what it's like to "be" that enemy. Perhaps you remember what it
feels like to be an impoverished child who grew up in a "third world"
country and whose family and country were exploited by foreign
superpowers. In the case of your current war, that other embodiment
over there in Afghanistan feels a particular way toward the United

States, and you who "remembers" things from all sides, are now motivated to "work it out" peacefully. Through your understanding and lack of self-righteous indignation, you are able to finally relate to your enemy, and so you can admit to your own foibles and how those foibles might have incensed another. You have grown up. You now embody what it takes to create peace, even while others attempt to slay you, for you finally understand the all of it from the perspective of the one who is doing the slaying.

You finally understand that for an "errant" characteristic or behavior to have shown up in your reality—and for it to bother you deeply, whether within the context of your individual or group relationships—means that you too embody that characteristic, either individually or collectively.

This is what is meant by as you sow, so shall you reap. As evidenced by your judgment, your inability to understand that other will be the cause of your creating a similar experience and embodiment for yourself, so that you *can* understand that other. What you have put out returns to you, not as a punishment, but through a vehicle that allows you to have an opportunity to gain empathy and compassion for everyone, everywhere, because you too will have been everyone, everywhere, but not merely through the vehicle of one lifetime following another lifetime, but simultaneously. Now you see the grand plan that allows for total acceptance of all beings. If you can't love another because of your judgment about that other, you will create an opportunity to be that other yourself so that you can.

This is why your personal relationships create the groundwork for mastery. The soul knows what it's up to and is always seeking for you to notice and heal the disowned parts of self.

It may be helpful to think of yourself as really having a whole team of you existing behind the scenes, each member of the team having an opinion, certain fears being particular to one member, and each "voicing" his or her input that "hit" you as conflicting thoughts, opinions, worries, and fears. When attempting to make an important decision, you will say, "A part of me is afraid to go forward, but another part of me feels courageous and wants to go for it." You have rightly understood that the superconscious, conscious, and subconscious have all had a "say" as well, and that is correct. But there is still more to the story. Life is still more complex even than that. You also have other embodiments, the personalities of whom all conspire in your totality of personality, in some form or another. You have felt the other aspects of yourself, but you have not been able to identify the source. The emotions and fears of those other simultaneous incarnations often come through one embodiment to another, which is why one part of you may choose and hope for a particular outcome, while another of "you" wants the opposite.

But then who wins out? Which part of "me" gets its way?

The answer will vary, depending on your ability to integrate or make peace with all aspects of yourself.

So we can actually meet our "twin" soul—in these instances?

You don't usually interact directly with other "embodiments" of your own soul, for to do so would be too potent. Instead you meet the symbolized versions of your own soul through your association with others, which for purposes of evolving your consciousness, *has the same effect as meeting yourself.* The challenge arises when your intellect refutes this and calls that other symbolized version of yourself your "enemy." Then, not only have you failed to integrate the disowned parts of yourself, but you have further alienated those aspects of self and have created an even wider chasm between all of you on your "team." In essence, by judging and assigning blame to another who most holds your criticism, you have doubled the magnitude of your assignment.

Remember, by the very act of your feeling induced to anger, irritation, judgment, etc., means *you are in the process of confronting yourself.*

In this way can you be motivated to find a way for your judgment to magically drop; in this way can you suddenly see the other as reacting in a manner that you can "relate" to. But most important, you now know that by refraining from being seduced into judgment, you avoid calling to yourself that other's exact experience *again* in the form of a "future" embodiment matching the one that you're judging and cannot understand.

Where We Are Going from Here

I become whom I judge?

In essence yes, not as a punishment, but as a means by which to understand and thus cease judging that other.

That scenario seems beautifully simple. We all become motivated to having compassion for each other, no matter the circumstances, because we might just wake up in that other's shoes tomorrow, no matter the location.

Jesus did say ye and your brother are one. There was no mention of geography.

Whether here or there, in America or Afghanistan, on this planet or that one, how do we know if those humans or extra-terrestrials whom we encounter are "good guys" or "bad guys"?

When you understand the nature of the dance in which we are all engaged, you cease labeling any entities as "good" or "bad," for you understand that all souls are part of your experience for a profound universal purpose. If you choose to transform any relationship in which you find yourself engaged, then use the tools suggested, noticing where you too might heal yourself. Then, forgive the other by noticing the gift brought to you, and then, that which you say annoys you can be miraculously transformed. This is why the answer to your question does not matter, for such context does not allow you to benefit from that soul's very existence in your experience. What does matter is that you cease judging another as the "monster" of the hour in your life, and begin to reconcile your own responsibility in creating the all of your experience in the first place, whether or not this experience is in your "normal" life or your "paranormal" life. There can be no separation between applying spiritual principles to healing your relationship with your co-worker, your sister-in-law, or your spouse—and applying spiritual principles to healing the nature of your encounters or other paranormal experiences. The process is the same with coming to terms or making peace with a relative, employer, neighbor—or a neighbor with gray skin who lives across the galaxy.

Okay, I understand how it is that we are calling the sym-bolized version of ourselves to us through all of our relation-ships so that we might heal the relationships and thus ourselves and that other. So then if part of the plan in which to do this is to have other physical embodiments simultaneously—and these are not limited within the constraints of geography—then encountering extraterrestrials would mean that experiencers are actually having encounters with . . . themselves?

Now you are ready to accept the unacceptable. You have come this far to see the perfection for what it is. Yes, precisely. As you grasp the ideas that several embodiments are taking place at one "time" in a general location, you can move to an understanding that simulta-neous embodiments are taking place elsewhere in the universe. Expe-riencers are simply becoming aware of themselves being elsewhere. It is not just that you as humans are becoming aware of your universal neighbors, but that humans *are* extraterrestrial neighbors—evolved. Since there is really no "time" in the way that you have understood it, all experience is happening concurrently and so you have the treat during this moment of now to meet yourself in one of your potential "futures."

That is why even those experiences that would seem to place you—as seen through the eyes of your misperceptions—in the role of victim or "abductee" are actually those experiences that your soul has called to itself in order to "interact" with the symbolized version of yourself. Now you finally understand how it is that we all truly share one universal soul.

So in our encounters with ETs, we are actually coming face-to-face with ourselves, who have come "back" from our future to meet us?

You'd be surprised to hear of how many encounter experiencers have already suspected that they have some very deep connection with extraterrestrials.

This is amazing. We really do get to meet whom we can be ourselves.

Welcome home to your new understanding of who you are—and

who we really are—and where you may soon be in the magnificent experience of your next evolution. Finally, you are beginning to understand all that is possible and all that is occurring, even while you sleep. But for those who dare, sleep no longer and awaken to your true lineage. For this reason can you know us, for we are not separate from you, but embody you, and you, us.

Many of you reading this book have struggled with issues pertaining to having encountered us. For you, this material has been provided. We hope it has helped. Others of you who have not yet met us, *will* meet us one day, for how long do you think it will be before you will come upon your neighbor?

For all of you, we await your outstretched hand whenever it is that you are ready to know us more fully—and therefore to know yourself—more fully. The emergence out of the cocoon of your isolation can now begin.

All of the universe awaits your invitation.

Author's Note

Thank you for joining me on this grand adventure, as I have shared with you my communications with extraterrestrials. My fondest desire is to have helped someone else feel better about what they too are going through in the process of meeting our otherworldly neighbors, and to support you in your understanding that this transition, although sometimes troubling, can be perceived of, and experienced as, the remarkable *spiritual* journey that it is.

For those of you who are also experiencers, I would love to hear from you, as I am in the process of collecting stories about others' encounters to include in a forthcoming book. Let us finally join hands and together announce to the world just how many of us are having these types of experiences. Please try to limit your submission to several pages so that I can include as many as possible. Tell me who you have met, anything interesting about them, what you have learned, and how the contact or communication has impacted you, or others around you. You may submit anonymously, but if you do, tell me why you need to do so.

For those of you who are presently in the stages of emotional trauma or upset as a result of your encounters or related phenomena, I would encourage you to find someone with whom you can share your feelings. I know from personal experience how difficult this can be, especially when you fear for your own sanity, or those around you do. For this reason it was important to me to provide here some encouragement from a representative from the "professional" sector who discusses the psychological profile of me as experiencer.

The following two appendices are written by Alan Ludington, M. F. T., and UFO investigator Joe Nyman. Although it appears that they are addressing my "case" individually, it is my hope that you too will feel encouraged by their words.

If you have been dreading finding a way to begin to tell your spouse or family about your own experiences and don't know how to start, you could begin by having them read Alan Ludington's essay. Simply open up this book to his appendix, hand it to them, and ask them to read it. You can then take it from there with your own experience.

We envision establishing a nonprofit foundation to further support and make practical ideas and inspiration that all of us have received from our contacts and communications. We envision that this foundation will establish a way to hold patents, etc., so that technical and other ideas can be researched, developed, and provided for the use of the betterment of humankind, rather than being owned by an individual, or the government, for reasons of profit or control.

Remember, these contacts are spiritual in nature. For this reason you will not be burdened with more than you can handle. Look to spirit for guidance, and above all, see yourself as the remarkable pioneer that you are. Together we can dramatically help shift our current paradigm.

Visit my website at www.talkingtoets.com. Contact me at lisette@talkingtoets.com, or write to Lisette Larkins, C/o Hampton Roads Publishing Company, 1125 Stoney Ridge Road, Charlottesville, Virginia 22902. Until then, warm regards on your blessed journey.

A Clinician's Psychological Perspective of a UFO Encounter Experiencer

By Alan Ludington, M. Div., M. S., M. F. T.

I am in practice as a licensed marriage, family therapist, not as an expert who specializes in paranormal features. I, and my colleagues, evaluated Lisette Larkins simply on the basis of testing, to include observing and assessing her in various clinical settings over a period of almost six years. I assessed her ability to achieve the quality and fullness of life that she is seeking. Lisette meets all the criteria—and she has had some experiences that are unexplainable in the standard form of psychological diagnosis. But most important, Lisette's case provides benchmark implications regarding the sound psychological makeup of other encounter experiencers who may now be able to step forward in greater numbers as my profession—and our entire culture—begin to consider that they are not crazy.

On March 9, 1990, I went out to the lobby to meet a new client with whom I had spoken on the telephone. She said that she had been referred to me by a friend and that she would like to come in and talk with me.

Lisette was a bright, attractive, redheaded woman of average size and weight. I took her down the hall into my office, where we began the first session of individual therapy.

From the very beginning, Lisette was not sure if she could tell me everything. She seemed to be waiting for an impending diagnosis that she was "crazy." She was anxious, wondering just how much she could confide in me. I sensed that she wanted to feel better, to get her life back on track after her divorce. Yet, she mentioned to me many times that if she really told me everything, I would certainly think she was nuts. She feared that if I found her to be emotionally impaired or mentally disordered, she would then lose the single most important thing in her life—custody of her beloved son, then three years old.

As Lisette began to trust me, she questioned me about my personal opinions regarding various "paranormal" phenomena. At times, she was vague, until at last, she asked me pointedly if I believed that there were such things as contacts with spiritual beings, psychic visions, clairvoyance, and encounters with extraterrestrials. I understood later that she was trying to find out where I stood, to see if, as a therapist, I could tolerate the tale of her own experiences. She wondered if she dared burden me with any kind of intangible mumbo-jumbo. Despite her curiosity about my clinical assessment of her, she seemed resigned to some form of negative judgment or pathological diagnosis that she felt would be forthcoming.

Slowly, Lisette's story of her life and the details of her paranormal experiences began to unfold. Her question was asked again: Did I now think she was impaired?

As her surprising experiences surfaced, I had to consider whether or not Lisette could be diagnosed with any significant disorder, while taking into consideration variable diagnostic information. Throughout Lisette's treatment, there were several different types of pathological disorders and acute diagnoses that I had to "rule out" or consider. For example, one of the seven key indicators of multiple personality disorder [Dissociative Identity Disorder] is when a person claims to have periods of time for which one cannot account. Some of Lisette's "encounters" are marked by these episodes of "missing time."

Throughout the past twenty-five years, I have counseled other clients who were clairvoyant or who have reported unusual paranormal experiences—and they were not disordered or psychotic. Lisette did not meet any criteria that would suggest a pathological diagnosis. She had one criterion for multiple personality disorder—episodes of missing time—but that was all. To be diagnosed with this severe disorder, a client would have to meet five out of seven specific criteria as stated in the *Diagnostic Statistical Manual*. Lisette did not meet any of the other criteria.

As part of my routine case management, I presented Lisette's case to the team of clinicians at the Conejo Counseling Center, a multi-disciplined mental health center, which I founded and where I was the executive director. At that time, we had a staff of twenty-six professionals, including psychologists, psychiatrists, and marriage, family therapists. I held case review sessions once a week, and we continued to discuss Lisette at these case conferences.

Despite her odd time lapses, corroborating feedback from my colleagues at these meetings maintained that Lisette could not be diagnosed with any impairments or disorders, including multiple personality disorder. No medication was ever administered to her. Over several years, Lisette consistently presented too many other sound personality traits. Although such a diagnosis could easily, from a clinical standpoint, explain her lapses of missing time, this was clearly not the case for Lisette.

A more intriguing and possibly disturbing alternative begged for consideration: Could Lisette's outrageous experiences be authentic? If so, a frontier was opening to humans that truly boggled the mind.

It would have been simpler to dismiss Lisette as unsound rather than mull over her remarkable experiences. But Lisette is a high-functioning woman. She is articulate, wonderful at mothering, and successful. Lisette was, and is, doing well in her life. This is an indicator of a truly "grounded" personality. Impaired and disordered clients often have an inconsistent and erratic job history and repeatedly struggle with unstable relationships with friends. Lisette, on the other hand, has maintained an employment history requiring significant, long-term competency, and she has maintained healthy, bonded relationships with many friends for twenty years and longer. Her period of emotional upheaval following the trauma of her initial encounter experiences were short-term and do not represent Lisette's behavior or personality in a general sense. The anguish these experiences caused was exacerbated by the additional weight of intense marital struggles during the same time period. We had to consider how any other person would react given her identical experiences. It is human to respond emotionally to catastrophic events.

After about two years of individual therapy, I invited Lisette to participate in one of my interactive groups, involving many sophisticated adults. Were Lisette impaired or disordered, psychopathology would have become very evident in intensive group therapy such as this. For example, if Lisette had multiple personality disorder, she would have inevitably "switched" into another personality—somewhere, sometime, and somehow. It might have been possible for her to "hold" one personality with me throughout the duration of our individual therapy, but if she were really MPD and placed in the midst of an extremely confrontational group of eight or nine people, something would have had to give. Lisette was in this group over an additional two-year period, and throughout this time, she behaved in a manner consistent with how I experienced her in an individual setting. She stayed very constant, despite significantly challenging events that were going on in her life during that time.

Appendix I

A colleague of mine also observed Lisette on an individual basis. A second followed, and I then invited a third therapist to join me in my group, one who had also observed Lisette during those two years. It seemed that any clinician who had any consistent, existential, or clinical experience with Lisette found her to be sound. Not only were there no personality switches, etc., but through the years, Lisette demonstrated behavioral characteristics in keeping with that of a truly mature, psychologically healthy individual.

From an objective, diagnostic standpoint, my supervision group and I had to weigh all these factors. Despite her odd experiences and missing-time episodes, after observing Lisette clinically over a period of several years, we concluded that Lisette's fundamental, psychological core is as solid as a rock.

Interestingly enough, during the initial part of treatment, I received a Minnesota Multi-Phasic Personality Inventory (MMPI) on Lisette from another psychologist. The MMPI looks for personality characteristics that might show mental disorders or problems. Some of Lisette's experiences within the realm of the paranormal are considered by the MMPI to be "deviations." The MMPI interprets visions (clairvoyance), time lapses, out-of-body experiences, hearing voices (clairaudience), and sensations of "probings" like those reported by UFO experiencers as mental disorders such as multiple personality disorder, schizophrenia, histrionic personality disorder, etc. Consequently, some of her answers were outside the norm. These answers could all be viewed as answering questions honestly, given the fact that Lisette reported having paranormal experiences. Keep in mind that any test is only as good as the criteria that it is designed to detect. This test does not have a deviation for paranormal experiences. Her claims do not fall within the standard codes relative to what we are assessing. So, the MMPI that she took does not allow for the answers of her own life experience.

The more we learned about Lisette's paranormal experiences, the more every answer that she had on that MMPI made sense. After evaluating her, we did not find it necessary to retest her. Lisette did not hear the voice of Jesus telling her to go shoot the president. The overall tone of her experiences proved to be life enhancing, never destructive. But she did have experiences that, when answered honestly on a standard MMPI, were "abnormal" responses.

Six years after Lisette took this first psychological test, another psychologist contacted Lisette, requesting that she take another test in order to participate in a research project on UFO-related phenomena. Lisette agreed. Coincidentally, she had not had any traumatizing encounter experiences for over two years. This time, it showed a "normal" result. It is interesting to note that by the time Lisette had taken this second test, the results bore out what was evident to both of us: She had made peace with her unusual experiences and had gained profound spiritual meaning from them—the very same experiences that had once turned her life upside down. If, in the future, Lisette should take yet another test while she is again witnessing unfathomable paranormal activity, the results may again show an "abnormal" result based on such happenings being read by this test as a "deviation."

Whether or not Lisette—or anyone else—obtained a supposed "normal" or "abnormal" test result, it is limiting to attempt to derive conclusions simply from contrived psychological testing. Such tests are designed by my profession and culturally standardized "norms," which are compiled from the perspective of a Caucasian, Anglo-Saxon, Western world. Any result outside that norm is then referred to as a deviation of norm, and it is given one type or another of adverse label.

History has provided us with many people whose lives have been marked by experiences that many of us have never replicated. Some of those experiences have been so unusual that to attempt to define them within the framework of any of our present-day psychological testing would show marked psychopathology. If I could have tested Thomas Aquinas, the Italian philosopher from the thirteenth century, his psychological test results would be way outside the norm. His claims of visions and mystical experiences had a sudden and dramatic impact on the remainder of his life. The same could be said of Florence Nightingale, Gautama Buddha, or any mystic. If Jesus of Nazareth would have taken an MMPI, he certainly would have shown a significant deviation from a normal personality. Psychological testing alone would indicate that they were all "abnormal"—not within the norm—but were they all crazy?

Is Lisette crazy? No. Is she outside the norm? Most definitely. Do we have a psychological "label" for people who have such experiences? No, but there are pat diagnoses we could provide to explain away such experiences as never really having happened. We could, for example, state that these people are delusional with characteristics complicated by paranoid features.

In some instances, this may be accurate. As the founder and former executive director of the Be Free out-patient program for substance abuse, I have often heard about a client's auditory hallucinations and "visions," which were clearly caused by alcohol and drug addiction. Substance abuse can often be noted as the underlying cause of some of these clients' so-called paranormal experiences.

But emotionally and mentally impaired and disordered clients do not present themselves like Lisette. They do not handle their life or interpersonal relationships like Lisette. They do not parent their children like Lisette. Clients presenting a plethora of emotional and mental diagnoses—including drug and alcohol addiction—just do not conduct the details of their lives as Lisette does. Despite her extraordinary experiences, no pathological diagnosis fits Lisette.

During the last ten years, the field of psychotherapy has become more and more inclined to see the integration of spirit, mind, and body, rather than just focusing on mental processes alone. As recently as twenty years ago, psychotherapists tended to view spiritual issues as almost abhorrent: a hocus-pocus, medieval ideology. Fortunately, this limited viewpoint is changing. I have found that as the field of psychotherapy grows, clinicians more readily accept that there are people who have human experiences that are not clinically diagnosable.

It is true that some professionals in the psychotherapy community still maintain that all perceived events or perceptions occurring outside of scientific explanation are simply rationalized dissociative disorders learned in childhood as a result of abuse or trauma; however, when attempting to arrive at a diagnostic conclusion, the full spectrum of one's experience and behavioral characteristics—mind, body, and spirit—also need to be taken into consideration. Even professional clinicians are not beyond society's general tendency to attack or label as bad, sick, or evil that which we cannot measure, identify, or comprehend.

Now, what can we say about Lisette—or for that matter, certain other experiencers of paranormal phenomena? If she and other experiencers are somehow experiencing and communicating with "others" whom most of us cannot see or hear, are they out of step—or are we—for not recognizing our own true natures? Are they simply using their God-given talents—abilities that we should have too but have somehow lost? Do Lisette and others who claim to have had a glimpse of another dimension simply have more attuned sensitivities? As a clinician, how should I diagnose her? As a society, how should we behold such claims?

In biblical times, she would have been called a healer. In aboriginal tribes, she would be called medicine woman or shaman. But in Western culture, we link her claims under the umbrella of the "bizarre experience" and call it "out there" at best.

It has only been about one hundred years since Freud developed the new discipline of psychotherapy. From the perspective of a historical time line, the professional psychotherapist is virtually brand new. Conversely, the "field" of spirituality preceded the formal study of psychotherapy by more than six thousand years. Surely, there is more to humankind's spiritual experiences and potential than what clinical professionals have approved of and categorized during the past hundred years. As a therapist, who am I to say that a person's paranormal experience is wrong or has not happened? I cannot say that extraterrestrial encounter experiences are not "real" experiences. Just because I don't have them doesn't mean that those experiences do not exist.

In addition, I do not believe that many people lie about their own paranormal experiences. The "reward" Lisette and others usually receive for coming forward with their experiences is ridicule. In Lisette's case, public exposure with respect to these experiences could be embarrassing, humiliating, and potentially jeopardizing. Admitting to her experiences is a bold act. It is much easier to never tell anyone of one's encounter experiences.

Interestingly enough, Lisette and others who have these types of experiences are often painfully aware of the degree to which their unusual experiences "deviate" from those of their friends and family. Lisette's initial challenge was to overcome a tremendous sense of shame and embarrassment when admitting her experiences.

From my observations of Lisette, I see a woman and mother who lives within the norm of human life—and yet she presents experiences that are outside of the norm. Her story does not frighten me, nor do her experiences compel me to label her as "sick" simply because I do not understand or share those experiences. I know there is more to human experience—spiritual experience—than what can be detected through standardized tests and other manmade instruments of measurement. History is laden with examples of just how limited a society's vision can be when it comes to accepting new ideas. We have often killed the messengers or dismissed them as absurd.

I encourage all of you to read this book. It is by a woman who has had life experiences that offer you a door to new thoughts and feelings. It is a reminder of our fullest potential, where the unity of mind, body, and spirit might ignite extraordinary human experiences that defy explanation.

For the past twenty-five years, Alan Ludington has counseled clients and has offered classes at Pepperdine University, Cal State Northridge, and Cal Lutheran University. His ideas have been published in several journals and magazines, and he is currently in private practice. You can write him at 875 S. Westlake Blvd., Suite 211, Westlake Village, CA 91361.

A UFO Investigator's Theory on the Nature of UFO Encounter Phenomena

Replacing the "Abduction" Model

by Joe Nyman, UFO Investigator

My understanding of the UFO encounter has come from more than thirty active years of investigating UFO sighting claims and related experiences. Although I used to be a UFO investigator for the Mutual UFO Network (MUFON), I prefer to work with people one-on-one, and so I have gone from trying to study UFO sighting claims to studying claims of unusual phenomena related to UFOs and their effects on the reporters.

UFO investigation has always been a complicated and frustrating endeavor. Claims are exotic; proof is nonexistent; and media noise level is high as well as potentially contaminating.

Since 1947, hundreds of books and countless articles have been written about the UFO phenomenon; numerous individuals have sold themselves or been exploited by the media in the name of "evidence"; films and television have unashamedly cashed in on partially investigated or totally uninvestigated claims; tabloids have printed wonderful photos of aliens shaking hands with presidential candidates; etc. If you can't prove it, you can at least sell it. The more sensational, the better.

Sensationalism aside, the sad lack of understanding of the nature of the UFO phenomenon is evident in the many boxes that hordes of "expert" writers and commentators have tried to fit it into. So, we have fairies, elves, angels, devils, extraterrestrials, time travelers, visitors from other dimensions, ourselves returning from the future, the spirits of our ancestors, sexual abuse transformations, and false memories induced by therapists and investigators—the list is as long as there are ideas and cultural categories.

The most relentlessly promoted theme is one of sci-fi extraterrestrials—beings evolved on another planet, much as humans evolved here on Earth, technologically advanced and arriving to do to humans much of what we humans would have hoped to do to them if we had gotten there first. This theme incorporates descriptions of flying saucers as seemingly manufactured vehicles with extraordinary performance characteristics transporting these alien beings. As an explanation, this meshes nicely with the direction human technology has gone in the twenty-first century. Unfortunately, it is an idea totally lacking in material proof to those doubters and curmudgeons skeptical enough to demand such things.

Personal encounters are the most spectacular aspect of the UFO phenomenon. UFO experiencers—those who harbor lifelong latent images of encounters with beings from UFOs and who, like Lisette, have also lived a life punctuated by anomalous and bizarre occurrences—may comprise a significant percentage of our population. My research suggests a number between fifteen and twenty percent. Unfortunately, these have been unyieldingly presented as a process of victimization based on emotional revelations unearthed during hypnosis. Unfortunately again, proof is lacking unless one considers that having one's story told in the media is proof or "information."

Investigators working this proof-by-publicity-angle have had two lasting effects: The subject has become firmly entrenched in American pop culture—which works wonders on public recognition and other potential payoffs—and it has sharply, perhaps irretrievably, polarized opinion on the nature of encounters with beings from UFOs. Credentialed individuals, those with higher academic degrees and college or university affiliations, are reluctant to risk becoming an embarrassment to their institutions by going public with their UFO interests.

These two obstacles, the barrage of media stereotypes and the lack of well-educated, scientific inquiry, have had a third less visible, but more important, effect. Work done by "therapists" and "investigators" who have prejudged the UFO phenomenon as victimizing is usually superficial and incomplete. The experiencers who are the patients and subjects of these "experts" are left feeling angry and used. They have been allowed only to confirm what they have probably already read or seen on television—that they are victims of uncaring alien abuse.

I used to consider that the study and treatment of UFO encounter claims properly belonged in the hands of credentialed mental health professionals. I must say that time has caused me to drop that chimerical notion.

Appendix II

I have no mental health credentials, and I make no pretensions to being a therapist. Although I am a retired software engineer, my authority on the nature of the UFO encounter experience results from twenty-five years' work with UFO experiencers. Having conducted more than five hundred sessions with these experiencers, I have developed a framework within which individuals can try to bring into conscious awareness what they feel is relevant to our joint efforts. I refuse to prepare them in advance with suggestions or explanations. I tell them instead that they must do the work to bring out whatever it is they wish. I know I have infuriated a number of people because I refuse to tell them anything in advance. Although people have been so inundated with encounter imagery in the media that they must inevitably arrive primed, at least they know that I don't expect them to perform in a prescribed way.

Even though I don't know what has happened to them, I know enough about the general structure of UFO encounters to allow people to bring to mind details within the structural stages. The process of individual recovery and assessment is up to the individual, and it can take as long or as short a time as the individual can handle. For about fifteen percent, the process never begins. No encounter imagery of any consequence ever emerges. Lisette was nearly one of these.

When I first met Lisette in 1993, she showed me how open and trusting she was. She had switched coasts for a week to see someone she hardly knew, to participate in a poorly specified procedure in the hopes of bringing to mind images that might relate to a number of vivid and upsetting experiences in her past.

Hers were details that I had heard described many times. They were details that were associated in the perceiver's mind with UFO encounter experiences. Lisette knew that, too, of course. She had read at least some of the UFO literature, attended conferences, and spoken with others. I had responded to her letters with some confirmations.

I admit I nursed slight suspicions about the nature of her trip since she had announced intentions of writing a book, and so, as we talked, I tried to assess her motivations. The UFO field, like any other, is in thrall to at least three ugly and indestructible demons—hype, hubris, and hypocrisy—the latter best known by its fellow traveler, self-service. Was Lisette after publicity? Did she feel she was bringing great truths to mankind? Did she intend to do well by seeming to do good?

I admit readily to being quite fallible. But as I listened to her, I sensed the same tentativeness, the same self-doubts, the same need to be believed and not to be dismissed that I remembered observing in dozens of instances before. As we lunched at a place across the road from her motel, her determination, buttressed by intelligence and vivacity, presented a formidable front. She wanted to know, to account for, and to explain; if she were crazy, I thought, so was everyone. Here was someone, I judged, who was independent, productive, and actively capable of normal human relationships, who was also determined to understand the nature of the unusual images that had burst into her awareness.

Lisette's case did not include a rich narrative replete with exotic other-worldly adventures and details; just the opposite filled our intense six-session exploration.

Was she searching in our work for the positive slant she believed I was going to help provide? I had expected that she would get into at least one completely structured experience with aspects of the first four stages of the encounter structure: anticipation, consciousness transition, examination, and communication/tour/trip. My expectations were not met. Neither the framework I had come to expect was evident, nor was any structure—only fragments attached to various ages throughout her life. It was ironic that Lisette appeared to have retrieved better encounter images from her waking experiences than she was able to glean through hypnosis.

However, our fourth session, on the morning of November 4, 1993, provided quick etiological insights that triggered in Lisette a deep spiritual and emotional response. There appeared to her a galaxy (" . . . lots of stars . . . ") and a female alien entity ("It feels like my mother.") Then, with heightened emotion, she reported, "I feel sad . . . I want her to come back. I want to see her right now." Then, there was a fade-out, the seemingly unconnected images of a clinically cold nasal implant, and herself on a table. The images continued in a disjointed fashion: seeing through the eyes of a newborn among alien heads and then admitting that she had censored her feelings about the alien mother out of consideration for the feelings of her natal mother.

Lisette realized at this moment that she had felt a longing for the mother whose form had appeared to her as the classic, inverted pear-shape alien head.

Lisette's acceptance of alien connection was relatively restrained—not the emotional temblor that needed to be quickly redirected to the unconscious, as I had seen in others. I wondered if she had been sneaking furtive mental glances at the alien head, or if she had long since suspected a connection with these beings these past couple of years without admitting it to me.

Lisette then shifted into thoughts about her life. She had a sense of a job, a sense of a mission, and a sense of origin elsewhere.

An image of the alien mother appeared again. "I feel I can accept it." Then she feels emotional detachment and sequentially, sadness, great humility, a sense of future joy, and the immediate presence of "Christ consciousness." I asked if this Christ consciousness was related to our investigation.

"Absolutely. It's the joining of the two in consciousness—the entities and the humans. Yet the consciousness has to be raised."

Lisette felt that coming into the limited human consciousness provided the needed counterpoise to allow her to realize the contrast with alien consciousness. This was accompanied by thoughts that the trauma of her human life had acted to allow her to step back in a kind of dissociation, to begin to be aware of her other self. In our final session I used a technique to bring Lisette backward a year at a time to review her encounter experiences back to her childhood. Lisette was happy at session's end.

The result of Lisette's life review, her spontaneous encounter awareness, and her work with therapist Al Ludington and myself has only reinforced her orientation that there is a deep and profound connection between "them" and her. Her experience of origin in the alien visage provoked tearful emotion in her. Despite aspects of fear, terror, and self-doubt, the lifetime summation remained unshakably positive, even though from experience, I know that critics of anything positive she might write about her experiences would accuse her of rationalizing her "victimization" either out of "alien brainwashing" or her need to avoid bringing the disturbing nature of these images to her normal, everyday awareness.

What can I say about her positive slant on her encounter experiences? From an investigator's point of view—my point of view—support for this kind of conviction, in the ordinary, material, and confirmable way is completely lacking. Yet, for the experiencer, it is an intensely personal, intensely authoritative conviction. It is not easily arrived at, yet when it does come, it overrides all ideas of victimization.

It becomes the nexus between the phenomenology of the encounter experience and the ontology of that experience. As a long-time investigator, I know how easy it is to leave experiencers feeling like victims and how difficult it is to allow them to come to the realization of "connection" without prompting or leading; however, I feel very strongly that encounter investigations must be undertaken with an unstated intention of having the experiencer arrive at "duality"—the feeling of the experiencer that one has a deep and profound connection to these beings—whether the experiencer reaches that state or not. Less conviction in this regard on the part of the investigator results in a great disservice to the experiencer.

Lisette's intention in writing her story, she tells me, is to hold out an alternative viewpoint to those experiencers who have been led to believe that they are, at best, victims of sci-fi aliens—that they are instead part of an ongoing, positive process. Once again, as a non-experiencer, and, hopefully, objective researcher, I can't make a judgment about the nature of that kind of conclusion, but from the point of view of enabling an experiencer to cope, it beats victimization by a long shot.

I wish I had objective proof to support this experiencer synthesis. I have only the observation that having reached this stage of realization, the experiencer loses a great deal of fear, anxiety, and self-doubt.

What I call "dual reference" is at the heart of the perspective shift that experiencers undergo during their explorations of encounter imagery. It is defined as the experiencing of oneself as both a human and an alien as one relives encounter imagery in the investigative setting.

Surprisingly, I have been told by my colleagues in the UFO investigative field that dual reference is "only a theory." That's simply not the case. It's a pattern in the data. More and more experiencers are coming to these conclusions on their own, discovering a feeling of deep kinship with the aliens. The inferences from what dual reference implies are hypothetical.

Let me make clear that "victimization" is also only a theory based on the pattern of encounter images that are expressed in terms of anger, fear, loss of control, and unwanted physical trauma. Unfortunately, it is a widely publicized one based on incomplete investigations.

The resolution of the traumatic stages comes when the feelings of connection and origination engendered in experiencing the duality provide a context shift for the experiencer.

Briefly, my work suggests that dual reference images in regression can be categorized into four classes: pre-human birth images as an alien; images of duality concurrent with one's life; general images of alien connection that suggest the dual nature of the experiencer; and images that pose the choice of possible return to one's alien origins.

Many of the images are those suggesting a "connection" with the alien beings. Lisette's are in this category. A number of dual reference images consist of experiencing oneself in alien form before birth, preparing to come into the human form. Less frequently expressed are images of oneself in an alien body concurrent with an encounter aboard a UFO. The rarest set of images involves having to make a decision whether or not to return to alien form and leave the human body.

Now, I want to emphasize as strongly as possible that the images in the four categories above are experienced in the same way as any of the other images concomitant with the encounter incident. They are active images as opposed to the passive ones of watching a screen or being "told" something. They are thus just as valid as any other active encounter image—table images, for instance, in which the experiencer tells about undergoing uncomfortable physical procedures under alien control while on a table. And these realizations of duality have an enormous emotional kick to them. Since I have kept this kind of material quiet for years, there has been no prompting in the media for experiencers to unconsciously incorporate.

There are those who wish to "save" the "abduction" hypothesis, which says that humans are victims of alien opportunity—randomly grabbed at random ages by sci-fi aliens for various purposes. To this end, the experiencing of duality has been dismissed as being merely a variation of Stockholm Syndrome—a phenomenon in which a hostage begins to identify with and grow sympathetic to his or her captors. Those who favor this view must either have no knowledge of the dual reference pattern or have completely misinterpreted it.

There are many ways in which the Stockholm Syndrome differs from dual reference. Here are five instances:

1. In cases of Stockholm Syndrome, as indicated from research after wartime, or with victims such as famous heiress Patty Hearst, the captives, initially fearful, gradually become acclimated through kindness, whereas, until dual reference is actually experienced by encounter experiencers, fearfulness is hardly resolved. Furthermore, the dual reference perspective is often not initiated by the aliens, but rather, is a consciousness that is often arrived at by the experiencer himself, rather than at alien suggestion.

2. In cases involving Stockholm Syndrome captives, there is a gradual shift in cultural identity to that of the captors, while with dual reference, there is a sudden sense of understanding of a connection to the aliens with no loss of human cultural identity.

3. With dual reference, the nonhuman state is experienced as the original state, but Stockholm Syndrome captives are always distinctly aware of their pre-captivity, and their post–Stockholm Syndrome lives are never viewed as their origins.

4. Dual referencers experience their forms as identical to those aliens around them and share an alien context. Analogously, Stockholm Syndrome captives should experience themselves immediately within the cultural context of their captors, which is never the case.

5. Dual referencers never feel a value conflict, such as is often the case initially with Stockholm Syndrome captives. Dual reference experiencers become more comfortable in their lives as humans, not less so, after experiencing duality.

"Abduction" saviors may object that the five states listed are the result of alien brainwashing—that these feelings have been induced to subdue unwilling victims. There are two objections to this point of view. First, if it is so easy to induce this mental state of submission, then why isn't it immediately present among all those experiencers who come forward? Why is it so difficult to find this state of duality if it is meant to mask the victimization process? Are the aliens, at bottom, incompetent?

Secondly, we must make note of a point previously mentioned—that the state of duality is experienced actively, and thus, it is logically impossible to draw an objective line and say that one accepts the trauma-ridden expressions as "real" and the positive expressions as "induced." All images must be accepted in one context or the other as totality; you can't divide them according to your prejudices or theories about the nature of encounters.

Finally, there is the issue of rationalization. The value of having kept the dual reference phenomenon largely unknown is now quite evident. Most subjects in the investigative setting experiencing duality for the first time and not having read it anywhere in the "standard issue" UFO literature, find it overwhelming and very difficult to accept. There is no glib statement of, "Oh, yes, that must be it. Now I feel better." Instead, there have been statements of fear for one's sanity. As one individual put it, it was safer to believe that one was crazy than to believe that experiencing oneself as a nonhuman being was true. The UFO books provided no supporting validation.

Critics of the dual reference theory would have us believe that "fear of madness" is in some twisted way an "empowering rationalization."

Let me also point out that what is suggested by "dual reference" easily accommodates certain findings about encounters that "abduction" has difficulty with. Experiencers frequently believe that they have been so throughout life, rather than from the random ages of their so-called abductions. This data is revealed in a number of encounter inventories similar to a session conducted with Lisette.

If there is any rationalizing going on, that is, attempting plausible but superficial explanations, then indeed, it is the attempt to save the "abduction" theory. The dual reference pattern contradicts that hypothesis and implies something quite different for the nature of UFO encounters.

However, admittedly, no objective, indisputable evidence exists to support any of the claims made; to the contrary, purported evidence that has been tested has proved "unconvincing" and non-supportive.

Experiencers of UFO encounters have been left feeling angry, violated, and abused, more, I fear, the victims of their UFO investigators, therapists, and the media than the aliens reported to be involved. This is, no doubt, because incompletely investigated encounters are inevitably measured against mass-media models—the victimization model.

The author of this book wishes to open the door to a wider perspective on the feelings that UFO experiencers have about the nature of their encounters. It is a perspective that goes beyond the stereotypical view of the world of science fiction. Even within the UFO interest community, alternate opinion about the nature of the phenomenon has a hard time emerging through the media din. At the risk of becoming part of the noise, it is necessary that this particular alternate view be heard.

Should readers be any less wary of what is written here then anywhere else? Certainly not. Nothing here should be taken without critical judgment or a suspicious turn of mind. But if the reader has ever considered that there might be an atom of truth in any other UFO-related work, then that reader should also consider the possibility of what is presented here.

Lisette writes to show, first, that she has gone through the same traumatic awakenings that so many other UFO experiencers have described, and secondly, that she shares a realization about the nature of the experiences unlike the science fiction staples of rape and victimization—just the opposite. She is also not proclaiming absolute truth because that may never be proved, but hers is a view consistent with my years of investigative work with UFO experiencers.

It is one woman's story. Readers will relate to what Lisette has to tell because her experiences could just as well be ours.

Index

Index

About the Author

Lisette Larkins first became aware of extraterrestrials in 1987, as a wife and mother of her then infant son. After more than a decade of processing her encounters—moving from trauma to acceptance, and then to transformation—she is dedicated to writing and speaking about the true spiritual nature of UFO encounters and offering an alternative perspective from which to view such events.

Hampton Roads Publishing Company

. . . for the evolving human spirit

Hampton Roads Publishing Company
publishes books on a variety of subjects including
metaphysics, health, complementary medicine,
visionary fiction, and other related topics.

For a copy of our latest catalog,
call toll-free, 800-766-8009,
or send your name and address to:

Hampton Roads Publishing Company, Inc.
1125 Stoney Ridge Road
Charlottesville, VA 22902
e-mail: hrpc@hrpub.com
www.hrpub.com